T4-ADF-453

The Best of
SCOTLAND *on* SUNDAY

The Best of
SCOTLAND *on* SUNDAY

edited by
Kenneth Roy

CARRICK PUBLISHING
Ayr

First published in 1990 by
Carrick Publishing
28 Miller Road, Ayr KA7 2AY
Telephone 0292 266679

Set by Communitype Communications, Leicester
Printed in Great Britain by Billing & Sons Ltd., Worcester

Copyright © 1990 Scotland on Sunday

All rights reserved. No part of this publication may be reproduced, stored in a retrieval system, or transmitted, in any form or by any means, electronic, mechanical, photocopying, recording, or otherwise, without the prior permission of Carrick Publishing.

British Library Cataloguing in Publication Data
The best of Scotland on Sunday
    1. General essays in English
    I. Scotland on Sunday
    082

ISBN 0-946724-25-3

CONTENTS

HANGOVERS	Alan Taylor	11
PIPE DOWN	Neville Garden	12
PLAYING FOR TIME	Kevin McCarra	14
BETTE DAVIS EYES	Allan Hunter	19
SCANDAL	Joyce McMillan	21
THE WALL	Rob Brown	23
THE CAMPBELLS KEEP MUM	Calum Neish	29
EXTRAORDINARY JOE	Robert Philip	31
FRAMED	Alan Taylor	33
WEEK OF JUDGMENT	William Paul and Kenny Farquharson	36
MR LIM'S CORNER SHOP	Joanna Blythman	42
MAY STANDS BY HER MAN	Sue Innes	44
URBAN VOLTAIRE	Kenneth Roy	47
SEXY'S CITY	Graham Spiers	51
TYRANNY AND AFTER	Alexander MacLeod	54
PEACE, IMPERFECT PEACE	Alan Taylor	56
LORDS OF THE RING	Ajay Close	58
CAUGHT ON A TRAIN	Joyce McMillan	64
DISNAELAND	Roddy Forsyth	66
CONFESSIONS OF A MEAT EATER	Derek Cooper	68
HANDS ACROSS THE SEA	William Paul	70
THE BIG M	Julie Morrice	75
EVERLASTING SUNDAY	Kenneth Roy	76
SMALL BUT BEAUTIFULLY FORMED	Rennie McOwan	78
INSIDE BARLINNIE	Keren David	80
DISCORDANT NOTES	Neville Garden	87
THE NEW MORALITY	Joyce McMillan	89
SCOTLAND 2050	Rob Edwards	91
POETIC JUSTICE	Kenneth Roy	94

THE WORM TURNS	Joanna Blythman	99
A WOMAN'S WORK	James Naughtie	101
A POW-WOW OF HELMUTS	Alan Taylor	103
IN SEARCH OF THE HARD MAN	Ajay Close	105
TRIAL AT TITWOOD (1)	Robert Philip	112
TRIAL AT TITWOOD (2)	Neil Drysdale	114
GHOST RIDE	Alan Taylor	116
LUCKY BREAKS	Roddy Forsyth	120
WAR GAMES	William Paul	121
THE KING AND I	Ajay Close	126
DYING FOR A SMOKE	Jeremy Watson	130
BRIGADOON REVISITED	Kenneth Roy	132
THE SURPLUS SEX	Sue Innes	134
GOGO AND BOBO ARE MISSING	Robert Philip	140
NOW FOR THE RUMBA	Kenneth Roy	142
TARTAN SPECIAL	Joyce McMillan	144
THE TRIAL OF JOHN BUCHAN	Trevor Royle	146
SINK OR SWIM?	Derek Bateman	152
GRANDSTAND FINISH	Graham Spiers	154
THE LAST SLEEPER	William Paul	156
RECIPE FOR DISASTER	Derek Cooper	158
THE FORSYTH SAGA	Michael Fry	161
ROYAL SOAP	Brian Groom	163
SEX AT THE FESTIVAL	Peter Cudmore and Alan Taylor	165
LOCKERBIE: A YEAR ON	Keren David	167
ARE YOU AN ORANGE PERSON?	Joanna Blythman	176
SEASONAL GREETINGS	Joyce McMillan	179
DIARY OF A SHOP ASSISTANT	Ajay Close	181

INTRODUCTION

Andrew Jaspan, Editor, Scotland on Sunday

Welcome to the first compilation of what we hope will become an annual feast of some of the best writing culled from a year in the life of *Scotland on Sunday*.

We have assembled a very strong team of journalists who are prepared to put in the homework and commitment to produce the best of weekly journalism. The dailies in Scotland serve us well in instant reactive journalism. We operate at a different pace and on a different cycle. We analyse, make sense of disparate events, speculate, opinionate, investigate and maintain a roving brief to report on our changing world as viewed from a Scottish vantage.

Not every journalist or writer either wants such a brief or is able to execute it. Such are the demands of a writer's paper. *Scotland on Sunday* must be informative, but above all it must be a joy to read.

The collection made by Kenneth Roy for this volume is an excellent representation of some of the most incisive and well-written journalism, reportage and social commentary to be found anywhere – not just in Scotland. That has been recognised by the national and Scottish press awards that the team won during the year.

I hope you will derive as much pleasure from reading this collection as we all did in conceiving, writing and executing the original. Here is Scotland's new writing force.

October 1990

ACKNOWLEDGMENTS

My thanks to Andrew Jaspan and the staff of *Scotland on Sunday* for their co-operation. I am particularly grateful to Brian Groom and Rae Kelly for their practical assistance with the project and Paul Overton and Katrina Hutchison for cheerfully undertaking the immense task of photocopying a very large number of articles. My thanks, also, to Carrick Publishing's Anne Hainey and Linda Holland, who typed the manuscript. Finally, I should like to thank the contributors without whom, as they say, this book would not have been possible.

K.R.

EDITOR'S NOTE

Kenneth Roy

There are 57 pieces in this collection. They were originally published in *Scotland on Sunday* between the beginning of September 1989 and the end of August 1990.

They vary in length: from 400 words (a short, sharp radio review) to 4,000 words (a compassionate account of the legacy of the Lockerbie air disaster). They vary in theme: from scandal on the Scottish bench (a model of detailed, objective reporting) to the fall of the Berlin Wall (a vivid eye-witness account). And they vary in style: from witty social observation to authoritative political commentary. Maybe these 57 varieties add up incidentally to a sort of portrait of the year – but the motive behind their selection was less lofty. They were chosen because they were especially interesting, or especially entertaining, or (often) both.

Arranging the pieces was unexpectedly difficult. Strict chronology – allowing them to arrange themselves – would have robbed the book of the swift juxtapositions of mood and subject matter that make an anthology enjoyable. Arranging them in subject groups proved unsuccessful for the same reason. So, in the end, the order was based on nothing more reliable than a compiler's hunch about what felt right.

Hangovers

Alan Taylor

So here they are, the Naughty Nineties. On the first day of the New Year the High Street felt as if Armageddon had arrived. In the early afternoon, men with complexions like over-milked scrambled egg went walkabout while the womenfolk prepared steak pies and defrosted peas. There was nowhere to place a bet, all the pubs were closed and if there were *Daily Records* for sale the Post Office was not open to sell them. It was a communal commiseration, that peculiar macho Scottish phenomenon of sharing and wallowing in a hangover.

Limp handshakes confirmed there was life after Hogmanay. It was a case of trump or be trumped. To be dealt a hand you had to have been up at least until after five in the morning; thereafter it was one point for a pint, two for a nip. Some made impressive scores but no one could beat the straight flush flourished by a Hole in Wa' habituee who, first-footing blind drunk, had mistaken pot pourri for Bombay Mix. He looked terrible but at least he smelled nice.

According to a posh paper it was not supposed to be like this. The Scots, it quoted an off-licensee, apparently were becoming even more like the English, bingeing at Christmas and toasting the New Year in alcohol-free lager and *aqua minerale*. Not in my neck of the bottle, they didn't.

Christmas is still a time to stoke up; New Year to soak in. But the adversaries of alcohol are beginning to make an impression. Where once upon a time you could get through the New Year by laying in whisky and sherry, with bottles or cans of beer as chasers, you now need to offer exotic tipples of more or less alcoholic potency. No one that doesn't want to drink should be made to feel inadequate or a wet blanket, they say, you can have just as much fun as sober as Cliff Richard.

No one really believes this. But it makes the pre-drink joust more entertaining. "You'll have a dram," you say, the brogue unfamiliarly peaty. Strange how at New Year everyone has just come down from the Isle of Skye. "No, not for me," he says unconvincingly. You wave the bottle hypnotically, like Robert Halpern's watch. "Well, maybe just a wee one to be sociable." You pour. "Say when." It's high tide before he signals to put a finger in the dyke. "I'll never drink all that. I better have a beer to water it down." Half the glass goes down in a gulp "to make room for water". More whisky and beer flows under the bridge, the one chasing the other, neither in danger of being overtaken. "Did you say you were driving?" he asks his spouse, now on her fourth or fifth Cointreau. If looks could kill, he would be in a sarcophagus. "Well, we'll just phone for a taxi, will we?" "We will." *Plus ça change, plus c'est la meme chose.*

January 7, 1990

Pipe down

Neville Garden

The world of nursery rhymes is full of unfortunate people – the worst example being, surely, the fine lady on the white horse at Banbury Cross. Not only does this luckless female have rings permanently attached to her fingers and bells to her toes. She is also required to have music wherever she goes.

"Wherever she goes." In my book, three of the most terrifying words imaginable.

I do not make, and have never made, New Year resolutions. But I am not in the least averse to making a wish at the beginning of a year, let alone a decade. My fervent wish for 1990 is that 'piped' music, taped music, wallpaper music, background music – call it what you will – will become less fashionable and a good deal less prevalent than it is at the moment.

It won't disappear. That would be too much to hope for. Maybe, though, some of the people who hit us with it day-in and day-out can be persuaded to try something else. Like silence.

Shakespeare's Lorenzo may have called for an excess of music. But then he, poor soul, was in love and romantically inclined. I doubt very much whether he would have wished an excess of the kind of noise all of us have to endure in the course of a normal day.

Over the past two or three weeks, loudspeakers in buildings everywhere have been wishing us Merry Christmases and Happy New Years through the medium of, at best, carols and at worst, quite dreadful pop songs with a seasonal message. In my case, they have not spread an iota of good cheer: they have merely made a stressful time of year 100% more stressful. Piped music is one of the most insidious of today's minor evils. Where and when we least want it, there it is.

The other day, in a department store lift, I heard a favourite piece of Liszt assaulted by what could have been Richard Clayderman's piano. If it wasn't his, it was that of an equally tasteless offender.

Only hours later, in the lobby of a big hotel, the taped music was so loud I had to ask the receptionist to repeat what she was saying. "It is a bit much, isn't it?" she agreed, doing nothing about it.

In one eating-house recently, I had to raise my voice to converse with a lunch companion because the ballet music from *William Tell* was engulfing the tables at a goodish fortissimo. "Could you please turn it down. Or, better still, off?" I asked the head-waiter. He looked apologetic but he said: "We've found, sir, that our customers like music with their meals – which is why we've had it installed." Since that seemed to be the end of the matter so far as he was concerned, I left before ordering – and shall certainly never return.

(I remember once a restaurant in Stirling which used to play a complete opera each day to its clients. But the music there was a feature of the place – and you went to listen as well as to eat.)

The use of piped music by airlines and dentists is no less abhorrent. The idea, of course, is obvious. The airlines are trying to tell you there is nothing to worry about as you sit waiting to take off. They plainly believe that a touch of James Last will take your mind off disasters. All they do is make you wonder if they know something you don't, and sow seeds of doubt that were not present in your head when you arrived at the airport.

Similarly, the dentists are attempting to take your mind off the fact that, at any moment, they will prod one of their fearsome implements into a nerve and cause you to jump to the ceiling. I have a friend who cannot listen to Schubert's Unfinished Symphony now because it happened to be playing when he had a perfectly dreadful experience in the dentist's chair.

Unhappily, the disease is spreading. Just before the year turned, I visited an old friend. All the time I was in his house, a tape recorder was playing music – oh, so softly – providing an amorphous and constant background. Eventually I asked him why. "Oh, I find it relaxing. It's never off." I felt that here was a soulmate for the lady at Banbury Cross if ever there was one. For me, it was a most unrelaxing experience. Because music that is at too low a level to hear properly is every bit as bad as music which is painfully loud.

Good music, quite simply, should not be used in a cavalier fashion. It was meant to be listened to and to be enjoyed. By the same token, if good music shouldn't be used carelessly, bad music shouldn't be played at all – which brings us back to the wonderful concept of going about our appointed tasks to the sound of silence. It would, after all, be splendid to think that today's men and women are considered intelligent and sensitive enough to exist – unaccompanied. Once, and only once, did I enjoy some 'piped' music – and the adjective was apt.

I walked into the luxurious loo of a Glasgow hotel where a tape was playing fairly discreetly. It was Handel's *Water Music*.

January 7, 1990

Playing for time

Kevin McCarra

The nation is about to be converted. Once again, for 90 minutes on Wednesday, Scotland will be independent, bidding for a place among the full-time countries in next year's World Cup Finals.

For some, football's central role in Scottish life is an affront. In this version, the game is the 'opiate of the people', soaking up vast quantities of energy and aspiration which would be better applied elsewhere. This, however, is to misunderstand the sport's true nature. It isn't an escape; Scots bring their deepest concerns with them to the match.

Many years ago, soccer historian Bob Crampsey described Hampden Park as the nearest thing Scotland has to a national assembly. Those who thought that whimsical should have been at the 1988 Scottish Cup Final. All round the ground, red cards were brandished at the unwelcome visiting dignitary, Margaret Thatcher.

It was far from an isolated occurrence. Scottish football always reflects its times. In 1909 Celtic and Rangers fans at the Scottish Cup Final replay joined forces to riot at Hampden when they discovered there would be no extra time. Inevitably they were denounced as ruffians but did they not also embody the militancy that was springing up in the wake of a depression?

In 1906 Glasgow returned its first Independent Labour Party member to parliament. The 10 years which followed that Cup Final included the Rent Strike of 1915 and the rudiments of revolution in 1919. That Hampden riot was influenced by more than mere hooliganism.

It isn't just a question of rebellious Glaswegians. No matter how the fortunes of the SNP rise and fall at the polls, nationalism has a strong hold on the terracing. Those 'Remember Bannockburn' banners may be preposterous but the message is potent too. Football isn't a mute, it's a microphone.

The football memorabilia to be auctioned at Christie's in Glasgow this week speaks of far more than the simple facts engraved upon them. The past is talkative. Lend an ear and you'll be there all day.

The inscription on the inner case of lot 19, a pocket watch, measures not only the height of fame but also the extent of a later fall. The time piece was presented to Manchester City's Scottish manager Tom Maley in commemoration of his side's FA Cup victory in 1904. Two years later, he was banned by the football authorities for making illegal payments to his players.

There is, though, little poignancy among the medals and mementoes displayed; this is the stuff of congratulations. A watch-fob, shaped like a football, opens to reveal a record of Arthur Geake's service to Queen's Park in the late 19th and early 20th centuries. The hordes cheering and stamping (one trusts) as they watch Scotland play Norway on Wednesday will be regrettably close to his principal achievement.

The present Hampden Park, the third, is all too obviously the same stadium as the one whose construction Geake masterminded between 1900 and 1903. Its tatty, crumbling fabric should not blind us to the majesty it possessed at the time of its opening. This was the greatest football stadium in the world, licensed to hold 125,000 in 1910.

The Nottingham-born grain merchant Geake was referred to as 'Uncle Arthur', but he looks a severe figure in the surviving photograph, the waterfall of his heavy moustache pouring down to a whiskery jaw. The aura of propriety, to be fair, was a necessity. Queen's Park's resources were slight when they began building the ground and they needed to maintain public confidence.

The award of watches and their paraphernalia to men like Maley and Geake is typical of the age. Time itself was an honour; the accumulation of years was to be welcomed. The team groups of the period show even young players mimicking respectable middle-age. They have the remote expressions of men engaged in feats of mental arithmetic.

Football, they seem to say, is only a phase they are going through. Life holds nothing more fair than the prospect of a position of office in the local Chamber of Commerce. It would all be incomprehensible to the modern-day star like Ally McCoist, willing to delight a youthful radio audience with his reading of the *Rangers Rap*. Yet, ironically, it is the current performers who are the true men of substance. If the watch was the ideal symbol for those Edwardians, the car phone must be its equivalent for the modern-day player.

It could be that the real fun was had by those men of the 1870s who stare grimly out of their photographs. The pleasure of inventing the SFA and the Scottish Cup fell to them in a meeting at Dewar's Temperance Hotel in Glasgow on 13 March, 1873. The copy which survives of the first constitution and rules has a "let's get this straight" tone about it. A handy Definition of Terms includes the following: "Hacking is kicking an adversary intentionally."

A little time was required for football to determine its own worth. The 5/- subscriptions of the member clubs in 1873 went towards the purchase of the Scottish Cup for £56-12s-11d. Its makers, Messrs George Edward & Sons, included in the price a modest set of medals. Christie's have the one which belongs to the victorious Queen's Park captain J.J. Thomson. It is made of silver and shaped in a Maltese Cross. By the time of the second final in 1875, the winners' medals were of a more precious metal; football had put itself on the gold standard.

Receiving one of those must be a moment of intensely personal achievement but the glow of satisfaction is more widely diffused down the decades. Medals are a family affair. The memorabilia of some sports, such as golf, move from dealer to dealer for tens of thousands of pounds. Football isn't like that.

The 1930 FA Cup winners' medal actually comes from the East Coast. It was won by Alex James, star of the 'Wembley Wizards' side which beat England 5-1 in 1928, while he was with Arsenal. The Final with Huddersfield was, quite literally, overshadowed. Just before half-time, the German *Graf Zeppelin* breached flying regulations and passed over the pitch at a mere 2,000 feet, dipping its nose to salute the watching king.

Arsenal won 2-0 and James sent his medal to Raith Rovers director Robert Morrison who had nurtured his talent during the early days at Kirkcaldy. "If there had been no Bob Morrison," an accompanying note said, "there would have been no Alex James."

Some items leave their owners' hands in more prosaic circumstances. One wonders what the strip worn by a Celtic player in their victory over Dundee United in the 100th Cup final will fetch. Has its value appreciated or dwindled in the light of subsequent career moves by its original owner, Maurice Johnston? He sold the garment shortly after the match.

The clubs and football bodies must covet some pieces of the auction treasure trove but this one clearly belongs elsewhere. Shouldn't Glasgow's People's Palace be raiding its budgets for one special purchase? This jersey was social history in the making.

Price, although comparatively modest, ensures that such keepsakes are not the province of the average football fan in any case. He must make do with the mass-marketed mememto. It has always been so. The club shops themselves are new but their merchandise is not. Plates, mugs, tea pots, handkerchiefs, badges and the like have

The Best of Scotland on Sunday

been with us for most of this century at least. The true entrepreneur could even attempt to harness two popular passions in one product. The Britannia Pottery sold figures of Wee Macgreegor, urchin hero of J.J. Bell's stories in the 1900s, kitted out in a Rangers' strip.

Medals mark the conclusion of a footballer's activities but souvenirs are just the start of the fan's life. The market in football programmes has grown to such an extent that it almost possesses an existence independent of the game itself. Programmes for inconsequential matches are sought after for abstruse reasons. Scotland v. Northern Ireland, 1928, is desirable only because it was, unusually, played at Firhill.

As Alan Cunningham, owner of Edinburgh's Football Crazy shop explains, each collector sets his own targets. "One will be looking for all his club's home games in Europe, another might want one programme for each senior side in Britain each season. We estimate that around 2,500 teams have issued programmes in this country at one time or another, so the permutations are endless."

While football memorabilia has not reached the price level of stamps and other collectibles, the desire to complete a programme collection will drive people to more painful expenditure. A Scottish Cup final from the 1920s might set you back £200. At least individual programmes don't taunt you with your failure to buy all their brothers and sisters. Not like football cards. Everyone can remember the quest for the two or three names that would make up a complete set. It always ended in penury or a bad mood; never in success.

They were very popular between the wars, but in Alan Cunningham's words: "Most of the series featured a guy from Celtic, a guy from Rangers, and 48 Englishmen you'd never heard of." The cards were given away with cigarettes, later with a whole host of goods including bubblegum. Nowadays they just come on their own – stickers with no accompanying sticky stuff. They give kids plenty to think about but nothing at all to chew over.

This development takes us full circle, to the scraps which were produced from the turn of the century onwards and sold in bags. These would be gummed into albums. J. Baines of Bradford whipped business along by offering prizes to the people who returned the most empty bags within a week of their issue.

Christie's have around 1,000 examples of his work, not always concerning football, but he claimed to have produced a total range of 888,888 different designs. That may be an exaggeration but his appealingly gaudy emblems do show signs of having been produced in haste.

Such curios can bring the last century alive but they also tend to point out our remoteness from it. Another of Baines' stickers bears the legend 'Well Dribbled'. It must have been a popular cry of the day but only a brave soul would give voice to it on the terraces now.

The shifts in language work like continental drift, easing us further from the past. No wonder we are fascinated by the bric-à-brac of another age.

Stickers, cards, programmes, jerseys, medals, watches – perhaps we are not drawn to them by the business with a football so much as by the extraordinary stories they tell of other people. A cap awarded to a Scotsman seems hardly worth a glance until you look again and notice he won it for Chile. Robert Cunningham worked for the Donaldson Shipping Line and lived in Valparaiso. After two years residence there, he was eligible for the national side and played for them 27 times in the 1890s.

The sport travels well; not only over oceans but also across wider boundaries of class. The crude rural versions of the game enraptured Sir Walter Scott. It was said that he would rather his son excelled at football than won the highest honours of Europe's foremost university.

The game also breaches the defences of chillier intellects. Indeed, it has been said of the philosopher A.J. Ayer that a profound scepticism was the inevitable consequence of his deep entanglement with the fortunes of Tottenham Hotspur.

There is a serious point to be made. Football, especially in Scotland, cannot be patronised as the senseless pursuit of a class who know no better. At its heart lies a mystery we can neither solve nor ignore. Whenever the ball is tossed out and a simple set of rules applied, a strangely compulsive spectacle emerges.

Edwin Muir grew up in Orkney, much closer to the values of Scandinavian culture than to the sporting obsession of Scotland's industrial heartland. His poetry has little to do with the superficialities of daily affairs. Yet in the waspishly affectionate biographical notes his wife Willa wrote about him in the mid-1920s, he is described as: "passionately devoted to football, although now too shortsighted to play...watches football for hours."

Later in the same piece she refers to his "unusual combination of clear thinking and passionate intuition". Who can doubt that football exercised both faculties?

The game's attraction is such that we find the circumstances of an individual and his era drawn into the confines of a small medal. These aren't inert pieces of bric-à-brac waiting for the auctioneer's hammer; these are signs of life.

November 12, 1989

Bette Davis eyes

Allan Hunter

When the young Ruth Elizabeth Davis arrived in Hollywood towards the end of 1930, few people would have predicted a career lasting six years, never mind one that would span six decades, 10 Oscar nominations and earn her the title of Hollywood Great.

She did not fit the accepted mould for stardom in the film capital. She was not conventionally beautiful and did not want to play the hero's girl or some other simpering representative of feminine decoration. She was an electrifying actress who wanted to illuminate the human condition in all its many facets and her long career was a battle to reconcile her aspirations with Hollywood's prejudiced penchant for women who purvey glamour rather than intelligence or character. Every serious actress from Jane Fonda to Meryl Streep owes her a debt of gratitude.

Towards the end of last month, she attended the San Sebastian Film Festival to receive another lifetime achievement award. In recent years, she had endured a stroke, breast cancer and a hurtful volume of autobiography by her daughter. A lesser woman would undoubtedly have succumbed to such combined misfortunes, but Davis was a fighter and a survivor. Told that she might never speak or walk again, she had metaphorically scrawled an inimitable "nonsense" and fought her way back to mobility and employment.

In Spain, she was but a frail reflection of her once-robust self. Her public appearances were sparing and journalists wondered what she had been doing with herself. She replied that she had been selecting outfits, working with a make-up artist and generally preparing herself for the scrutiny of a press conference. Tireless professionalism was inculcated in her generation.

Dressed in black and puffing on her perennial cigarette, she greeted the assembled throng with a jocular "Buenas Tardes" and then proceeded to belie her appearance and age by conducting a long and lively conference that touched on every aspect of her life. She paid tribute to directors like William Wyler who had conducted her through some of her finest performances in *Jezebel*, *The Letter* and *The Little Foxes*. She recalled co-stars like Errol Flynn and Ronald

Reagan ("He wasn't much of an actor but I miss him as president, he made the country feel good again"). She diplomatically dissembled when it came to the subject of an alleged life-long feud with Joan Crawford, but was readily candid on the topic of Miriam Hopkins ("I'm not sure if I can say the word but she was a bitch, which was a shame because she was a very good actress but incredibly jealous").

She claimed a preference for playing 'naughty' women because of the dramatic possibilities they offered to a hungry actress. Asked whether she had been naughtier in life or on screen, she paused for effect and replied, "fifty, fifty". Her sense of humour was evident once more when a Spanish colleague had the temerity to inquire whether she could confirm that she had been asked to pose nude for a film just a few years back. She fixed him with an amused stare, sighed a regal sigh and responded: "My dear fellow, I'm 81. A few years ago, I was in my seventies. Who in their right mind would want to see me without any clothes on!"

From more than 100 roles on film she selected such classics as *Now Voyager*, *All About Eve*, *The Private Lives of Elizabeth and Essex* and *What Ever Happened to Baby Jane?* as her personal favourites. Critics and filmgoers are unlikely to disagree with any of these choices and would probably add her moving portrayal of the dying heiress in *Dark Victory*, the evil one-eyed widow in *The Anniversary*, the icily-memorable murderess Regina in *The Little Foxes* and her Emmy-winning performance in the TV film *Strangers* to a long and illustrious list of celluloid achievements.

She would have liked to film with Spencer Tracy and spent a lifetime awaiting the opportunity to co-star with James Stewart in the 1983 euthanasia TV movie *Right of Way*. ("He was at Metro, I was at Warners so we never worked together. He is one of our most beloved stars. If I'd gotten to him when we were much younger, life might have been very different.")

After San Sebastian, she had intended to update her 1962 volume of autobiography. It was entitled *The Lonely Life*, suggesting that there had been a personal price to pay for enduring professional success. Married and divorced four times, she reflected that it was difficult in her day for a man to accept a place on the sidelines of a woman's career.

If anyone merits the claim then it can truly be said of Davis that we shall not see her like again. The circumstances under which she became a star no longer exist; the Hollywood that was her kingdom is long gone. She once suggested that her epitaph might read: "Bette Davis – She Did It The Hard Way." In San Sebastian she was asked what would now give her pleasure and she replied without hesitation:

"A good script with a good part." That, too, might stand as a fitting farewell.

As her press conference ended, an entranced crowd rose to their feet and applauded her not only for the previous 90 minutes of her company but for a lifetime of indelible images; sharing a cigarette with Paul Henreid, shaming Henry Fonda as a Southern belle, serving a very special meal to a crippled Joan Crawford and advising us to fasten our seat-belts as the immortal Margo Channing. We started to leave the conference room. With the exit blocked, Davis stood acknowledging the crowd. Suddenly, I found myself before her. I took her hand, kissed it and congratulated her on what turned out to be her last award. She fixed me with her still-potent Bette Davis eyes and thanked me. Memories are made of this.

October 8, 1989

Scandal

Joyce McMillan

It is 26 years now since the Profumo scandal broke over the Macmillan government, sending shock-waves to every corner of the British establishment; in that quarter century, the face of private life in Britain has been transformed. One in four of our babies are now born outside wedlock, many of them to loving couples who choose not to marry. Homosexuality has been legalised, and despite continuing prejudice is no longer "the love that dare not speak its name". And divorce has become so commonplace that the only man whose career could still be wrecked by it is, in all probability, the Prince of Wales.

In other words, we're living in a society in which the idea of sexual scandal should have lost a good deal of its power; there is not much evidence that the public is really shocked any longer by, say, Anne Diamond's illegitimate babies or Princess Anne's separation. Yet as the Tory Party in Scotland discovered to its cost last week, when the Scottish edition of the *Sun* took the wraps off a series of humiliating call-girl allegations about its president Ross Harper, sexual scandal is by no means a thing of the past. Given the wrong set of circumstances, a good-going 'revelation' can still threaten career and credibility, wipe a presidential candidate out of the race, force a minister out of the cabinet or an MP out of the House; and every time it happens, a predictable siren song arises from the establishment about 'invasion of privacy' and the hounding of good men out of public life on account of behaviour which is nobody's business but their own.

Now it is clearly true that the British tabloid press has plumbed new depths of intrusiveness in recent years. They doorstep, they pester, they barge through private grief and pain with an insensitivity that beggars belief. Even more seriously, they've been known, in certain cases, to fantasise, to invent detail and quotes, to create deliberately misleading impressions. If the government – as seems likely – introduces strict legislation against the invasion of privacy, then the rags will have richly deserved the inconvenience.

All the same, it seems dangerous to me to confuse outrage and the way in which the tabloid Press goes about its business with objections to its going about it at all. To say that the Press should not invent lies about the private lives of public figures is one thing; to say that they should never discuss or investigate personal lives is another, and to my mind much more debatable. For I come from a generation formed by the realisation that the personal is political, and that there is no way of separating the inadequacies and oppressions of private life – or for that matter its joys and fulfilments – from conduct in the big world outside. We are a generation unimpressed by the idea that Hitler was fond of children and animals, or that there is no relation between (say) a judge's attitude to his wife and his administration of justice in cases of domestic violence.

Looking back to the most dangerous crisis of our lifetime, we make the link between the cold, relentless, athletic womanising of Jack Kennedy and the dangerous machismo that took the world to the brink of destruction over Cuba; we are not convinced that the American people had no right to know of the reality behind the Camelot facade.

Because the truth is that the idea of this rigid boundary between public and private affairs is one of the most dangerous and alienating features of our culture. It's this boundary, this block in the mind, that enables loving husbands and fathers to commit hideous atrocities or quiet cruelties in the line of work; it's the boundary that enables a nice man to drop a bomb called 'Little Boy' on 60,000 innocent citizens of Hiroshima, and fly home whistling.

In less extreme terms, it's the boundary that for centuries has allowed men to dismiss 'women and children', their concerns and their needs, to the periphery of 'real' life as it was lived in the factories and law courts, in clubs and in parliament. And it's the boundary that has allowed sex itself – that central creative force in the human personality – to be consigned at best to the low-status world of weekend recreation, and at worst to a grubby sub-culture of secrecy and 'naughty' practices.

But the game is up, because in our new permissive society, it is not so much what people do sexually that makes them vulnerable, but the sense of secrecy and furtiveness with which they do it. Public figures like Anne Diamond or the new proud-to-be-gay Ian McKellen, who make little secret of their circumstances and try to integrate their private experience with their public persona, have little to fear from any transient public disapproval. But those old-fashioned men, those Gary Harts and Joe Bakkers who still treat sex as a naughty, secret business to be dealt with in hotel rooms by paid help, and who try to sustain a full public life – and perhaps a marriage – while keeping such a vital part of their personalities concealed and separate; those men are increasingly recognised as sad hypocrites, whose pronouncements on the family and morality are a sham.

If last week's *Sun* allegations are false, then it's hard to imagine what kind of compensation could match the depth of the injury inflicted on a reputation and a career. But if they prove true, I can't find it in my heart to say that the public has no legitimate interest in them; or, for that matter, to support any return to that conspiracy of media silence which, for a century and more, protected the British ruling classes from the moral judgment of the people, and from the need to practise the standards of family morality they have not been slow to preach.

September 10, 1989

The Wall

Rob Brown

Friedrich Strasse Station, the last eastern stop on Berlin's East-West underground line, used to be known as the Palace of Tears – by East Germans who were forbidden to travel beyond it and by their Western relatives, friends and lovers who were forced to bid them farewell there before re-surfacing in West Berlin. But on Thursday evening, as the clock ticked towards the usual midnight visa deadline, there were only tears of joy.

As a long queue of passengers wound its way slowly up the stairs to pass through passport and custom control, a cry went up from the crowd: "Die Mauer ist weg! Berlin ist wieder Berlin!" – The Wall is gone. Berlin is Berlin again.

Cheers of jubilation instantly rang out around the dank orange-tiled concourse. Total strangers started hugging each other. A few even looked for a human reaction to the pistol-clad East German border guards, who remained characteristically stony-faced but made no effort to check travel documents or otherwise impede anyone.

"This is history. The days of state serfdom are over," exclaimed Tana Pinkowski, a young hotel receptionist who a few hours earlier had sat in her East Berlin apartment and watched in amazement as Guenter Schabowski, a spokesman for the beleaguered communist government in East Germany came on state television and announced unemotionally that citizens of the GDR were free to leave through any checkpoint in the German border – even the Berlin Wall.

In one administrative stroke, the teetering SED (Socialist Unity) administration had rendered obsolete the most cruelly resonant symbol of the Cold War. Although they announced no plans to dismantle physically the lethal boundary that has claimed more than a hundred lives and separated millions of people for 28 years, Die Mauer is already psychologically emasculated. Apart from the new crossing points created yesterday, it seems only a matter of time before it is brought down or it collapses under the weight of the jubilant crowds which have since converged on it, some of them already trying to destroy it.

Of all the convulsions in the communist bloc since Mikhail Gorbachev came to power in the Kremlin, this is by far the most breathtaking. Just over a year ago, in a speech in West Berlin, Ronald Reagan challenged the Soviet general secretary to "tear down this wall". That, said the US president, would be the true test of Gorbachev's resolve to bring peace, liberty and prosperity to the Soviet Union and Eastern Europe.

But as she headed for the Friedrich Strasse on Thursday night, 24-year-old Tana Pinkowski was determined to test her government's sudden commitment to free travel. "I want to make some surprise visits to my friends in West Berlin. I know it's very late and I've got to get up for work in the morning, but who cares?" She giggled, thumbing theatrically through the visas in her dark blue covered GDR identity document. "Look, I've been everywhere in the Eastern bloc, but I've never been west of Friedrich Strasse."

Elvira Rehnert, a 56-year-old shop assistant, was just going along for the ride. She had never seen the bright lights of West Berlin, but she was going tonight even if it meant turning up bleary-eyed next morning at the state store where she works. As the train trundled towards the commercial heart of West Berlin, she joined a group of young compatriots who had struck up a celebratory song in the cramped carriage. *So ein Tag So Wundershon wie heute!* went the chorus line...what a wonderful day!

At the upstairs exits tonight, there were no armed guards waiting, no fierce patrol dogs, just noisy crowds of equally delirious – and equally stunned – West Berliners waiting patiently to embrace friends and total strangers alike from the East.

Michael Vossen, a balding young student with pebble glasses, wasn't sure if his friends from East Berlin would be coming across (like most East Germans they didn't have a private phone) but he was prepared to stand around for hours in his thin denim jacket. "For 40 years it has been opposite situation," he said. "People in the East have had to wait for us coming across."

Out later on the Kurfurstendamm, West Berlin's most fashionable shopping thoroughfare, Rheinhard Teuile, a 21-year-old blacksmith, stared in awe at the forest of neon lights. He would also get back for work the next morning, but for now he was going to savour the ambience of this convivial boulevard with its all night Kneipes (bars) and open-air cafes.

Car horns blared till the crack of dawn in the Ku'damm, as East Berliners revelled in their new freedoms on the Western side of the Wall. A cheer went up every time an East German Wartburg or Trabant cropped up among the more customary BMWs and Mercedes. These tiny state-produced vehicles, which lend a whole new meaning to the term basic mobility, have been regarded with fresh respect since they started chugging through Hungary and Czechoslovakia two months ago.

It was primarily the huge human exodus from East Germany which forced the country's besieged communist leadership to pass a new liberalised travel law. Even as Schabowski delivered his deadpan address, East Germans were spilling over to West Germany at the rate of 250 an hour, swelling the total number of refugees over the last two months to almost 200,000. The crippling effect of such wholesale emigration in a country of just 17 million citizens is best demonstrated by the fact that soldiers had to be drafted in to help out in hard-hit hospitals and public transport depots.

How many East Germans were still defecting this weekend was hard to tell. None of the tiny cars flooding through the checkpoints in West Berlin seem to be carrying much luggage, suggesting that their passengers had come across the Wall simply to experience life on the other side or to savour a slice of history.

If they were looking for the latter, the place to be on Friday morning was by the Wall, preferably beside the Brandenburg Gate. Washed and battered repeatedly by the violent tides of German history, this triumphal arch was where Soviet troups hoisted the hammer and sickle on 'liberating' Berlin in 1945. East Germans marched beneath its Doric columns bearing traditional black, red and gold flags – with the GDR state symbol cut out – during the last, failed workers' revolt in 1953.

On Friday the Brandenburg Gate proved the perfect backdrop for the television news crews which had streamed in from every corner of the globe as news of momentous developments in the GDR unfolded. Without any direction, thousands of people – most of them, but not all, German teenagers – clambered on top of the Wall.

Perched precariously among them was Anna Muck, a 20-year-old East German student who had driven all night with a college friend from her home village 125 miles north of Berlin on the Baltic Sea. She would be going back to the East after a few days, but she would only happily stay there if the Communist Party relinquished its leading role. Like virtually all East Germans she wants to settle for nothing less than full-blooded reforms and free elections and the dismissal of the new general secretary of the SED, Egon Krenz.

Climbing on to the Wall was not at all difficult for Anna or anyone else, not just because some public spirited reveller had provided a small aluminium step ladder for the less agile. The 15-feet concrete barrier has always been the least daunting feature of West Berlin's 99$^1/_2$ mile boundary. What made this the world's most lethal frontier line was the surrounding panoply of security measures: machine gun towers, dog runs, tank traps, concealed trip wires, fences rigged with electronic wires and listening devices, infra red cameras – all controlled by the Grepos, the grim faced border guards trained to kill their own countrymen and even their own colleagues if they made a bid to escape.

By Friday morning, however, all this terror technology had been effectively de-commissioned. The Grepos relaxed and joked with the crowds glowering down at them, seemingly intent on preserving public order. The youngsters who slipped off the totally cramped Wall ledge into the Eastern sector were humorously helped back up.

'Peace and love, East and West' read one hand-drawn banner, reminiscent of the psychedelic '60s. 'Test the West!' appealed a placard carried by a bunch of American high school girls, clearly bowled over by all the attention their handiwork was receiving from the international press corps. "Hey, are we going to be on the front cover of *Time* magazine?" they shouted down.

The Best of Scotland on Sunday

The extent to which the American media appropriated, and indeed almost ended up stage directing, the celebrations was a sight to behold: the way the big US television news crews jostled for camera positions was breathtaking even to one who thought he had seen their worst antics in the movie *Broadcast News*. All the big networks had flown across their star presenters to front live coverage of the historic developments. Dan Rather, chief newsreader with CBS and the highest paid anchorman in America, was there.

Germans, however, were in no doubt as to the hero of the hour. There was an ecstatic reception for former West German Chancellor Willy Brandt when he arrived unannounced on the scene and started mingling with the revellers. The man who was mayor of West Berlin when the Wall was erected in 1961, who stood beside John F. Kennedy when he made his famous (if grammatically foolish) declaration "Ich bin ein Berliner", accompanied the new SPD mayor of the city to the Brandenburg celebration.

"Willy auf die Mauer" (Willy get up on the Wall) was soon the chant as the crowds flocked around the elder statesman. But Brandt declined their raucous invitation, preferring to gently salute them with a symbolic red rose a little girl had thrust into his hand.

After delivering a few words through an inadequate megaphone, Brandt was cornered by the American TV news crews. CBS, NBC and ABC were by now practically killing each other to persuade the architect of Ostpolitik (West Germany's patient policy of gradually-improved relations with the East) to say a few brief words to US breakfast time viewers.

Brandt duly obliged. "These are very moving times. It is especially moving to see families reunited again. We are very close to ending the period of artificial division that was so cruelly symbolised by the erection of the Wall," said the former Chancellor, suggesting, however, that it might be wise to preserve a section of the Wall as a monument to the hindrance of the movement of people.

What did he have to say to Americans this morning, asked Rather, plainly sensing that this was all getting a bit philosophical for the viewers back in Peoria. "I think the first thing Americans should understand is how grateful everyone is," responded Brandt. "We wouldn't have been able to survive the siege after the war or to come through the crisis that led to the Wall without American support."

Then the German question reared its inevitable head. Asked about the prospects for reunification, Brandt gave a calculatingly vague response. There could be one Germany again but it need not necessarily take the form of a single nation state. What kind of co-operation could only really be decided once the people of the GDR were free to exercise self- determination.

Reunification has been a goal of all Bonn governments since the post-war division of Germany – an objective enshrined, indeed, in the Federal Republic's Basic Law – but translating Sunday's speechifying into administrative reality will prove a momentous task for even the most seasoned diplomats. Last week, as the prospect for reunification at last looked real, the cry for one Germany started to sound increasingly Augustinian: unite us, oh Lord, but not yet!

The West German authorities seem to have enough on their hands for now coping with the sudden avalanche of East German visitors, without beginning to ponder the horrendous practicalities of reintegrating two polarised economies, societies and political systems. While emphasising that the West Germans would not turn anyone back, interior minister Wolfgang Schaeuble appealed to East Germans to think carefully before heading across the border. He told a hastily convened news conference on Thursday that the Federal Republic was struggling to provide shelter and accommodation for immigrants, despite having set up 140 emergency centres with space for 46,000 people.

The West German government is also upholding its practice of handing out 100 marks in welcome money to every East German who visits the West. The GDR, desperate as ever for hard currency, has still not dropped its much resented visa requirement that Western visitors exchange and spend 25 marks during their day trips to the East. The official exchange rate is one East German mark to one West German mark although a West German mark can fetch up to seven times as much on the streets of East Berlin.

In its appeal to the East German population, the West German government was plainly mindful of the concern among some of the West Berliners – contained to under-breath grumbling in the current euphoria – that the present tumultuous events could eventually prove financially costly to their hitherto cosy half of the city.

Isolated in the communist bloc, West Berlin has been heavily subsidised by the Federal Government in order to sustain its population and preserve its status as a capitalist showcase. But Federal funds could be diverted to the other side of the Wall, if the present trend continues and Bonn turns its attention to a reconstruction of the East German economy.

West German economic aid will not be restricted to what the state supplies. Major manufacturing companies, including Daimler Benz, Volkswagen, and the chemical giant BASF, have not concealed their eagerness to explore the possibility of setting up new branch plants inside East Germany. Politburo officials in East Berlin last week promised new legal safeguards for companies entering into such cross-border ventures.

"If the reforms are implemented and the capital becomes available, East Germany could become an extended work bench for West German industry," according to Heinz Vortmann, an East German specialist at the German Institute for Economic Research in West Berlin.

Whether this is the idea of freedom East Germany's opposition groups have been struggling for, is open to dispute. Although thoroughly disillusioned with the existing communist hierarchy, most seem far from enamoured by Western capitalism.

Many, however, remain cautious and watchful. Annetta, a 23-year-old nurse who fled from East Germany three months ago, is not itching to go back despite the events of the past few days. She left, she says, because her boyfriend lives in the West and because she had wanted to go to university in the East but was barred from doing so because she did not accord with the party ideology. "I left because the only people who have a chance in that country are people who conform with the communist system. You cannot say what you think."

November 12, 1989

The Campbells keep mum

Calum Neish

It has become an annual event over the past decade. Ever since the Campbell family reached double figures, the national and international media have been trying to get them to come out of their croft house overlooking Loch Bracadale on the Isle of Skye to tell their story. The answer is always the same, and will not change. Jessie Campbell will again keep mum when she returns home with her 20th child, a 10lb boy born in Inverness last week.

On the birth of No. 18, the family, now 12 boys and eight girls, were offered £3,000 by a women's magazine to talk and be photographed at the house that has been enlarged around them. The answer, as always: No. The desperation of the media to get the story counts for nothing with the head of the household, Skye-born John Campbell, a sturdy man in his early fifties, who looks out on the world through strict Free Presbyterian eyes. He will not allow television or Sunday newspapers into the house.

As a fundamentalist, he has a literal acceptance of the Bible, and if the good book says 'Go forth and multiply', John and Jessie obey. Local legend has it that John was once advised by a doctor to desist because, he said, the Biblical command to populate the earth was not intended to be achieved by one man.

As a layman, John preaches in his local church along the road and across the loch near Carbost. He is often seen shopping at Portree, the biggest town on the island, invariably of cheery disposition. He is a popular character, who has a number of nicknames in Gaelic and English associated with his prolific fatherhood. No-one would dream of using them face-to-face because of their distinctly earthy connotations.

Jessie, 44, who hails from Bonar Bridge in Sutherland, is less well known, but by all accounts is held in high regard within church circles and more widely by mothers in general for the appearance and well-being of her children.

Tabloid newspapers, in the absence of an interview, recently whipped up a story about the huge amount of child benefit the Campbells are entitled to claim, but even the more sensational among them would not print the rumour about the main post office on Skye ordering an armoured van to handle their cash deliveries. However, it is true that the Campbells' nearest sub-post office prefers not to have to deal with the amounts involved. The nearest shop would love to have their grocery account, but it is denied the opportunity because it is licensed for off-sales, and the family stay well away.

The Campbells have made life hell for this reporter, who in the past has been the medium engaged to make contact and to attempt to persuade them to go public – but not any longer. There was the over-confident American television network all set to send from New York a camera unit and ace interviewer to film "your quaint Scotch family with all the children" for prime-time broadcast coast-to-coast. They were advised not to bother, and didn't.

More recently, soon after the birth of the 19th child, a London-based producer commissioned me to ask the Campbells to travel with the new baby to London, all expenses paid, to appear on *Wogan*. Despite bluntly telling the producer the idea was a non-starter, she insisted. Jessie courteously listened on the phone, before asking: "Terry who?"

The eldest children are now in their twenties and, almost certainly, when the first Campbell wedding takes place, the photographer will have to agree to no commercial gain from the image of the family group – whatever its size. *January 28, 1990*

Extraordinary Joe

Robert Philip

New Orleans has always offered sanctuary to the Merchants of Menace: the Chitimacha Indians posed a greater threat to the early settlers than yellow fever, voodoo queen Marie Laveau plied her trade amid the brackish bayous of the Mississippi River, and the notorious pirate Jean Lafitte ran his business from a blacksmith's shop in Bourbon Street.

Tonight, The Big Easy will witness violence and mayhem of a 'sporting' nature, when the San Francisco 49ers and the Denver Broncos contest Superbowl XXIV, the climax of the American football season, with all the razzmatazz one would expect of an occasion which unashamedly bills itself 'the greatest show on earth'.

Forget Wimbledon, St Andrews, Yankee Stadium: if you like sport distilled of all artistry, invention and grace, the Louisiana Superdome, site of the 1988 Republican Convention, is the place to be. Sure, Superbowl XXIV will provide feats of strength, athleticism and courage. So would 22 Clydesdales if you gave them a football.

That said, the occasion does offer a rare opportunity to see a genuine all-American hero at work, San Francisco quarterback, Joe Montana, and also an excuse to visit the birthplace of jazz, ride the tram which inspired Tennessee Williams to write *A Streetcar Named Desire* and sample the best in Cajun food.

Those wise in such matters insist Montana is the greatest quarterback in history, better than Joe Namath, better than Johnny Unitas, better than Batman. When learning to count, American children reel off the figures 13, 14, 15, Montana, 17, 18...number 16 belongs to Joe. "He's football's Fred Astaire," says Namath. "So smooth, you don't notice the difficulty of what he's doing."

Three times a Superbowl winner, Montana, 33, has been with the 49ers for 11 years. During that time he has displayed near-mystical powers, leading seemingly hopelessly beaten teams to outrageous victory in the dying seconds of a game. For this talent, 'Comeback Joe', who lives with his model wife Jennifer and three children on the edge of the Pacific in California, has a contract worth $2 million a year plus the love of a nation – well, almost.

"A lot of people in Monongahela hate Joe because he's turned his back on his roots," explains the man who discovered Montana, former Ringgold High School coach Chuck Abramski. He also criticises his former protege for depending on his father, Joe senior. "Hell, if I was in a war I wouldn't want Joe at my side...his dad would have to carry his gun," says Abramski.

Monongahela, Pennsylvania (pop. 5,900) is an economically deprived area in the coal and steel valleys to the south of Pittsburgh, and 'Mr America' fell further from grace when, on 'Joe Montana Day 1982', the great man claimed travel expenses after 1,000 people turned out for a motorcade and chicken dinner.

After two failed marriages and a high profile nightlife, there have also been the inevitable rumours concerning 'sex, drugs and rock'n'roll'. "I'm probably not a lot different from the average guy," says Montana. But, unlike the average guy, he appears in television adverts for everything from underwear to soft drinks, and proposed to his present wife by having a plane fly overhead trailing a banner reading "Will you marry me?" while they picnicked in a San Francisco park.

"Unfortunately, my life is played out on a stage," says Montana. "When you go out for dinner, some gossip columnist isn't going to pay a waiter to find out if you put French or Italian dressing on your salad. I have to watch everything I do in public. I even stopped going to the rest-room in restaurants for a time because I knew if I went more than once people would accuse me of taking cocaine."

What remains unquestionable is Montana's valour. Unless hit by a moving train while looking the other way on a level crossing, the 'average guy' is unlikely to savour the unique experience of being smacked by 300lbs of angry, snorting nose-tackle. "I get banged up pretty bad but the linebackers play in a different pain zone. Their arms and shoulders are purple...and that's the bruises which are healing. The new welts, which run from wrist to neck, are somewhere between lipstick and fire-engine red."

The 49ers' locker-room has a rich tradition of raw animal instinct, like fearsome tight-end Jack 'Hacksaw' Reynolds, whose single-mindedness on match days included eating breakfast in full uniform – guiding huge forkfuls of scrambled egg through his helmet.

Away from the 52-acre, Louisiana Superdome (the dome measures 680ft in diameter), New Orleans has much to offer, from topless, bottomless bars which stay open until dawn – with waiters and waitresses – to a maze of picturesque streets in the French Quarter, providing jazz in every doorway. Assuming you are immune to the effects of calories and alcohol, it is possible to spend a 'perfect' day wandering the narrow alleys, with their three-storey wooden houses painted every pastel shade and featuring filigreed balconies, shutters and gables, with the occasional stop for sustenance along the way.

Let us start with the world-renowned 'Breakfast at Brennan's' for a bloody Mary and eggs Benedict, followed by mid-morning refreshment at the Pontchartrain Hotel where the speciality is Mile-High Pie – 8in of peppermint, vanilla and strawberry ice-cream, meringue and chocolate sauce.

Since we are saving ourselves for dinner, a light lunch of shrimp Creole and salad in the Palm Court Jazz Cafe will suffice until our arrival at Galatoire's, where the late Duke and Duchess of Windsor lined up like everyone else for chicken jambalaya before going on for a post-prandial cognac at Benny's Blues Bar.

None of this, of course, is for the players. When asked which of New Orleans' fabulous restaurants he would patronise, Montana answered: "Room service".

Finally, while Crocodile Dundee was a figment of Hollywood's imagination ...Alligator Annie is not. Annie Miller runs boat trips into the swamps and marshes of south Louisiana, attracting the reptiles into camera range by calling out their names – Smiling Sam, Toothless Tommy, and the deliciously named Larry Limb.

Montana should feel right at home among Sam and co. His favourite form of "relaxation" is to film sharks off the coast of Santa Barbara...in and out of the protective cage. As he says: "A quarterback has to be a little bit crazy. Anyone who is set to have his ribs broken every day can't be playing with a full deck."

January 28, 1990

Framed

Alan Taylor

The women's magazine *Marie Claire* is the last place you would expect to find Ronald Frame's name, except perhaps anomalously included in the round-up of 'fast reads for the beach'. But here he is, however, in the July issue, credited as a contributor, sandwiched between the confessions of a 33-year-old virgin and the sad stories of couples who married in haste and promptly wished they hadn't. Frame's contribution comes under Comment: 'Momentous Truths in Public Places'. "It is my only foray into journalism," he pleads in mitigation. "Scottish writer Ronald Frame," froths *Marie Claire*, "is often inspired by eavesdropping."

"Why is it," asks Frame, "that we choose to make highly serious disclosures and offer momentous truths in such places," by which he means "restaurants and cafes where you can sit comfortably on a padded stool, preferably with some kind of spinal support and which swings for ease of observation." He has the answer to his own question: "I suppose because we hope that the presence of other customers will help to contain the damage, discourage verbal fallout."

Sitting in a Glasgow restaurant, loud with lunchtime diners and the ubiquitous Pavarotti, I suppose I am hoping the same. But if he is a 33-year-old or, to be accurate, a 37-year-old virgin, Ronald Frame does not volunteer the information. Nor does he mention marriage, though I suspect he might have liked to eavesdrop on the couple who stuck it for 10 days before she slapped his face and he tapped her with a Mike Tyson. There would have been a short story in that.

Instead, we talk about swimming. Every day Ronald Frame, manacled to routine, swims at his club. His habit is to get up early and work. His method is laborious. He handwrites his increasingly lengthy books before entrusting them to typists. "They're very good at what they do." For the book he is currently working on, he abandoned cursive script and measured out each word in capitals, a process that makes one fear for his sanity. ("All writers should be a little mad," says Frame.)

Apparently the novelist William Boyd passed on the tip. The thought that he may have been sending Frame up occurred to me, though it's more likely that it was a vain attempt to dam the flood of books from the prolific Glaswegian. Since his debut with *Winter's Journey* in 1984 there have been another seven books; short stories, novels, plays, and a solitary article for *Marie Claire*.

The swimming pool is Frame's regular social outing. There he chalks up the metres, making astute observations about the weather to fellow doggy paddlers. Though mathematically precise in the way he talks and works, he has trouble keeping count of the lengths. His thoughts drift towards work: "Inspiration can come anywhere." The pool attendants, he says, speculated on what he did for a living. Though he has never worn a stethoscope (either inside or outside the pool), they have decided that he must be a doctor. He has not put them straight. Now he gets inquiries from infirm bathers about their ailments. "I usually prescribe fresh air," says Frame, patently pleased to be of service.

Were these arthritic, breathless men to find their way into his novels, however, one wonders if the prescriptions would be the same. For Frame, like Anita Brookner and Thomas Mann, both favourite authors, has a penchant for spas, watering-holes for the tubercular, where lives fade like curtains exposed to sunlight. The glamour of spa life, conspicuous in *Bluette*, his latest novel, is undeniably appealing to Frame, a scion of Bearsden, where little tragedies lurk behind lace curtains and "tumultuous truths" are uttered over afternoon tea and shortbread.

For Ronald Frame is the poet of *the dansant*, obsessed with the minutiae of women's lives. He could read a dress label, one suspects, through a fur coat. But he dismisses what he calls the Ovaltine style of writing, dropping brand-names to evoke the past. Where he is guilty of it, he confesses, in *Penelope's Hat*, his last novel, and in *Bluette*, even in *Winter's Journey*, is in the matter of sports cars. "There were so many British makes around in the '50s," he says addressing an auto-illiterate. "Anyway, I like the idea of putting people in cars. They're incredibly dangerous mechanisms, you know. The business of being apparently in control of your own destiny while being at the mercy of this power is quite appealing."

Cars, however, are simply props in sinister, sensual dramas. In the novels, and in stories like *Paris* which was dramatized for television, Frame paws over women's pasts, the homoerotic obsession with clothes, silk stockings, evening dresses, even hats. Half-open doors, unfinished sentences, a child's eye view attract readers like gatecrashers into worlds where lives are cracking like glass, splintering those in their orbit. Romantic music, the cinema, foreign places, invade Ronald Frame's fictions like adultery until, ultimately, anywhere becomes everywhere, the product of imagination. The externals may be Bath or Glasgow or Paris but what is created is "an odd dimensionless city". "What interests me," he says, "is this business of collecting a life together, amassing all the truths and evasions, the enigma that people make of themselves."

Enigma in Frame's book is a priceless asset, adding mystic to authorship. "I've always been interested in writers I knew very little about; what you should be doing is cultivating anonymity." Consequently, you can fatten a cv with facts but you will be no nearer to the man. In Glasgow, he seems out of place but his accent is *echt* Bearsden, and even when he is not writing about Scotland there are hints and allegations of his Scottishness. Yet he does not fit in with the world's eye view of what makes a Glasgow writer. In surveys and critical articles he is ignored or mentioned *en passant*. "I think a lot of the London coverage of the Glasgow literary scene has been extremely patronising," he comments. "Very much a pat on the head." He is not working-class, has never been to a greyhound track (or one assumes he hasn't), does not habituate pubs; the buroo, dowts and the *Daily Record* are alien to his vocabulary. "There is a whole area of the city," he says, "that isn't even treated. I'm as Scottish as anybody else that is writing here. It's just that I do it in a slightly different way."

Could he write anywhere else? Where he writes, he says, is immaterial. "Hotel bathrooms, preferably," he says, stroking his manicured beard. "I love bathrooms without windows and ventilators. Shut me in there for nine months and I would come out with a book."

July 1, 1990

Week of judgment

William Paul and Kenny Farquharson

No words were wasted when the resignation of Lord Dervaird was announced by the Scottish Office on Friday, December 22. A single sentence press notice recorded the fact that he was to step down from the bench on the first day of the new year. It was hoped that would be the end of the story, but the curt statement begged one question which intrigued legal, political and media circles: Why?

Why does a 54-year-old judge, universally regarded by colleagues as a highly intelligent, fast-rising star, suddenly decide to quit after less than two years in the position that advocates work all their lives to achieve?

No-one in authority was prepared to say. And as the speculative rumours gained force, Dervaird – formerly John Murray, QC – retreated to his cottage at Craigcaffie, near Stranraer to spend Christmas with his wife and three adult sons. Reporters from a number of newspapers visited the cottage but all requests for more information were steadfastly refused by Lady Dervaird. Scottish Office spokesmen were equally unforthcoming, adding only that the resignation had been deferred to January 1 to allow Dervaird to deliver a particularly complex judgment on a case involving British Coal and the South of Scotland Electricity Board, the last case he was to preside over as a judge.

Rumours had been circulating among advocates and lawyers in the corridors of Parliament House and in the Jolly Judge, Quill,

Snatchers and Valentines public houses where, in the words of one observer, the rules of evidence are interpreted more loosely than anywhere else.

The recent rumours first surfaced early in November but gained further currency during an embezzlement trial at the beginning of December associated with the collapse of an Edinburgh solicitors' practice, Burnett Walker. The firm's senior partner, Ian Walker, a practising homosexual, hanged himself 18 months previously during Law Society investigations into book-keeping irregularities. During the trial homosexuality became a central issue and the names of certain judges were mentioned in behind the scenes discussions. The trial ended on December 18 last year with the acquittal of Colin Tucker, 35, of charges of embezzling £46,000 from two elderly female clients of the firm.

Dervaird's resignation was announced three days later and the rumours quickly spread to a wider, less circumspect audience. Court clerks and reporters recalled one of Dervaird's few criminal trials, a side of the law he preferred to avoid, when he was apparently brought close to tears as he sentenced Edward Slater, 24, to life imprisonment for murdering a man who had made a homosexual advance to him. Observers were puzzled by his emotional response.

Scotland's professional circles were gripped with rumour; no lunch or dinner party was complete without speculation as to why Dervaird had resigned. Soon the rumours concerned not only Dervaird but other judges. The majority of the speculation centred on a cottage in the south-west of Scotland, and another in the Borders, where wild homosexual parties were said to have taken place with some of those present being under-age boys from London. This had led to the Metropolitan Police in London asking for assistance from Scottish police in investigating an alleged vice ring. This link is alleged to have led to an unnamed judge being questioned by police.

The inescapable implication was of scandal and cover-up. The rumours would not go away. The legal establishment clearly did not want to reveal the reasons for Dervaird's resignation. The situation was fast running out of control and causing increasing damage to public confidence in the judiciary.

Last week *Scotland on Sunday* broke the conspiracy of silence in a front page news story in which Menzies Campbell, QC, the MP for North-east Fife, said: "Rumours of this kind are damaging if they proceed unchecked. The public must have total confidence in its judges. Any hint of the risk of compromise is unacceptable. The public's anxiety needs to be allayed."

The story stung the legal establishment, reaching the highest echelons and triggering an extraordinary series of events.

A few days later, the editors of Scotland's principal newspapers, with controllers of radio and television, were asked to a briefing at a private home in Edinburgh's New Town at 3pm. They arrived from all over Scotland, many with little idea as to why they had been summoned: most had not even brought notebooks or paper, but all were curious given the source of the invitation.

As each editor entered the Georgian hall, their names were carefully ticked off at the door before they were ushered into a large book-lined study where a long oval polished mahogany table had been extended by the length of a smaller table to accommodate the 25 men. The atmosphere was tense and curiously nervous. There had never been a meeting like it and no-one knew what to expect.

After a futile 20-minute wait for David Scott, Scottish Television's controller of news and current affairs, the briefing, given by an influential member of the legal establishment, started with a request that the information about to be revealed was on a strictly unattributable basis – as is the case with Downing Street briefings by Mrs Thatcher's press secretary, Bernard Ingham. Everyone agreeing to those terms was asked to raise his hand. Every hand was raised. When Scott arrived later, he was asked to give the same pledge. It is because of that undertaking, which *Scotland on Sunday* has been told is still in force, that we cannot name the person who gave the briefing.

It was explained that the meeting had been called following the publication of *Scotland on Sunday's* front page article 'Worry over judges rumours', parts of which were read out by way of an introduction. Over the next 90 minutes the astonished editors were candidly told what was officially known of the rumours and the way in which they had been dealt with. The editors, most of whom had thought their reporting days were over, furiously scribbled away. Arnold Kemp, editor of the *Glasgow Herald* used the covers of his cheque book and then borrowed some writing paper. Magnus Linklater, editor of *The Scotsman*, had to tear sheets of paper from his notebook for colleagues on each side of him.

The editors were aware of some of the rumours but were amazed by the detail they were told. In addition to Dervaird, the rumours surrounded the behaviour of four serving judges, listed anonymously as judges A, B, C, and D.

The allegations had reached Lord Hope, who was only installed as Lord President and head of the Scottish judiciary last September, through his principal clerk Hugh Foley. Hope, one of the youngest men to hold the office, had been Dean of the Faculty of Advocates since 1986 where he had earned a formidable reputation as a reformer. He also introduced measures to tighten the code of conduct to safeguard professional standards. He is regarded as a "new broom" and his appointment over the heads of the old guard of sitting judges came as something of a shock, given that he had never sat as a judge himself.

At first, Hope had been minded to ignore the rumours and take no action. However, the editors were told that on December 20, officials of the Crown Office and the Scottish Courts Administration – after arranging a lunchtime meeting by telephone – placed certain allegations about Dervaird before Hope.

The allegations were of a homosexual nature and Hope deemed them worthy of swift action. Dervaird was summoned to appear before him later that afternoon when court business had finished for the day. When challenged, Dervaird conceded that there was some substance to the allegations. The following day Dervaird submitted his letter of resignation to Hope though it was addressed to the Secretary of State, who formally appoints judges.

On Friday, after agreeing a resignation timetable which would allow the judgment on the British Coal/SSEB case to be delivered by Dervaird, came the terse public announcement. Dervaird had done "the honourable thing". The editors were also told about four other serving judges. Judge A was also interviewed by Hope but strongly denied allegations that he had been to a gay bar in Glasgow with a junior member of the bar involved in the same High Court circuit. The person was, Judge A claimed, his godson and they had been having a drink before going to dinner and it was clearly a case of mistaken identity.

Other allegations, also covered by the first denial, were that he had attended a gay disco, and a cottage in the south-west of Scotland where criminal conduct with under-age boys is alleged to have taken place. The Lord Advocate had carried out checks into the last allegation and could find no evidence of criminal conduct. Some rumours about Judge A were so wild that one suggested he had resigned, another that he had died.

Judge B had not been interviewed but alerted to the rumours circulating about his conduct. The only specific allegation was that he went to a gay disco in Glasgow before leaving "in disgust". Judges C and D were also the subject of unspecified rumours but nothing that warranted investigation.

Questions were then invited from the editors prompting a discussion on just how promiscuous a homosexual judge could be before attracting the displeasure of the Lord President. A stable relationship was considered acceptable, but at the same time it was unwise of any judge to go into a place frequented by homosexuals. Were judges A to D keen sailors, it was asked. Judge C has never been to sea, was the reply.

"The problem in dealing with rumours is that you can only counter them by telling what you know," the editors were told. "The way in which you present this material will have an effect on the country's judicial administration."

As the meeting broke up at 4.30pm, Steve Sampson, editor of the *Sun* in Scotland, told the senior legal source that he would be "going big" on the story. The reaction, he claimed, was one of genuine surprise. In the street outside, Sampson slipped into the back seat of his chauffeur-driven white Mercedes shouting into his portable telephone: "Clear pages 1 to 3. This is the big one."

Reports of the meeting broke on the radio news at 5pm and Scottish Television's *Scotland Today* news programme led its 6pm bulletin with a report. *News at Ten* ran it as the second item, Sir Alastair Burnet announcing that: "A Scottish judge is forced to resign." In the House of Commons, demands for a statement came from the Scottish Nationalist member Jim Sillars. That was refused.

The next morning's newspapers included screaming tabloid headlines with the single word 'SCANDAL' emblazoned across the *Sun*. *The Scotsman* front page had 'Judges in homosexual inquiries' and the *Herald* 'Judges questioned on vice ring claims'. The undertaking not to name the source of the information was broken by English papers who were not present at the briefing.

Later that afternoon in the Commons, Sir Geoffrey Howe, who as Leader of the House is responsible for the day's business, rejected another demand for a government statement. Sillars, arguing that the public had a right to know the reasons for Dervaird's resignation, could provoke no response from the Scottish Secretary, Malcolm Rifkind, or the Lord Advocate, Lord Fraser of Carmyllie, the government's chief law officer in Scotland, who advises the Queen on judicial appointments.

That night, a statement was issued to *The Scotsman* by Lord Weir, a High Court judge since 1985, denying that he is involved in homosexual activity. The statement, issued through his solicitors, said: "The Honourable Lord Weir wishes it to be known that he was one of the judges interviewed by the Lord President of the Court of Session, and in relation to whom the Lord President made reference in his statement to representatives of the press on Wednesday, January 17. There is no truth whatsoever in any allegation that he has engaged in homosexual conduct, associated with homosexuals or otherwise behaved in a manner unbecoming a judge. He makes this statement in order to dispel rumours relating to him which have been brought to his notice. He will not hesitate to take appropriate action should there be any repetition of such defamatory rumours which, by their very nature, are distressing to him and his family. No further comment will be made."

Following further press inquiries, the Crown Office felt it necessary to issue a statement on Friday explaining that checks on the rumours of misconduct by judges had been made and had revealed no basis for further investigation. It concluded: "Allegations of non-criminal conduct by judges are not matters for investigation by the Lord Advocate."

Formal disciplinary matters have never previously been a problem at the highest level of the law. Before Dervaird no judge in Scotland has ever resigned in tainted circumstances.

This weekend Lord Hope is isolated at the pinnacle of the legal establishment, striving to control the biggest legal scandal ever to break in Scotland. Within legal circles, some regard the decision to call in the editors as a brave move, designed to meet the rumours head on, rather than let them go unchallenged. Another school of thought is that the matter has been handled badly and that there should have been no briefing at all. Opinion is also divided over what the briefing was intended to achieve.

The briefing strategy was based on advice that Hope had received from the Lord Advocate's office. But this weekend questions remain as to whether the Crown Office's attempt to check the rumours of criminal activity was unable to unearth the full story in the absence of a formal complaint which would have allowed the launch of a more comprehensive inquiry. But as the editors were repeatedly told, it has not been possible to "look behind every bush and crag". Should any specific allegation be made, the Lord Advocate has promised a full investigation. But while the only remaining evidence is rumour, the verdict will always be not proven.

January 21, 1990

Mr Lim's corner shop

Joanna Blythman

Saturday mornings in Thiam Lim's Chung Ying supermarket have a certain rhythm. Up until 11am the staff scurries around, purposefully labelling and pricing that morning's consignment of fresh shrimp and chive noodles, rice sticks, char sui dumplings and spicy chicken feet, while a few non-Chinese Scots look around in a desultory fashion.

Around 11.15 the first wave of Chinese women arrive, homing in on the new fresh additions to the 600-line supermarket. There is a lot of chat. Mr Lim's presence is required out front to answer questions about freshness and quality. Once reassured, the women drift to the till where they stand and discuss, or browse through yesterday's copy of the *China Daily* or *Sing Tao*.

"They are shopping for their lunch," explains Mr Lim. "There is no pattern to Scottish shoppers, they seem to come in at different times each week, but the Chinese are like clockwork." In fact, it is fairly obvious that the local Chinese community from the area around Garnethill (a miniature Chinatown, according to Mr Lim), uses Lim's not as a supermarket, but as a corner shop. They come to see what fresh fish has been bought from Peterhead and Aberdeen that day, crabs, lemon sole and grey mullet being the favourites. Or, on a Wednesday, to buy labour-saving dim sum snacks for steaming sent up from Liverpool. Here they can be sure of getting the sort of chicken they prefer, with head and feet still on, either young for stirfrying and braising, or old for boiling to make a broth. They can rely on finding fresh buns and dumplings from the Night Palace Chinese Bakery in Drumchapel.

But where Mr Lim's emporium differs from the daunting Chinese supermarket where you might well be met with inscrutable blank faces and come away with the feeling that unless you are a Chinese restaurateur, your trade is largely immaterial, Mr Lim takes Scottish retail custom extremely seriously. In Mandarin, Chung Ying means Chinese doing business in Britain, and since he took over what was primarily a wholesale operation 18 months ago, his custom is now almost exclusively retail and at least 50% non-Chinese. "Most Scottish customers wouldn't come in before. It was orientated only for the Chinese and there was no customer service." This achievement has come about partly through Lim's own commitment to integration and also the efforts of Margaret Lim, his Scottish wife, who is an articulate advocate of Chinese cooking.

"We get people coming in who are intrigued about all the things they see but who don't know what to do with them. We explain to them simply how to go about things and encourage them that once they have understood the basic principles, then they can make anything," says Margaret. The Lims, who eat exclusively Chinese food at home, realise that it is hard for Scots to get used to fundamental Chinese approaches like steaming. "When Chinese see a fish, they want to steam it, but the Scots want to fry it. Scottish food is all fried – chips, chips and chips. It's not healthy."

It is what Mr Lim calls the 'old lady stuff' which most baffles the Scots. Items like century eggs, granite speckled and salty (for soup broths) or dehydrated sugar cane (a cooling drink for hot days) or bamboo tea (to promote energy on a cold day), or lotus seed cake with a whole salted duck egg inside (to celebrate full moons) are not found in the accessible pages of Ken Hom's BBC cook book.

Thiam Lim, of Chinese descent but born in Malaysia, speaks three Chinese dialects, plus Malay, German and English, and makes a point of catering for a broad South-east Asian community. In Lim's you will find Indonesian favourites like sweet soy sauce, Vietnamese chilli paste with basil leaves, Thai lemon grass and Singaporean chestnuts.

Old habits and bad habits are hard to break as much for the Chinese as for Europeans. 'White taste powder' or 'flavour enhancer', better known as monosodium glutamate, is still on sale, but relegated to small, discreet packages on a low shelf. "I feel it's my duty to explain that it isn't all that healthy and offer non-MSG substitutes, but the Chinese much prefer the MSG ones," says Lim. Reading the labels is essential. Spicy steamed Chinese sausages made in West London contain the white powder, those made by Vietnamese in Strasbourg do not. Junk food comes in the form of pot noodle look-alike tubs of 'Instant Noodles with Artificial Beef Flavour' retailing with refreshing candour at 42p. Cans of 7UP and Irn-Bru jostle with grass jelly and lychee drink.

Even for timorous cooks who have yet to crack Chinese cuisine, supermarkets like Lim's are the place to buy larder items like peppercorns, cardamon, top grade long grain rice from Thailand, or dried mushrooms. Seen there as basics, they do not attract premium prices. This is the best venue for purchasing a wok and at the same time getting lucid instructions on the courageous business of seasoning it properly so that it doesn't rust irretrievably within a month of purchase. And shopping for Christmas presents is painless (and cheap) here, with dainty six-tin sets of mixed green teas for under £3 and stocking fillers of crunchy, sweet black sesame snacks, or jars of Tianjin Preserved Cabbage at £1.29.

Irrespective of what the cabbage tastes like, the aubergine-glazed ceramic pot with its straight-from-the-mummy's-tomb lid is worth it just for appearances. Lateral thinking can pay off. Chinese tramlines need not prevail. Why not buy some spring roll skins to stuff with anything from ratatouille to mincemeat or chop some fragrant pink Thai shallots over your potato salad, or make a sorbet with Jasmine tea? If in doubt what to do, just ask Mr Lim.

October 15, 1989

May stands by her man

Sue Innes

I really meant to find something cheery to write about this week. All this brooding on the state of the Scottish male psyche that I've been doing recently does a gel not a lot of good in the long run. But with the escapades of Romeo Ron, as he is now known, all over the headlines it has been rather unavoidable.

The tabloids and sections of the Leith Labour Party have decided Ron Must Go (the papers, I suspect, as much for the internal rhyme of the headline as anything else). It would seem that it was his refusal to be even remotely contrite – especially the champagne episode – that has most bothered people.

But it won't be too surprising if Ron survives; sex doesn't hurt a man's reputation too much and it is that that has become the issue. It may all reinforce his self-defined role as an anti-establishment man. Though actually this *is* how the Establishment behaves; only it has more experience in not losing the heid and being found out.

And the case has revealed undoubted political skills. Anyone with the capacity to call black white (as in being fined for smashing up a flat and calling it a moral victory) and more importantly getting that definition into every headline in sight with the strong implication that you've won something, surely deserves a place in cabinet.

If he survives it will be more to do with the conspicuous support of his wife than anything else. Women standing by their men are – understandably enough – taken as a crucial test of truth and character. The starring role of the "fragrant" Mary Archer, made explicit by the judge in the *Star* libel case is a notable recent example. Nor does Ron Brown underestimate May Brown's role; he believes his constituents are realistic enough to take the same line as his wife.

And indeed there is something attractive in her robust realism. She has been described as masochistic yet she is clearly not so, but a strong woman who knows her own mind. Warm, motherly, tough and not overly inhibited – it's not just the name that gives her a resemblance to Ma Broon.

May is considered to be the brains, the organising force, and the worker of the family. She is both his (paid) secretary and the treasurer of the Leith Labour Party; her tireless work behind the scenes is credited as the secret of his reselection; she is responsible for a very great deal of the constituency work and it is his attention to constituents' concerns which is the main reason for his local support. A number of party activists have suggested that without her behind him he'd have an even harder time surviving and that she would make a better MP than him.

Then why isn't she? The real puzzle about her stalwart support is: what's in it for May?

No doubt she has come, long ago, to some accommodation; but it is hard to believe that she has not felt jealous and humiliated and angry. No doubt she's no oppressed saint. (Indeed one can only hope that in recompense she has a nice fella on the side – though given the double standards on sexual adventuring it's a bit unlikely.) The parallel of Newcastle-under-Lyme MP Llin Golding is perhaps relevant; when her husband John, who was MP, resigned over a sex scandal she – already credited with doing most of the work anyway – took the nomination and then the seat.

It would be a bit over the top to say that behind *every* great man is a woman who should have his job – but the phenomenon of the wife who does the work or has the ideas and the man who gets the credit is a very common one. Nonetheless, in the still male-dominated networks of politics, no matter how hard they work, no matter their own gifts, those women can lose their role and identity if they lose the man.

And women, rather than expressing ambition directly, will often do it through a man. If men benefit from the support and work, women benefit from the ultimate let off – when it hits the fan he's first in line; she can both hide behind him, and gain a few brownie points for her selfless devoted support into the bargain. But it is time more women were both braver and better supported to get into that front line, with all its risks and rewards, for themselves.

Scottish women are proud that they stand by their man – personally I prefer the Liz Lochhead version to the Tammy Wynette.

'If you love him you'll forgive him, bite your tongue and pass a can

/ and if you love him be proud of him 'cos after all he's jist a man.'

"I don't need to forgive him, because men do have affairs with other women," May Brown has said. "If you are a wife you just accept it." It is the classic view that men can't really be held responsible for their actions, poor dears, and we just have to be tolerant of their inadequacy. Robust realism and compromise does have something going for it – but within the traditional marriage a view of men that is far from flattering subsists beneath the apparent glorification of his role and virtues. It is manipulative and motherly and ultimately patronising; women do the hard work, keep things together and get precious little thanks or credit for it, but that's the way it is. "They're just wee laddies, aren't they" (said in an indulgent, self-satisfied tone). Women who think like that think women who call for change are naive and immature. But a belief in egalitarianism at least gives men the credit that they're up to it.

Women, it seems, will still forgive men next to everything. Think of the assorted wives of sex criminals, murderers and so on, loyally observing he's a nice chap really apart from this difficult-to-understand tendency of tearing young women apart.

One motive, I guess, is that suddenly he really needs you after all. Sweet forgiveness is power of a sort. It can be hard to resist a chap when he's down but it would be more flattering to both him and us to relate a little more honestly when he's up.

Another double standard has been evident throughout Ron Brown's trial. Just as in rape trials – though it's now supposed not to happen – the details of Nonna Longden's sexual relations and her taste in lovers and their previous offences have been as much at issue under cross-examination as Ron Brown's conduct.

In the reporting of the case it has also been presented as very much a moral issue, to do with adultery and the proper sexual behaviour of people in public life.

What arrangement or accommodation Ron and May Brown have made is up to them. The public and political issue is domestic violence, the harassment and intimidation of a woman, the smashing up of her home. In celebrating being found guilty of that, but not of theft, Ron Brown has made clear he sees it as a relatively trivial matter. Adultery is a private matter, but domestic violence and harassment must not be.

It is not to excuse those crimes to feel that the endless parade of women standing by their men, no matter what, both makes the male behaviour acceptable and makes it harder for ordinary women to fight against domestic violence and humiliating behaviour. In the words of a colleague of mine: "She's taken us back 10 years". Maybe that's what Ron Brown found worth celebrating with champagne.

January 14, 1990

Urban Voltaire

Kenneth Roy

It is noon in Heraghty's Bar, and the self-styled Urban Voltaire of Scottish journalism sinks the first of the day's whiskies. By the end of the night, he will have consumed half a bottle of the stuff, smoked 60 cigarettes, and battered out another 900 words of invective for his *Glasgow Herald* column. The column is written in less than an hour – 40 minutes is his record – but the drinking is more sustained. He expects to die young.

When I first met Jack McLean, he was an art teacher in Glasgow, a part-time contributor to educational journals, and even then – this was the early '70s – a prodigious drinker. He was the flashiest toff I had ever encountered. He is still.

"Why shouldn't you act the toff? Put on the style? It's a very Glaswegian thing, don't you think? Glaswegians like vividness and colour. We're gypsies."

There are, it has to be said, precious few gypsies in Heraghty's this particular lunchtime: only a camel-coated punter talking about his forthcoming appearance before the Sheriff, and a scattering of wee men in bunnets. How splendidly incongruous he looks, the extravagant figure in the corner by the door, nearest the buses that trundle along the Pollokshaws Road. Jack is wearing one of his immaculate light grey suits with matching tie and hankie, and an absurdly expensive watch. On the table are other essential props in his repertoire: his felt hat, his whisky and cigarettes, and a brown envelope containing a publicity picture.

He sends autographed copies of the picture – a terrible parody of a Hollywood tough guy – to his fans. But I wonder if his fans might not be vastly outnumbered by his enemies. When he won some media award a year ago, he was described as "a controversial, but much-loved columnist". I confess that until then I had never thought of McLean as a much-loved anything.

"You hate a lot, don't you?"

"You could do an awful boring column about the things you like. Everything I write has passion in it. I let the words rule the logic. I'd hang myself for a good phrase. Because of that, I'm a bit cruel sometimes."

"What are your main targets?"

"I was offensive about single parents not so long ago. Modern education, I hate. Modern anything. Hate television. Hate certain attitudes to the arts – this view that high-up forms are something beyond the wit of common man. Fact is, the people who go to Scottish Opera are a collection of jumped-up insurance salesmen."

"You don't like media women either, do you?"

"Well, so few of them are any good. All that soft stuff about health and bloody yoga. But I certainly support women's rights in every way. If they want to be just like men, let them go right ahead. But I don't see why the rest of us should have to accept their theory that all men are beasts or that anyone who goes even slightly against the feminist grain has to be some macho bastard."

"Do you like women at all?"

"Not only that," he boasted, draining a second whisky, "women like me. But one thing is for certain. I'd never dream of getting married, and I'll never live with a woman again. Never."

"Why not?"

"You can't get away from them. You know that great Scottish phrase, 'Your life's no' yer ain'? That's so true, isn't it?"

"If you love somebody, you don't want to get away from them."

"How long's that gonna last? They don't want you out huntin', they want you in that bloody cage with the boulder in front of it."

"So you prefer living on your own?"

"God, yes."

It was not always so. Until her death a few years ago, Jack lived with his widowed mother. Unlike the other women in his life, Mrs McLean made no demands on him. She was "a very shy wee girl" who fed him and polished his shoes every morning. I must have looked askance at this revelation, for he added that he was in no sense a mammy's boy. Then he said: "That sounds like a protest, doesn't it?" Yes.

Her death, slowly and distressingly, from Alzheimer's Disease, made Jack McLean very lonely. In his grief, he wrote a direct, simple little tribute, all the more moving for being shorn of the writer's usual spectacular effects.

His father was a regular soldier turned school janitor. "I was close to him as well. No, that's a lie. I loved him dearly, but he used to knock hell out of me." Jack McLean's father was another of that vanished generation of working-class Scottish patriarchs so often encountered in these interviews: a man with an almost sacred belief in education. Jack was sent as a bursary boy to Allan Glen's School – "the only high school of science and technology in the whole of bloody Britain, and I could hardly count."

He disappointed his father by doing badly at school. He had a succession of jobs – apprentice welder in a Clyde shipyard ("I might have brought the yards down single-handedly"), bus conductor, barman, cleaner. He went to London for a while during the swinging '60s, but found that London did not swing for him. Then he discovered that in Lanarkshire there was such a shortage of teachers they would put a monkey in front of a class. He got a job as an uncertificated teacher of art. He liked that. People called him Mr McLean.

"Were you a good teacher?"

"Bloody excellent for the first few years. People say I'm a failed art teacher, but for God's sake I taught for 20 years. These are the same people who're looking for early retirement at 45. When I started, people were 70 and still working at it, still enjoying it. But nobody wants to stay now."

"What's changed?"

"The teachers don't know what their real role is. There's this sentimental idea of child-centred education. For a while, I was rather good at writing this sloppy, left-wing, intelligentsia drivel myself. But schools aren't set up for individual children, they're there to make sure the kid can earn a living and add something to the rest of society. It's as cold as that."

Not only cold, but narrow and bleak as well. What about education for education's sake? Jack thought that was a grand idea: up to a point. But I should not delude myself that the majority of children who couldn't cope at school were sorry wee lads. They were a reluctant proletariat because they refused to be anything else. They were little bastards. He spat out the word with some relish. Another whisky bit the sawdust.

I could forgive Jack McLean practically anything, but not his occasional shrill demand for the restoration of corporal punishment in schools. Had he belted a lot? He thought maybe a couple of times a year, as hard as possible – but generally he had been a bit of a softy. He invited me to consult any of his former pupils for confirmation. When I asked why, then, he would bring back the belt, he replied that it might help to reduce truancy and housebreaking.

"It was institutionalised sadism."

"I don't think so," he said cautiously. "I think there were some teachers who went over the top. But that was a lesson to be learned as well."

"What lesson?"

"The lesson that some people are bad bastards."

"Bastard is one of your favourite words. What is a bastard in your book?"

"A bastard is somebody that doesn't actually care about the other guy. Somebody who disnae give a damn. Schoolteaching is full of shocking people. The polis, too. A lot of them start off as decent young lads and end up as fascists. And look at our profession. Packed to the gunnels with bastards. Canopies of cynicism. No let-up. Nothing's ever fun. Everybody's out to do everybody else. It's no' true, is it?"

"Are there journalists you admire?"

Jack had a long think about that, and reeled off a few names without enthusiasm. Then he settled upon his *Glasgow Herald* colleague, William Hunter. "Willie goes beyond flippancy. Goes beyond seriousness as well. He reaches heights of utter poetry. Put that in."

Bastard apart, Jack's favourite word is sentimental. He uses it pejoratively almost always, except when he is talking about Country and Western music.

Modern education is sentimental bad. I suspect he is beginning to believe that socialism is sentimental bad, too. He hasn't voted in years, and once advised his readers to support the Tories. But still, for some reason, I think of McLean as an old-fashioned authoritarian left-winger. Of course, maybe that is just being sentimental.

"Despite everything, do you remain a socialist?"

"I don't know. What's socialism now? I'm in favour of the sale of council houses. Better bloody idea than getting messed around by the council. And a meritocracy is a good idea. Why shouldn't the most talented people rise to the top?"

"Socialism is about humanitarian values which don't put capital first."

"Socialism," he retorted, "is about a pleasant sentimental notion that we should be rather nicer to each other. Bit Christian, isn't it?"

"What's wrong with that?"

"It's not hard enough. It's not going to solve much."

It is now 2.30 in Heraghty's Bar. The camel-coated punter has gone – to face the bookie or perhaps the bench. The wee bunnets have disappeared as silently as they arrived. Outside, it is offensively sunny. Jack orders more whisky, and the pub talk moves effortlessly from politics to religion, as it surely must in any self-respecting Glasgow pub.

"Do you believe in God?"

"Not at all," he said, with a kind of half-laugh. "Wish I did. It would be an awful comfort, wouldn't it?"

"What happens when you die?"

"My deepest suspicion is that nothing happens. Finish."

"Did you feel that when your mother died?"

"Yes. But I wish – more than anything else, I wish – that my mother was up there. Not so much because I want to be united with her again – I had a good 40 years with her – but so that she could see how I'm getting on. But I don't believe it. Do you?"

"Probably."

"Is that a comfort to you?"

"Not if God is another of your hard bastards."

"Looks like He is, doesn't it?" said Jack McLean.

He is 45. He reckons he will be dead by 55 – 500 columns from now and heaven knows how many whiskies. Before he goes, he does not intend to write the Great Scottish Novel – "why imagine all these people in your head, when you've got real people in front of you?" But he is already planning an early autobiography, in preparation for the fatal heart attack and obliteration. It should be a funny book.

April 1, 1990

Sexy's City

Graham Spiers

It rained hard, almost spitefully, as if the gods had it in for us. Palmerston Park last Wednesday night was no place for anyone, except perhaps those with a demented fixation for football. Hot tea seared between teeth, while cold pies sagged wet through tissues. Awful.

Hop aboard the Brechin bandwagon, someone had suggested. Brechin, whose tearaway lead at the top of the Second Division had those in the First bracing themselves for next season. Brechin, whose last 10 games had permitted just one defeat. Yet the self-same Brechin were about to be well and truly gubbed, as they say in football.

The script was to go most decidedly wrong. But the idea needed investigating. Glebe Park had spawned another troupe of fixers: engineers, cleaners, marketing men; students (two of them), one doing accountancy, the other business studies; and most of all, a father and son partnership, a rich symbiosis, one in the dug-out, the other wearing the No. 9 shirt. This was a side that had to be seen.

All it required was a telephone call.

"Hello, can I speak to John Ritchie, manager of Brechin City?"

"This is John."

"Would it be possible to join the team for their trip to Dumfries for the Queen of the South match?"

"Certainly, we'll pick you up. Look out for the Bean's coach."

"Ah, what was that, sorry?"

"The Bean's coach. You know, what you eat. It's the firm, Bean's of Brechin."

"Right..."

The Bean's coach it was. Pick-up point, half-way down the M74. This was its umpteenth stop, following those at Dundee, Fife, Edinburgh and assorted roundabouts in between. A gradual assembly of talent. This time four figures: the players Candlish, Hill and Sexy (Paul Sexton to those who don't know him so intimately), plus a bedraggled journalist.

It was, appropriately, a coach full of goodness. Footballing goodness. The top of the Second Division table confirmed as much. Up at the back, cards were dealt, jokes were fired, and everyone individually was held up for ridicule. Meanwhile at the front, a manager, sombre and pensive.

John Ritchie is a man of steely determination. He can also reel off the manager's stock-in-trade phrases without so much as a scratch at a sideburn: his team "took nothing for granted"; there's "no room here for complacency"; success has been down to the players, "and all credit to them"; nor has the board been obdurate, "and all credit to them, too".

He's also bought wisely, which accounted for his team's supremacy. Apart from changing almost completely the personnel he inherited three years ago, two names in particular have been astute acquisitions: his son Paul, bought from Dundee for £12,000; and of course Sexy, fleet of foot and wonderful in name, whose football odyssey hitherto had landed him at Stenhousemuir.

"But we're a no-gimmicks team," says Ritchie snr. "Last season we were in a strong position round about this time, but then fell away and eventually missed promotion. We've learned from that. No gimmicks, no complacency."

Palmerston's floodlights finally loomed through the drizzle. A *frisson* of excitement shot through Bean's coach. Cards were shuffled away. Conversation became dulled. Sexy was up and getting his coat on hurriedly. It was another big night for Brechin's players. Paid a basic £30 a week, it would be double that if both points were won.

Into the dressing-room, and an impassioned, discursive team talk. Ritchie, wearing the long-established mantle of a manager hollering at his players, once again confirmed the similarities between his role and a preacher's: a general introduction, a slight warming to the theme, a sudden outpouring of emotion, and finally fists banging everywhere. We need this, we need that, we need the other! Short, sharp jabs before an attentive audience. Ralgex hung in the air like smog.

But it was to be a disaster. After three minutes, Queens were awarded a penalty. "A bloody disgrace," shouted Cardo Gallaccio, Brechin's aged vice-chairman. Dave Lawrie, Brechin's business-studying goalkeeper, was adjudged to have brought down a forward. "But he had the ball clean in his hands," Cardo continued to lament. And he was right. It was a perverse decision. A bloody disgrace.

Cardo's face is almost concave, like that of a boxer who has taken too much punishment. His Italian lineage gives him an aura of mystique. Having survived in Scotland on ice cream parlours and restaurants, his billiard hall in Brechin is populated by the local 'gunslingers'.

"A den of iniquity," one local describes it. But there is nothing iniquitous in this man. He is a good man, a great man. Only this night, as he looked on, his 77-year-old face was grizzled with pain.

Brechin were never to come back. At half-time, Ritchie nearly blew the roof off. "I warned you about the conditions, so what's all this fancy football," he roared. "You play this, you play that, then you get it up the field. The last third. Woomph!" That final bit lost us, but the volume was frightening. Players looked on askance. I cowered in the corner of the dressing-room.

Queens went on to score two more. Yet how different it might have been. Just before the interval, Sexy went on a brilliant run, rounding three players before setting up Lees. He dithered. "God, he's wanting it gift-wrapped!" The voice might have been Cardo, but it was probably someone else. We all felt flat, heads sunk in hands.

Defeat, and irony as well. Both Sexy and Ritchie jnr, arguably Brechin's two best players, were to depart the scene before the referee's final whistle. Substitutions were essential on such a heavy night as this, but their being called inside summed up the visitors' predicament. Brechin's fuse was extinguished.

Back on the motorway, recriminations were mild. It's behind us now, claimed the manager. Saturday is another day. It's how we react that counts. The league leadership was intact. The First Division still beckoned. All yet to play for.

The M74 was dark and ghostly. The rain, still incessant, seemed unwilling to let up in its misery. Again, four of us piled out, dumped at midnight and hurdling the central reservation. Where were our cars? What a night, what a trip...

February 11, 1990

Tyranny and after

Alexander MacLeod

To say it has not been a good year for dictators is the wildest of understatements. So many of them have been dragged or pushed from their pedestals that now it is necessary to scour the darker reaches of Africa to discover examples of the species alive, well and going about the business of oppressing people.

The latest to meet his fate (though precisely how kismet will treat him remains unclear) is Nicolae Ceausescu, a tyrant in the classical mould, complete with an extensive clan (including a granite wife) and a savage apparatus of subjugation. He goes to join other tyrants in the pantheon of those who turned politics into a form of suffering for the masses.

The style of despots, of course, is all too familiar: arrogant exercise of power and ruthless denial of rights to anyone except themselves and their hangers-on. It is commonly said that dictatorships contain the seeds of their own destruction.

Nonetheless, the Stalinism of Ceausescu, Honecker, Husak, Zhivkov and their ilk appeared durable, despite *perestroika*. Their regimes seemed set in concrete. Even in Hungary and Poland it was apparently too much to hope for the total collapse of authoritarian rule. Why did such cruel regimes come to grief so quickly and, apparently, so easily?

A year ago, we were all getting used to the idea that the rigidities in the world system fostered by superpower confrontation were melting. This was producing areas of peace in quite unexpected places: Afghanistan, the Gulf, Cambodia, Angola. We were able to say new patterns of diplomacy were asserting themselves, creating the prospect of a world from which the old tensions and rivalries would be drained. What hardly anyone anticipated was that the easing of the Cold War would have another, equally welcome by-product.

It would make survival difficult – indeed impossible – for totalitarian governments which had prospered in the era of inflexible alliances. It would erode the ground on which dictators walked. As with so much else, the origins of this remarkable process are to be found in the ideas and attitudes of Mikhail Gorbachev.

When he passed the word to Honecker that he could no longer rely on Soviet tanks to keep him in power, the East German leader's essential prop was removed. The message was quickly appreciated in Sofia and Prague. Supposed iron men began suddenly to appear tarnished and obsolete as people power came into play.

The tyranny in Romania was a different case because it did not depend on Soviet support, but it now turns out that the domino effect created by so many oppressed peoples in neighbouring countries shaking off their shackles was irresistible there, too. Romania's singular tragedy lies in its near-total lack of a democratic tradition and the specially vicious character of its secret police. The carnage of the past week illustrates just how profoundly divided Romanian society had become between the people and the clique which ruled them.

Unfortunately, the jubilation that has greeted the toppling of so many tyrants in so short a time seems likely to give way rather soon to disillusion.

In East Germany it already is becoming clear that New Forum, the mass movement which began the tidal wave against Honecker, will be unable to mobilise its members in a coherent way. Next year's promised East German elections are more likely to be dominated both by the smaller parties which were held under for so long by the communists, and by the communists themselves, operating under their new name.

In Czechoslovakia, likewise, the way ahead is unclear. The difficulty of smoothing the path of the playwright Vaclav Havel into the presidency, in the teeth of hardline communist resistance, suggests that next May's elections will not produce anything like a clear-cut result. Poland and Hungary, too, are heading for a period of uncertainty as politicians of many stripes jockey for position.

None of this means that the communists merely have to wait until opportunities present themselves to batten new Stalinist-style dictatorships on the people. The system represented by the former regimes is well and truly discredited, and it is hard to imagine it returning. That, however, is not to say that democracy is certain to enjoy an easy ride.

Ironically, President George Bush is beginning to learn much the same lesson in Panama. Manuel Noriega may have been a petty tyrant compared to the strongmen of Eastern Europe (though there was nothing negligible about his involvement in drug trafficking). The mess created by the American decision to expunge him from the leadership of Panama illustrates, however, the difficulty of replacing a totalitarian regime with something more palatable.

In Panama's case there was a democratically elected president, in the ample shape of Guillermo Endara, ready to take over, and yet chaos is occurring. In Eastern Europe the prospect is that the elation of the past few weeks will give way to anxiety as people denied democracy for half a century or more, and in some cases with no experience of it at all, struggle to create new and stable forms of government. It is easier to get rid of tyrants than to replace them with institutions answerable to the people. Eastern Europe's experiment with liberty and democracy is only just beginning.

December 24, 1989

Peace, imperfect peace

Alan Taylor

No Scottish city is capable, as E.B. White observed of New York, of bestowing the queer prizes of loneliness and privacy. In Edinburgh, according to W. Gordon Smith, adultery is out because no matter where you go someone is bound to know you. In Glasgow, as William McIlvanney says, you never know "where the next invasion of your privateness is coming from".

Both Aberdeen and Dundee are not cities in the modern sense; they are still inflated villages, unlike Donne's island, entire of themselves. Size has something to do with it. In a lifetime you bump into a lot of people and a lot of people bump into you. Some remember you, and you remember some. Together it must add up to a decent crowd at Murrayfield.

Talk of getting away from it all is tosh. Take a walk through Lairig Ghru if you doubt it. After a long day on the hill I collapsed into the Corrour Bothy with a mouth as dry as a birdcage, my stomach rumbling like an avalanche. A silent night stretched ahead with a thriller and a flask of something colder and warmer than soup. To my chagrin, a couple had got there ahead of me and had settled in like field mice. That was bad enough; worse was that I knew the girl. In such situations in the city you would make your excuses and leave; 20

miles from nowhere the best you can do is sacrifice the flask.

This yearning to be alone is double-edged. After a week of yeast-wet air, buses bulging like Hong Kong junks, telephones ringing and the insidious flop of buff envelopes, you want to scream, jump off, get out. What you need is "the invigorating effects of silence", to quote a commission from the editor of a New York paper to the essayist Edward Hoagland. But after driving alone for eight hours Hoagland goes up the wall in his own company: "Loneliness is my middle name at the moment," he writes. "I'm 'dying' of loneliness; can't seem to live with people or without them."

If only he'd known that he could have had it both ways in New York. At least in the city you have the option; in the country you are on your own, left to your own devices. There is no turning back. In backwaters like Orkney you find refugees from the 'Gold Belt', the gilt-edged South-east, who have burned their boats. I can never decide whether they're happy or not, whether they're at home in their new habitat. But you hear a lot of backbiting about White Settlers; they are invariably the ones who agitate for better education and transport, are voluble at nuclear inquiries, and rough up the ineffectual island councils who are happy to have rusting cars blight the verges. Just the kind of thing you might have thought they wanted to escape from. Is it because the incomers care more because they have chosen to live there and know what the alternative is? Or are they inveterately restless?

A little energy in the country is much more conspicuous than it is in the city. Even in a town like Peebles, which is hardly the back of beyond, the shop assistants move like Daleks with flat batteries and the air, though fresh, is languorous. For city workers, towns like Peebles seem to me to be the worst of all worlds, preserved for commuters who weekend like fury and then drudge back to work on a Monday. It is half a life.

The charm of Peebles used to be its close-knit remoteness. Now, even by bus, the journey from Edinburgh takes less than an hour. Cars whizz up and down in half an hour. What was a compact town is burgeoning. Rude new expensive housing has usurped prime grazing land, much of which is being lost to timber-planting. Hectares of what was once sheep country are pockmarked with baby firs that make hill-walking impossible. Develop or die is the cry.

Last Wednesday, on a freezing morning, high above Glentress forest, the wind blowing and snow falling, the gift of loneliness and solitude was grudgingly bestowed. I accepted it graciously but gratefully got aboard the bus back to town, and people.

January 21, 1990

Lords of the ring

Ajay Close

Nine-thirty pm at Falkirk Town Hall. The Round Table is having a charity dinner in aid of the local hospital. A classy affair: black tie, three courses, coffee and mints, followed by three hours of boxing.

Two ring card girls – one white, one black – parade inside the ropes. The all-male crowd are in dinner jackets, but the girls would look underdressed anywhere. The white one, teetering on black stilettos, wears a G-string half-heartedly masquerading as a swimsuit. The black one (yellow stilettos, white fringed bikini) plays to the crowd, clambering through the ropes rump first to a chorus of appreciative whistles.

After the first couple of bouts, attention at the tables wavers. But up above, in the packed gallery, old men in bunnets and teenage boys whose trousers have yet to catch up with their last growing spurt crane forward with parted lips, eyes riveted to the ring. Their hoarse shouts spill over on to the desultory chat of the elegant diners below: *jab him... one-two, one-two...go for him, son.*

Thirty years ago you could see a public boxing contest every week in Scotland. Like football, boxing was a national religion; its mecca, Glasgow, home of the spit and sawdust street-corner gyms.

The 1960s brought the exodus to the housing schemes, and the rise of rival amusements. Boxing is still a traditional way up in the world for the fighter whose punches are powered with the frustration of the dispossessed, but nowadays he entertains a different crowd: the deal clinchers and carphone users, with their expense account chins.

Increasingly now, boxing is a sport to be savoured with a £30 meal, rubbing shoulders with the rich and famous. It's not an entirely new phenomenon. Boxing has always straddled high and low life; patronised by peers and public schoolboys in the privacy of the club, notorious for roughnecks and ne'er-do-wells in the public halls. What has shifted is the balance. Last year there were 38 professional boxing tournaments staged in Scotland and 31 of them were wine and dine evenings. Only seven delivered no-frills displays of fighting.

Tomorrow night, the St Andrew's Sporting Club at Glasgow's Albany Hotel will host the junior light welterweight world title fight, an occasion hyped as an honorary event in the Year of Culture celebrations. It's the sort of claim which provokes Outraged of Bearsden to fire off a volley of sarcasm to the letters pages of the Scottish press, but boxing is in fact a highly appropriate sport for the new Glasgow: its mix of artistry, showmanship and brute force pulling a glitzy crowd whose sharp suits cannot conceal an unreconstructed streak of machismo.

At the last count there were 128 professional fighters on the books in Scotland, perhaps 50 of them active: a sharp decline from the 200 around in the early 1960s when there were more than 20 gyms in Glasgow alone. Today the city has just two professional gyms, serving the rival stables of fighters managed by Tommy Gilmour jnr and – for the time being, at least – Alex Morrison.

Last week the British Boxing Board of Control fined Morrison £1,000 and revoked his manager's licence for 12 months. It appears that one of his fighters, a Mancunian known as Tony Dore, enjoyed a successful career in the ring under the name of Lance Williams until 1982 when he failed a medical and was banned from the sport. Morrison insists he knew nothing of Dore/Williams' past and has won 21 days' grace from the board while he prepares an appeal.

Morrison and Gilmour are the big boys of Scottish boxing. Tommy Gilmour jnr has 16 fighters on his books; most notable among them Ronnie Carroll, soon to fight for the European bantamweight title. He also nurtured Stevie Boyle to British lightweight champion status but lost him to Frank Warren in London a few months ago. Morrison manages 30 boxers including Scottish bantamweight champion Donnie Hood, former British lightweight titleholder Alex Dickson and Pat Barrett, the British light welterweight champion.

Standing 6ft 1in tall, a powerfully built 17st, Alex Morrison is not the sort of man you would pinch a parking space from. A former boxer, he retired from the amateur ring at the age of 26 ("drinking and wild living," he says regretfully), but made a comeback when he was 41, to carry off a clutch of amateur heavyweight titles.

Striding through Falkirk Town Hall with his barrel chest and boxer's strawberry nose, he exhibits the classic, not to say clichéd, contradictions of the tender-hearted tough guy. One minute he is cheerfully announcing "if someone's offended me, my instinct is to hit them", the next, confessing he is a vegetarian who gives cockroaches safe conduct out of doors on a folded newspaper. It occurs to me that it would be unwise to trust this sensitivity of spirit too far. He and Reg Kray maintain a penfriendship, drawn together by their common interest in charity work.

After a varied career which has included spells as a scrap metal dealer and Kleen-E-Ze brush salesman, he now runs a haulage firm for the money and a stable of boxers for love. Until last year he also promoted fights, but since the Board of Control banned managers from wearing both hats, he has handed Prime Promotions over to the care of his 21-year-old daughter Katherine and the former world featherweight champion Walter McGowan.

All three businesses are run from an office above an oil-drenched garage in Glasgow, its walls crowded with photographs of fighters with identikit broken noses and those circumflexes of thatched scar tissue boxers have for eyebrows.

One of Alex's boys is fighting in the Falkirk Round Table show: Matthew, a gentle giant of 18 with a tendency to stutter in unfamiliar situations. Alex fondly believes he has cured him of this. "I told him 'if you do it again, I'll smash your fucking face in'," he says, adding disarmingly: "Excuse me swearing, it's lack of vocabulary."

Alex explains that Matthew is a bit of a coward. This may or may not be his problem; the point is, the boss believes it – and that *is* his problem.

The journey to Falkirk from Glasgow has been something of a trial. Six of us in a Landcruiser (the Roller is in the repairshop), with Matthew sandwiched between trainer and supporters in the back, smiling unhappily at quips like "You know why he's in the middle? So he can't jump out when we stop at the lights."

Once the boxing begins, I am surprised to discover that, although opposed in principle to the idea of hitting people, I watch the slower bouts with mounting impatience, interest only quickening in the more aggressive fights.

Matthew's spell in the ring is pretty low on excitement. He wins the fight but the balcony is not impressed. A man with a concave face mutters to me: "You'd have beaten him yourself, eh hen?"

As the evening progresses, Alex explains the finer points of the sport. Eyesight, reflexes, knowing how to punch – being a 'banger' – they're all important, but ultimately temperament is what makes a boxer. "You'll get a guy who's very aggressive in the street but in the ring he hasn't got it. It's the ability to fight back when you're losing. When you're whacked on the chin with a good punch it's not a very nice experience. It flashes, you see lights, then you recover. When you're fired up you don't feel the pain the same way, but it's a terrible thing when you're in the ring and you're tired and the crowd are laughing at you. Imagine running a mile and somebody hits you in the body and the whole power goes out of your legs and you've got to hide it."

Put like that, it's difficult to see why anyone does it, but Alex has a theory on the sport's appeal. "When I was boxing I just liked hurting people – I just got a pleasure out of inflicting pain on people," he says guilelessly. "I think a lot of people like getting up and dishing it out."

Then there's the money, of course. A journeyman boxer will get £2,500 to £3,000 for a fight of eight three-minute rounds. At the top of his class he can make much more. If a number of promoters are interested and there's an auction, a boxer can walk – or stagger – away with a £60,000 purse. But even the best only get four or five good years. The trick is knowing when to get out. One day the sharp, hungry, young fighter with everything to play for becomes the musclebound, punch-drunk veteran with nothing left to lose.

Spend any time with boxers and sooner or later the touchy subject of brain damage will come up. The stock response runs along the lines of *boxing is not at the top of the list of dangerous sports/it's also risky crossing the road/and what about smoking, anyway?* Alex uses the latter retort, but it's clearly an issue which troubles him. "I don't know whether it's old age but I forget things," he admits. "I used to be very, very good at mental arithmetic, but I can hardly do the most simple mathematical problem now."

If Tommy Gilmour jnr did not exist, Alex Morrison would have to invent him. And vice versa. The two men revel in their contrasting personal styles. While Alex sports a knuckleduster of a diamond ring and a vivid green sweater that could knock you out at 15 paces, Tommy jnr, 38, favours the discreet grey suit and tie. Each regards himself as the true custodian of boxing in Glasgow, and is cheerfully magnanimous about his rival's operation.

Unlike Alex, Tommy jnr did not break into the business with his fists. The third generation of a family of boxing grandees, his face is much as nature gave it to him. "I was always the fellow that had the sharper pencil than he did a jab," he says; not, I'd guess, for the first time.

A printing engineer by trade, he climbed the boxing ladder by doing every job in the business. "When the club opened in 1973 I worked in the corner handing the bucket up, and washing up the gumshields," he says. Now he's a businessman. He has a Mercedes and a fax machine and an ivory letter-opener in the shape of an alligator, and an office on the mezzanine floor of the Albany Hotel with a framed photograph of himself and Leslie Grantham on the wall.

Until that inconvenient rule change by the Board of Control, Tommy jnr combined the roles of manager and promoter. Now he sticks to managing and the fights are promoted by St Andrews Sporting Club, a subsidiary of Clansmen Sporting Clubs Ltd (managing director: T. Gilmour jnr). Corporate and individual members (more of the former than the latter) subscribe £100 a year for the option of buying tickets for a dozen formal, five course dinners with ringside entertainment, held at the Albany Hotel. These are exclusive occasions, but Tommy jnr grows agitated at the suggestion that boxing has been taken away from the working class.

"One of the last public shows in Glasgow was £75 for the ringside seats," he says. "We provide top class entertainment cheaper than if you watched it in the public halls. It works out at about £21 a night for a five course meal and total entertainment. It'll cost you £12 to watch football teams in the European Cup and you don't even get a packet of crisps."

There is one thing you have to get used to about Tommy jnr: he speaks like a publicity brochure. St. Andrews provides "a facility for closing a deal in a first class atmosphere, in a nice, friendly, but prestige environment, with five star cuisine"; "an avenue for corporate entertainment with something to suit everybody's taste."

Well, not quite everybody. Despite intermittent threats of action under sex discrimination legislation, women are not allowed. He has nothing *against* women, but this is a business environment. Don't women do business too? Only in daylight, apparently. "Women will take clients out to lunch, but the biggest majority of them have got a life at night-time. It's not always entirely suitable for the woman of the household to do entertainment at night-time. Like it or not, boxing is primarily a male-oriented pastime."

In a way he's right. Boxing defines manliness without reference to the opposite sex; it is an expression of machismo with no interest in the mating game. But he's also wrong. Male or female, who wouldn't feel the fascination of the shadowy world beyond the gleam of silver and crystal on white napery?

Like every sub-culture, boxing has its own argot and legend. There are tales of professional losers who have won perhaps a dozen of their 100 fights; 'divers' who take on matches for the money and hit the canvas at the earliest opportunity; 'carry jobs' where hard-up boxers agree to hopeless fights on the promise of a gentle ride. I am told of visiting boxers running up four-figure champagne bills entertaining armies of escort girls; thousands changing hands in illegal bets...uncheckable stories from unattributable sources.

Boxing has always attracted the underworld. Alex Morrison cheerfully admits that his punters include bank robbers and fraudsters: "People who break into houses and sexual offenders – I'd get them exterminated – but people who do a bank are welcome to come to my shows."

We are in a territory familiar from countless episodes of *Minder*, but then, in this world of seedy glamour, life and art do display a certain interdependence. Boxing is the biggest B-movie never made, and everyone has a starring role.

When Tommy jnr reminisces about the days when "you weren't a boxing promoter unless you went about with a fedora and a camel coat and cigar you could choke on", it's unclear whether he's talking about Tommy snr or Edward G. Robinson. Last year he acted as fight consultant for the Scottish Television mini-series *Winners and Losers*, the occasion of that photograph with Leslie Grantham ("super guy"). At the Falkirk fight I meet a man who claims to have introduced Willie McIlvanney to a number of Glaswegians who appear, thinly disguised, as characters in his books; characters who are, in turn, played by their Glaswegian friends and acquaintances in the forthcoming film of *The Big Man*. The boxers in Tommy jnr's stable even work out to the theme from *Rocky*, and no location scout could have bettered his decision to site his gym in the Melbourne Street meat market.

This is the traditional face of boxing – broken nosed, cauliflower eared. Windows steamed with condensation, a ghettoblaster thumping out disco hits, leather punchbags strung up like liverwurst long past its sell-by date. Bodies skipping, toe-touching, squat-jumping, sparring, in a steadily intensifying fug of sweat.

Over my two-hour visit a series of men wander in, until the room is filled with lumpen-faced former fighters, streamlined professionals, hangers-on who never remove their anoraks, kids dressed for the beach in day-glo Bermudas and novelty T-shirts and, a hub of stillness amid all this activity, Duncie Jack in his lambswool cardi and cloth cap. Duncie, "the best cut man in the business", is 64-years-old, and has spent 44 of them in boxing. When he worked for Tommy snr, he trained the last of the Scottish big men, the legendary Chic Calderwood. Tonight, the object of his attentions is Ronnie Carroll, a bantamweight due to fight for the European title in Italy next month.

Tommy jnr, with a manager's eye for good publicity, has sold Ronnie to me as a Runyonesque character: cocky, cheeky, but with a heart of gold. In conversation with the fighter, I learn that he is 26, lives with his mother in Drumchapel, and works in a youth club...not exactly Sky Masterson. But in the ring, Ronnie undergoes a transformation. In cherry red gloves and black headguard, face smeared with an uneven mask of vaseline to protect it from marking, a gumshield forcing his upper lip into a Neanderthal snarl, he squares up to the first of a succession of sparring partners.

Ducking and swerving and feinting with the economy of an

Astaire, his neat movements unerringly take him just out of range of his opponent's gloves. Suddenly he's closing in with an arpeggio of punches. From outside the ring, Benny the trainer calls instructions, but Ronnie seems to inhabit a different world. It's a witty, spellbinding, animal performance.

Watching me watching him, Tommy jnr smiles faintly: boxing has made another convert.

February 18, 1990

Caught on a train

Joyce McMillan

On Thursday evening, I took the 1718 train from Edinburgh to Dundee. The price of a day return had risen by a cool $12^{1}/_{2}$% since the previous week, and as usual ScotRail flatly denied the existence of the train – the 2300 to Euston via Waverley – that I would have to return by; but those were routine irritations compared with the grief and angst of the journey itself, which by the time we reached the Tay Bridge, seemed to encompass a whole world of contemporary woes.

To begin with, the journey took place aboard a piece of rolling stock called a Sprinter, proudly introduced by ScotRail a couple of years ago. What the publicity failed to mention is that Sprinters are radically unsuitable for most of the purposes to which they're being put. For one thing, the trains are simply too small to cope with rush-hour traffic on an InterCity route; as usual, it was standing-room only on the 1718 before it even left Waverley.

But even without standing passengers, the internal design of the Sprinter is a disgrace. It's a nasty, noisy, skimpy little train, with an interior like a badly-made bus. Its sliding doors rattle and clatter, and admit savage draughts once it gets up speed. Its two toilets are not enough. Worst of all, the width of seat space provided for each passenger is about 15in, as measured out on my copy of *The Scotsman*.

When the train is full, it's impossible even to read a newspaper without seriously invading your neighbour's privacy; in fact, it's difficult for an adult of normal girth to do anything except sit with arms folded across the chest, praying that the person next door will get off at Dalmeny, and won't exhibit any unusual personal habits.

Well, we thundered north over the Forth Bridge; we heard the boom of the great metal girders beneath the wheels, even if we couldn't see through the steamed-up windows. But at Inverkeithing, things took a turn for the worse when the lady wedged up against my left side was replaced by a youngish male drunk en route for the offshore fleshpots of Aberdeen.

He was short, aggressive, curly-haired and Liverpudlian, with a smell of booze about him that would have stopped a tank at 10 paces; and he had reached that condition of drunkenness where he wanted a bit of attention. He lurched, he grunted, he cavorted like a demanding toddler; and every time we pulled in to one of the little stations along the Forth, he thrust his face into mine, and bawled: "Where's this? Aberdour? Where's that? Are we near Aberdeen?"

And after a while, I couldn't see why I should put up with this reeking imposition any more. "Look," said I to him, feeling sick, "you really smell of drink, and it's horrible with the train so crowded, and I just don't want to talk to you, I'm sorry."

I spoke quite quietly and ingratiatingly, because I didn't want to start a fight; but all the same, I could hear the sharp intake of breath from the eight or so people close enough to hear, see the exchanged glances, sense the faint indignation that I had refused my palliative role as the drunk's chosen victim. And of course, they were right; enraged by rejection, Curly rampaged about a bit, trampling on toes and yelling at the guard, before he finally subsided into an alcoholic stupor.

A few of my fellow passengers started chatting among themselves; but to me, no-one said a word. And so we rattled on into the night, cramped, embarrassed, wreathed in Curly's alcoholic breath; and myself crushed not only with anger and discomfort, but with guilt.

Now what this glum little tale shows, if anything, is how matters of public policy come together with much more subtle and intractable social forces to make up what we think of as our quality of life.

Of course, the government is much to blame for the squalor I've described. On the most obvious level, its blinkered and destructive railway finance policy is fast becoming a Europe-wide scandal; less obviously (but only because we've come to accept it as normal), the government is implicated, through lax taxation of the booze industry, in the extraordinary growth in casual drunkenness we've seen these last 10 years.

But what saddened me most of all, about my trip to Dundee, was the fact that 20 years on from *The Female Eunuch*, a woman with the gumption to say "boo" to a drunk on a train is still an object of wariness, unease, and mild disapproval.

I suppose I'm beginning to wonder whether a tolerable life as a woman in our culture isn't fundamentally incompatible with the kind of independence and self-assertion that my generation was encouraged to develop. I keep thinking of a pair of colleagues who heard me speak at a conference once, and sniggered, "Well, no need to send you on an assertiveness course," as if my lack of timidity was somehow comical.

I see before my eyes a row of sweet-faced, high-achieving thirtysomethings on the BBC's *Family Matters* programme, considering motherhood by donor insemination because comparable men won't have them as partners; and I wonder whether the prizes of independence, self-respect and professional achievement are worth so much social friction and private pain.

So I sat on my train, wishing I could have produced one of the "appropriate" female responses of tears, flight, or compliance. I felt the long-distance loneliness of a particular generation of women, who never learned the right submissive gestures in their feminist youth, and are too old to acquire the knack now. And about that, I'm afraid, the government can do nothing at all.

February 11, 1990

Disnaeland

Roddy Forsyth

I never heard a more compelling beginning or end to a one-sided conversation than that uttered in a Glasgow pub – Tennent's in Byres Road, as a matter of fact – by the middle-aged man, a complete stranger, who planked himself down heavily in the seat next to me about half past five one Friday afternoon last year.

With the tips of both index fingers he positioned his whisky precisely on the centre of the table in front of him, swivelled slowly in my direction and asked, in a voice resonant with the tone of authority: "So what do you think, my friend?"

This sonorous inquiry was followed by the barest pause, then he said: "Before you say a word, I don't give a fuck what you think."

He raised his glass, surveyed the teeming scene around the bar and sipped elegantly. It was Fool's Mate in two moves and a Zen masterpiece of economy which deserved suitable applause; the sound of one hand clapping, possibly.

That charming scene leapt to mind last week with the revelation that Saatchi & Saatchi had thought to emphasise Glasgow's advent into cultural heaven with a full-page advertisement depicting an open razor, of the type formerly favoured by those inhabitants who liked to inquire of passers-by whether they knew the way to the Royal Infirmary, before giving them a compelling reason to get there in a hurry.

Naturally, when the city fathers were exposed to this reminder of their manor's lively past, they were speechless with outrage and ordered the artwork to be carted off and buried in an unmarked grave. One cannot, after all, have people getting the wrong impression of a municipality where the opera house performs to 90% capacity audiences and a one-man play by Dario Fo fills the King's Theatre every night for a week. Well, maybe, but as Captain Dreyfus would no doubt have observed on his return from Devil's Island, it's a lot harder to shed an ill reputation than to get credit for the sparkling new one.

The trick is to make the grim face pay. In Whitechapel, they queue to stroll around the alleyways where Jack the Ripper passed his evenings mutilating prostitutes. In Chicago, they lead you proudly to the cinema where John Dillinger, in his final incarnation as Public Enemy Number One, was shot to pieces by the Feds. And what does every foreign journalist who visits Glasgow ask to see first? The slums, James, and don't spare the rodents.

But the slums have gone, gone to motorways every one. So rebuild a few. Or take a couple of stonecleaned blocks and turn them into the Glasgow Heritage Park. Wanted – Experienced Sootblasters, willing to restore old mankiness. The donation of a single Bottle Bank would be sufficient to scatter a square mile of back courts with broken glass. Graffiti? Ask the local secondary for a morning's loan of the remedials.

Rats and rickets are an obvious problem but there should be enough unemployed actors to man the street corners and bawl virulent abuse at the tour buses. And when the visitors arrive they will divide according to gender. The women will discover how to borrow a poke of sugar, hing oot a windae, and say: "That wan? She keeps a dirty hoose."

For the children and old folk, the Midgy Bin Treasure Trail should offer an absorbing couple of hours, while few men could fail to savour the ambience of the public house, where the clock still stands at five to ten and the drunks line up four pints, ready to be downed in wanners. I anticipate no difficulty securing drunks, incidentally, on account of the number of journalists who are apparently bursting to take a walk on the wild side of our cultural capital.

Some Glaswegians will cry, plaintively: "It used to be like that but it disnae happen noo!" Well, in order to emphasise the difference, they could call it Disnaeland. It is only an idea but it is offered for earnest consideration. After all, the advertising artwork already exists, courtesy of Saatchi and Saatchi.

So what do you think, my friends?

March 11, 1990

Confessions of a meat eater

Derek Cooper

I was doing something on Sky television this week, talking about the virtues of good food with an old friend, Patrick Anthony. His fellow presenter was Tony Blackburn who surprised me by announcing that he was a vegetarian. I felt a sense of envy, rather like meeting someone who's given up booze for Lent. You admire their strength and determination and you also feel a bit resentful because you know that they'll feel all the better for it.

My thoughts were compounded by a reader of this column who wrote from Inverness to ask whether I was a meat eater and if so didn't I think it out of keeping with my moral stance about compassion towards animals. That gave me furiously to think. The debate about the morality of eating animals has been going on for centuries.

The finest exposition of our ambivalent attitude to both plants and animals has been written by Keith Thomas, a former Oxford Professor of History. In *Man and the Natural World* (Penguin, £7.99) he reminds us that by the beginning of the 18th century all the arguments which sustain modern vegetarianism were already in place. And the arguments sound surprisingly contemporary; slaughtering animals was considered not only to have a brutalising effect on humans but the eating of animal flesh was considered to be bad for health.

Quite a few kenspeckled folk were vegetarians. It was the Scottish Pythagorean John Williamson of Moffat who made a convert of the 16-year-old James Boswell, not that his conversion to the joys of vegetarianism lasted very long. The future minister James Gillies as a student at Aberdeen in the 1770s discovering that he could live quite happily without eating flesh immediately gave it up altogether.

There was plenty of inspiration in those days of colonisation. The radical Scot John Oswald acquired his vegetarian habits from the Hindus while serving with a Highland regiment in India in the 1780s. An American of Scottish descent, Sylvester Graham, who promised to save souls through the stomach in Philadelphia in the 1820s, was also the inventor of the Graham cracker made from wholewheat. In those days, many radical vegetarians believed that if mankind only gave up eating meat there might be an end to violence and war.

Although that hasn't happened, the vegetarian movement in Britain goes from strength to strength and its arguments are as compelling as ever. Indeed in these days of intensive farming, with its attendant overuse of antibiotics, eating meat at all must seem like an act of gross self abuse.

In March the *Journal of the American Medical Association* produced more evidence that a high consumption of saturated fat increases one's risk of suffering some form of heart disease. In the typical American diet, rich in dairy produce and high-fat meat, fat accounts for 40% of all the calories consumed.

If we all moved to a diet of grains and pulses, fruit and vegetables, how healthy we might be. And how bored. That's my own personal Achilles heel. I actually like eating animals. What a shaming confession to make in print. I know that beef tea killed more people than Napoleon but there's nothing like a good broth on a cold day. Living up to being a non-meat eater can be a trial even in the most considerate household.

Professor Thomas recalls the anomalies of life that confronted Shelley when he embraced the vegetarian code. Mrs Shelley perversely retained her liking for tiny corpses. "Mrs Shelley's compliments to Mrs Nugent," she wrote in 1812 when her husband had become a plant eater, "and expects the pleasure of her company to dinner, 5 o'clock, as a murdered chicken has been prepared for her repast."

To enjoy the subtle, delicate taste of cock-a-leekie soup, a chicken has to die. A breakfast of bacon cannot be had without killing a pig. A Burns Supper is no supper at all without a haggis and without the slaughter of sheep you just can't have a proper haggis. At this time of the year, when the Easter lambs are gambolling, the thought of lamb chops brings ambivalent responses; the saliva may flow but the moral fibres are brought up with a jolt. Could one really *eat* such an innocent little thing?

Animal eaters have always been illogical about what they can bring themselves to eat and what they can't. The creatures which excited most sympathy were the ones whose cries of pain when *in extremis* sounded most human. And that's probably why fish have always been regarded as fair game – cold-blooded, conveniently mute in their death-throes, deemed to be lacking in the ability to feel pain.

That's probably why a new breed of demi-vegetarian has appeared; caring folk who would no longer dream of chewing steak but dine quite happily on a cod cutlet or a filleted haddock. I don't know what Dryden would have said about that. "Take not away the life you cannot give," he wrote, "for all things have an equal right to live."

I shall remember that when next I pluck an oyster screaming from its shell or send my hooks down into a shoal of mackerel. I remain an unrepentant predator. Compassionate, of course, and especially kind and grateful to lobsters.

April 8, 1990

Hands across the sea

William Paul

A story is told about the island of Vatersay and a visitor who had a reputation for the second sight.

He was a man from Uist and he was among a squad of workers who had come to build the island's first and only road. One day, some 50 years ago, he was at Caolis on the north side when he chanced to look over his shoulder and see a red car driving over the rocky hillside on the neighbouring island of Barra.

The point of the story is that there was no road there, not even a footpath, and no reason then to believe that there was ever likely to be one.

The road appeared only in September last year. Still unsurfaced, it leads a mile and a half from Castlebay up and over to the edge of the Tangaval peninsula where a new causeway stretches 200 yards across the sound to Vatersay.

"I wouldn't believe the story myself except it has been around much longer than any campaign for the causeway," says one crofter. "I don't know what the people thought then but I think it surely proves the Uist man did have the second sight after all."

The road and the causeway are real enough and are likely to be completed this summer, months ahead of schedule, at a cost of £4m, half of the money coming from the European Regional Development Fund.

Vatersay, population 70, the most southerly inhabited island of the

Outer Hebrides and the last to be provided with vehicular access, is grateful that Big Brother Barra, population 1,600, is holding out a helping hand across such a narrow piece of Atlantic Ocean. The people of Castlebay are rather taken with the idea as well. Since the beginning of this month when the causeway finally spanned the sound, every Sunday has meant cars of every colour coming up and over the hill to park on the north shore and people stepping carefully through the boulders from island to island. It has become a family outing.

In Castlebay I am informed I can easily walk across to Vatersay but the wind is high and the rain is horizontal so I decide to take the ferry instead. It is a small fibreglass boat owned by the islands council which runs four times a day but will almost certainly not be doing so by this winter.

The ferryman these last 12 years has been John Allan MacNeil, a former cox of the Barra lifeboat, and he is resigned to the fact that he will lose the job. If the causeway hadn't been built, more people would have left the island and the service would have been cut anyway, he rationalises philosophically.

There are two other passengers in the tiny wheelhouse, literally rubbing shoulders as the ferry dips and dives through big waves whipped up by a 35 knot wind on the 10-minute crossing.

One is Mick Sinclair whose parents came from Vatersay and who is going back to visit relatives. He was born and brought up in Glasgow and it is hard to know if he is being serious when he says he wants to live on the island, speaking one moment in broad Glaswegian and the next in fluent Gaelic, a language his parents did not let him forget. Do we know, he asks, that the latest Miss Scotland's mother comes from Vatersay? Wouldn't it be fine if she did the opening ceremony for the causeway?

The other passenger is Father Calum Maclennan, parish priest, former councillor, and persistent campaigner for the causeway. There is a church on Vatersay, a wholly Catholic island. It is Our Lady of the Waves, constructed from wood and corrugated iron that used to be painted a vivid blue until the building was refurbished and harled a few years ago.

"I am happy for the islanders that this is happening," Father Maclennan says. "Actually, if you look at it demographically the island has a very healthy population spread over the age groups. It is not all old people by any means. There are seven children at the primary school on Vatersay and eight travel on the ferry to Castlebay. The causeway can do nothing but good for the island. It is not before time either."

Vatersay's problem is depopulation, a common complaint in the Hebrides. The number of residents has fallen by half in the last 10 years. In 1908 land raiders from Barra in the north and Mingulay, now uninhabited, to the south squatted on the island until crofting reform laws enabled the government to buy it from the absentee owner for a price then considered quite extortionate, £6,250. In the 1920s and 1930s the population peaked at 350 but more recently it has become increasingly difficult to find people prepared to live there. Empty croft houses are everywhere in the landscape.

The long-awaited causeway is confidently expected to halt population decline by making transport especially, and life generally, so much easier. Last weekend a furniture van bounced its way over with a delivery that previously would have had to be done by a moonlighting fishing boat.

At the Vatersay landing, built in the late 1970s as a Job Creation project, I offer to pay the ferry fare but am told it will be collected on my return later in the day. The boat turns round and is heading back to Barra before we reach the stacks of lobster creels at the top of the slope. The postman, Donald Duncan Campbell, father and grandfather among the land raiders, is waiting to collect the mail and the chat is all in Gaelic. Twenty yards away stands the co-chomunn shop and cafe, a co-operative run by the islanders.

Grey-haired Margaret Dickson serves in the shop and drives the community mini-bus. The engine sounds a bit rough and there is a bash in one door, but it goes well enough. She was born on Vatersay, trained as a nurse and then worked in Africa and several other far-flung places including England. Her husband is English. They came back on what was supposed to be a visit three years ago and decided to stay.

"It was my husband who didn't want to leave," she explains as she negotiates a tight corner. "I wasn't too bothered at first but now I wouldn't want to go away again. When you come here you know what it is like with the isolation and the transport difficulties so you can't really complain. When the causeway is ready, perhaps that will allow us to finish the house we have been building for three years."

On the bus, on her way home, is Flora Gillies. It is her 16th birthday and she has just sat her Gaelic O grade at Castlebay and will be going on to Linaclete school on Benbecula in the autumn. She is one of 10 Gillies children, only two of whom are not living on Vatersay, but she has ambitions to be a primary teacher and will probably move away, causeway or no causeway. In the meantime it will be good to be able to nip into the youth club in Castlebay at nights, or anytime she wants to. Not so boring.

The bus stops and I step down into thick, oozing mud on the road outside Joe MacDougall's modern house. A cross-Hereford calf born at 2am that morning is sheltering from the rain in the lee of its mother's body under the living room window. MacDougall, 63, used to be a foreman joiner in the Clyde shipyards. Known as Barra Joe, he learned his trade on the Waverley paddle steamer and then helped put together the QE2 before taking part in the famous UCS workers' occupation.

His father was one of the original Vatersay land raiders before eventually settling back to Barra. MacDougall met his wife Morag when they were both returning home on the ferry from Oban; he to Castlebay and she to Vatersay. They married, had six children, and eventually returned in 1975 to live on a Vatersay croft where they built a new house for themselves, even making their own bricks out of shingle. Morag works as a nurse in Castlebay and the shifts mean she has to stay overnight for days on end. With the causeway, the hospital will be a five minute drive away.

"This island would have gone the same way as St Kilda if nothing had been done," says MacDougall, a former chairman of the community council. "I really believe that. I would have left, definitely. This was a terribly neglected place but now maybe it will get better here. Our next problem will probably be an influx of tourists."

He offers to take me on a tour of the island in the rather rusty left-hand drive Fiesta he bought from the vet's Dutch assistant a year ago. The floor is littered with straw, there is no door handle on the driver's side and no tax disc on the windscreen either. Castlebay folk say some Vatersay islanders were against the causeway because it would mean they would have to pay their road tax. MacDougall laughs. "It will be a change to have more than one road to drive on."

First stop is a derelict house about half a mile away. It is, he proudly claims, the most westerly croft in the UK and the birthplace of his wife, also of the ferryman John Allan MacNeil, who is her brother and who owns the sheep on the land. "You will find that everybody is related to somebody around here," he confides.

The road runs for about four miles over the island, past the church, and past the wreckage of the plane that has lain untouched since it crashed at the end of the war, past the school that will probably close soon, past the £60,000 community hall where one bit of the wall has collapsed, and past the memorial to 350 Scots and Irish emigrants who drowned in 1853 when the *Annie Jane* out of Liverpool was driven ashore in a violent storm.

Vatersay village is the main township, made up of a clutch of

Scandinavian-style wooden houses which the council provided rather than grants to renovate the crumbling croft houses scattered around them. There are two other townships, both entirely deserted.

On the way back, the engine begins to overheat and MacDougall pulls up. He gets out and picks up an old beer can at the side of the road, fills it from a ditch and pours water into the radiator. As he is doing this a car draws in beside us and the driver emerges to hurl a black plastic rubbish bag towards the sea. It lands at the foot of low cliffs among a scree of household rubbish piled round the skeleton of an old car. "No refuse collection on the island," MacDougall explains. "We burn ours."

Vatersay in recent years has had the knack of attracting publicity out of all proportion to its size. In 1987 there was the celebrated case of Bernie the black Aberdeen Angus bull who expired on the shore where the causeway now makes landfall, after attempting to swim the sound to service 40 waiting cows. Swimming was the traditional way of getting a bull to the island and three crofters were later acquitted of causing the death of the ill-starred, one-tonne beast. Bernie, by the way, was a name invented by a *Sun* reporter. The animal, owned by DAFS and rented out to crofters, was more properly, but less alliteratively listed as H9.

In 1984 came the story of the Vatersay bachelors, more than 20 of them, who were stranded on the island without a single woman of marriageable age for company. The cure for their ills in this sad story that went round the world was to be a causeway – a road to romance, the newspapers delighted in calling it.

"The more publicity we got the better it was for the causeway campaign," says MacDougall. "We would not have got it without the press. I have had at least two calls from London papers asking me to get the bachelors together again, but I don't think I could do that. It was different when there was the prospect of a causeway but we have got that now. There have been a few marriages and a few children born since that story went out."

Down at the causeway, fishing boat skipper Donald MacNeil and his partner Donald Gillies, one of Flora's brothers, are sitting in a car watching the rocks being rolled into place by the heavy earth-moving equipment. About 500,000 tonnes is being blasted out of the hillside and spread across the sea.

Both deny membership of the 1984 Vatersay bachelors' club, although Gillies is unmarried, while MacNeil is recently wed and even more recently became a father. The thing they are looking forward to is being able to stay on Barra for a drink at nights and know they can get home in a matter of minutes. That will make all the difference.

I have missed the last ferry so there is nothing for it but to feel guilty about not paying the fare and walk back to Castlebay in the rain. I go over the causeway, through the avenue of yellow lorries and diggers and up the steep hill. Half way up, I stop and look back to Vatersay and the scattered crofts of Caolis. When I turn and look forward, a vehicle comes over the crest of the hill. It is one of the contractor's Toyota pick-up trucks. Second sight is not necessary to see that it is bright, shining red.

March 18, 1990

The Big M

Julie Morrice

Forget Derek Hatton, Alan Ayckbourn and even the Moderator of the General Assembly, the most listened-to interview on the radio this week was with Madonna Louise Veronica Ciccone, fitness-freak, teen-idol and pop-star.

Madonna – The Breathless Interview was the first the steely blonde has given for three years, and Radio 1 could not have been more pleased if they had discovered John Lennon alive and well and living in the basement of Broadcasting House. While the fans tugged impatiently on their baby-reins, the presenter stalled the tape of the star herself in order to interview the interviewer, early-morning DJ Jakki Brambles. So what was it like, Jakki? Jakki was tongue-tied with recollected excitement. "I knew I was in the presence of someone really, really big – in the true sense of the word."

No sign of an incisive interviewing style there, and, sure enough, this was the Real Thing, an hour of over-packaged, adulterated, easy-to-swallow marketing. To the continual accompaniment of her own records, hissing in the background like a leaky Walkman and cutting up the conversation into manageable spoonfuls, the Big M talked about her music, her family, her current romance, her money, and her philosophy of life: "I think the most important thing in life is to be happy and to have friends and to find at least one person that you can be really intimate with. That's it."

Apart from pop phenomena and past winners of Miss World, no-one could pass this stuff off as communication, let alone interesting radio. Even the eager 12-year-olds, fired by the image that combines *femme fatale* with gum-chewing hustler, must have been disappointed at the lack of spark. Only once did the self-importance slip. "I'll never have rollers in my hair and I'll never have children that scream," growled the misnamed Madonna, "I'll tape their mouths."

Second in the running as popular hero of the week was Benny Lynch. Glasgow's obsession with their flyweight champion is matched only by the Radio Scotland drama department's obsession with Glasgow. By my reckoning, five out of seven of the new play series have been set in Culture City.

Patrick Prior's *The Hardest Wee Man In The World* (Radio Scotland) was a verbal rollick that Dylan Thomas would not have blushed at. Sinuously weaving past "the parish-bred and the means-tested" and "the Paisley patterned legs" of "sweetie-wifes with snibs on their drawers," Prior's play was more a personal celebration of the back-streets than an autopsy of Lynch's psyche. Annoyingly over-produced and ultimately unsurprising, this was, nonetheless, a pleasure to the ear.

May 27, 1990

Everlasting Sunday

Kenneth Roy

On a warm, overcast summer day, as Edwin Muir drove through the industrial towns of Lanarkshire, it occurred to him that Motherwell and Airdrie were the most improbable places in which to be left with nothing to do: that only work could reconcile anyone to living in them. They brought to his mind "a disused, slovenly, everlasting Sunday".

Is the prospect of Monday any closer? On another warm, overcast summer day, I took Edwin Muir's *Scottish Journey* with me on the train to Motherwell. "Ravenscraig decision is final, says Scholey," announced the *Glasgow Herald*. I opened the book. "A silent clearance is going on in industrial Scotland," Muir was saying, "a clearance not of human beings, but of what they depend upon for life." He was writing 55 years ago. It might have been today.

By the time I reached Motherwell, Muir's lyrical prophecy of post-industrial Scotland had depressed me. I followed the sign to a coffee shop behind the station. It turned out to be a converted church run by an evangelical organisation. The pulpit was surrounded by cafe tables; uplifting muzak had replaced thundering sermons. After a sip of hot gospel coffee, I fled across the road to Aquatec, Motherwell District Council's new leisure centre.

"Just go to the top of the hall and you'll see everything," the attendant promised. He was right. The jacuzzi was overflowing with jolly, overweight women, a sewing bee consumed by the great flood. In the restaurant, you could buy a portion of chips for 45p. Next door in the ice disco, boys and girls skated, held hands, and looked happy. On the way out, I said to the attendant that it was all very impressive. "A good facility, sir," he agreed.

I asked at the bus stop in Merry Street how to get to Ravenscraig. Take the bus to Cleekhimin, they said. Cleek where? Merry Street, which was so long that it almost met the doomed steel plant, had a defiant ring, but Cleekhimin was baffling. When I left the bus, I was confronted by the Alamo Lounge, a block of empty, vandalised flats, and a hazy view of Ravenscraig. It was belching smoke listlessly into the leaden air.

In the Alamo Lounge, there was impassioned talk about absolute garbage – not Bob Scholey's latest pronouncement, but the performance of Scotland's footballers. "Eleven aff the street would have played better," said a customer. He was half-heartedly completing a pools coupon. "Goin' to the racin' the night, Joe?" he asked. "It's Saints and Sinners night at Hamilton. Take yer wellies and a big fat wallet." No one was sure how Cleekhimin had got its name. One theory was that this was the spot in the old days where they bridled the horses before the big push up the hill to Carfin. But one thing they *were* sure about, these lugubrious punters: Ravenscraig had had it.

"Is there much of a campaign locally?" I asked. "Oh, aye," one said with a sour laugh. "*Daily Record* stickers everywhere."

People in the street gave me helpful advice. If I wanted to meet the union leaders, I should go to the golf club for lunch. If I wanted to get injured, I should go to Motherwell Cross. In the pedestrianised shopping centre, the travel agent's had closed; windows once reserved for offers of cut-price holidays in faraway places now contained "Fight for Ravenscraig" posters. The Labour Party rooms were shut too, and the hotel was serving only soft drinks. If I cared to come back next week, the barmaid said, I would be guaranteed alcohol.

At the offices of Motherwell Enterprise Trust, I asked to speak to someone about the town's future, if any. A friendly secretary told me that the director was in a meeting, but volunteered copies of the trust's giveaway newspaper. It carried a symbolic picture of five girls getting their skates on to face "the challenge of the nineties". The director's name is Mr Hope.

Outside, I bought two gas lighters for £1 from an entrepreneur in a tartan bunnet. He explained that candy apples were his main line; on a good night, he could sell 100 outside the chip shop. "It'll be murder when the Craig goes," he said.

A group of sullen middle-aged men stood aimlessly at a street corner. But when a lorry with a long trailer tried and failed to turn the corner, the group was galvanised at once. They hurried to the driver's assistance, directed the traffic, reorganised the bollards and saw the vehicle safely on its way. For a few purposeful minutes, there was a glimpse of how Motherwell might react to glad, confident Monday.

June 17, 1990

Small, but beautifully formed

Rennie McOwan

Sometimes hill gangrels argue about which hill is the most northerly on the mainland. The Munro-baggers have a clear-cut case: Ben Hope, above Strath More, is clearly the most northern Munro, followed by Ben Kilbreck (pronounced kee-bree) and both can be reached via the A.836 Lairg and Tongue road in Sutherland.

I once participated in a light hearted discussion at Cape Wrath over whether a nearby swelling constituted a hill, but aesthetically one of the most northerly mountains of stature is surely Morven in Caithness. At 2,313 feet it is not big and for those who love categories it is not even a Corbett (2,500 feet needed), but it is *very* big when seen from the terrain where it belongs – the flat lands of Caithness, the rolling brown moors besprinkled with lochans, the small fields with their 'fences' of Caithness slabs, the big skies, the little fishing villages that have known other, more prosperous times and the many ruined houses, relics of changing patterns and enforced eviction.

The expansionist Norsemen gave us the name Sutherland, their south land, and Caithness derives from old Norse, Katanes, the naze or nose of the Land of the Cat, from the Gaelic Cattey or Cattadh. When they looked south across the flat lands, they saw a blocking wall of mountains which forced the trade routes, as they still do, down the eastern coast.

The Best of Scotland on Sunday

Morven takes its name from the Gaelic for big or great mountain and it dominates this area, has magnificent views over wide moorland and wild glens and is flanked to the west by the long cut of the Strath of Kildonan. Two lovely rivers, the Berriedale and the Langwell, flank it on the north and south.

Here I have to declare an interest. My mother was born at Langwell and my grandfather, Johnnie Ross, and my great-grandfather, old Donald Ross, were stalkers on the Duke of Portland's estate. Donald Ross was known all over the northern counties as a head stalker of great experience, a man who thought nothing of using his tongue on guests who would not accept his instructions and a friend, as well as an employee, of the Duke.

Donald Ross once threatened a guest with a gralloching knife after he had called him a fool. The guest demanded that he be sacked, but it was the guest who left that night. He also had a fight with the French chef and sat on his head and shouted: "Waterloo! Waterloo!" The Duchess wanted Donald sacked. The chef left. Donald stayed.

Guests in White's Club in London crowded to the window to watch him walking down the street, wearing plus-fours and carrying a crook and saying "good morning" to everyone he met, in the same manner as Crocodile Dundee in New York.

His son, Johnnie, contracted tuberculosis in the days before it could be cured and the Duke sent him to Rhodesia to start a tobacco farm in the hope that the climate would cure him, but he died there. Granny Ross must have had a big heart to travel there by ox wagon, found a home and with the only other male her eldest son, then aged 14. My mother said she sometimes wept thinking of the chuckle of the Caithness burns and she longed for the feel of rain on her face. But she returned to Scotland and died here after a long life.

Morven is special to Caithness people and so are its neighbours, the long ridge of the Scaraben and the sharp-pointed, lovely, small peak, the Maiden Pap. Morven is a landmark to sailors and a weather barometer for local people.

Caithness people of my mother's generation, such as author Neil Gunn, took a pride in local people 'getting on'. I read in an old history that seven distinguished Edinburgh Caithness students early last century had formed themselves into a kind of self help band which they called the Corriechoich Brotherhood, named after a bothy and part of the glen on the Braemore side of the mountain.

The modern landowners, the Welbeck Estates, now have a popular gardening centre at Langwell and water from the hill burns is bottled, canned and exported, surely one of the most cost-effective businesses in Scotland.

The estate prefer hillwalkers to climb Morven from the northern, Braemore side where a minor road runs west from Dunbeath. Cars must be left beside the phone box at Braemore Lodge (checks are requested during stalking). A track leads to Corriechoich, from where the mountain can be gained over rough ground. The southern route up the beautiful Langwell glen is also very attractive and both glens have produced poetry and songs of praise from Caithness people.

Morven cannot be put in a mathematical category. Like Bennachie in the north-east or Dunchuach at Inveraray it has a special character for local people, but it has a size, stature, setting, history and vistas that make its name truly appropriate, the Great Mountain.

January 28, 1990

Inside Barlinnie

Keren David

Dignity is the first thing you lose at Barlinnie. The black police van takes you through Glasgow to the gate in the high walls surrounding Scotland's biggest prison, and a brisk humiliating ceremony turns a free man into a numbered prisoner. You step into a 'dog box', a tiny cubicle which some terrified first-timers take to be their cell. On a busy day several men could be crammed in together. You strip off and walk naked up a narrow corridor to hand all your personal belongings to an officer. He gives you a bundle of clothing. In a few minutes you're wearing denim or thick serge trousers, a red shirt for a convict, a blue one if you've still to stand trial.

A thorough medical examination follows. You hold out your arms to be checked for drug needle marks. No one talks to you or asks for personal details. There is little counselling about prison life, or what to expect in the cells. "We'd like to make the process more human, but sheer weight of numbers makes it impossible," says Bob Luke, an assistant governor. About 12,000 men go in and out of Barlinnie every year.

Once processed you are assigned a cell – a small dark space with a concrete floor. Daylight filters weakly through a window covered with a grid of bars. You probably inherit walls plastered with pictures of naked women. There's little furniture except two iron beds and a slop bucket, no sink or toilet. The hall smells of men and disinfectant.

If you've had a morning court hearing you might be in time for lunch, the main meal of the day, which you'll eat from a metal dish in your cell. If it's later you may just have supper – a slice of cake or a bun. During the day, the halls are deserted – most prisoners are at work. Later you can mingle for recreation, TV and videos – mainly crime films, with inmates rooting for the baddies.

Arriving at Barlinnie may be traumatic for a prisoner and bleak for his visitors, but there's a warm welcome for outsiders. The staff are keen to let people see the changes that have taken place in what was, until recently, Scotland's most notorious jail.

It's hard to forget the scenes which appeared on the nation's TV screens and front pages just two and a half years ago – the masked prisoners on the roof shouting and brandishing banners, demonstrating against overcrowding, poor conditions and alleged staff brutality. They were there for five days and took three prison officers hostage before the riot ended. Three of those involved are now serving an additional 22 years. They would hardly recognise Barlinnie today.

The seeds of discontent were sown years before the riot. According to a 1986 report by the Inspectorate of Prisons, Barlinnie "frequently has an inmate population 50 per cent above its rated capacity". Tiny cells were stuffed with up to half a dozen men. It had to cope with more prisoners than the rest of Scotland's jails put together.

Drug-taking and violence were rife. Staff morale plummeted to its lowest ebb and many officers preferred to go off sick than work in a place where, as one senior officer bluntly put it, "We had lost control." In June 1986, prisoners took part in a roof-top protest over the crowded conditions. In November, an inmate brandishing a metal bar spent 13 hours on the roof, and several fires were reported in prison buildings. Then, in January, the five-day riot began.

But Barlinnie's troubles did not end there. In 1987 and 1988 officers took industrial action on overcrowding, several prisoners were released by mistake and a number of others were found dead in their cells. There were reports of fires in prison buildings and of 'incidents' involving officers and inmates. In December 1987 more than a fifth of officers were on sick leave, many complaining of stress-related illnesses. In the space of a week, 12 officers and an assistant governor were injured in attacks by inmates.

One man was given the task of saving Barlinnie. When Alan Walker took over as governor in the summer of 1987, the prisoners were kept in their cells 24 hours a day. He has been described as the man with the toughest job in the country. It hasn't been easy, but according to inmates and officers, policy changes he has instituted are finally beginning to take effect. There is less tension and morale among staff and inmates is higher than ever.

Deputy governor Peter Withers says, "There are various strands to the new policy. One has been restoring control and that has been very successful. Second, there has been a significant improvement in staff training. Staff are being encouraged to apply for promotion and we've had very good results from this." New limits have also been placed on the prison's intake. Until recently, Barlinnie accepted all male prisoners committed by courts in the west of Scotland whether convicted or on remand. Many of these men are now being sent to other prisons.

Everyone – staff and prisoners – is full of praise for the new regime. Alan Walker is, they say, tough but fair – and they respect him for this. No one is punished without good reason, but any inmate who steps seriously out of line is sent to the prison's segregation unit to cool off. Good communication – between governor and officers, officers and prisoners, the prison and the public – is central to Walker's philosophy. We were warmly welcomed and told constantly, "Speak to whoever you want, go wherever you like."

Barlinnie may be coping well with its most immediate problems – the overcrowding and staffing difficulties – but many others remain. Some are social – Aids, drugs, alcohol and an increase in the number of sex offenders, many of whom have to be kept apart from their fellows for their own protection. There is also a growing number of mentally handicapped people ending up in the jail because there's no other place for them.

Then there are the physical difficulties of catering for hundreds of men in crumbling buildings. Improvements like installing a toilet in each cell can't take place until a long-awaited economic assessment by the Scottish Office is completed. The size of the prison and the high turnover of inmates exacerbate Barlinnie's problems. Few stay for more than two years, and many are there only days or weeks before being freed or moved elsewhere.

Myths surround prison life, and few people who haven't been inside know what to expect as they approach the jail. Scenes from the BBC's prison sitcom *Porridge* and the gritty Borstal drama *Scum* mix uncomfortably in the mind as you search for a space in the overcrowded car park.

Barlinnie is a study in ugliness. Four grim Victorian halls dominate the 18.5 acre site, towering over the squat modern additions. The smaller structures are decorated in the nastiest imaginable shades of green and beige government surplus paint. In the grounds, monotonous grey concrete is broken only by well-kept flowerbeds which look ludicrously out of place. Inside the administration block, the carpets are covered with psychedelic Sixties' swirls. The echoing halls, currently home to around 800 prisoners, are painted putrid yellow.

Visitors line up outside for their half-hour of chat and quick kisses. In the visiting room, used by hundreds of people in one afternoon, black cameras swivel on the ceiling, all-seeing eyes watching for drugs. It used to be common for visitors to pass them to prisoners concealed in a loving kiss or in a baby's clothes. Walker's policy of increased surveillance and strip searching visitors who are believed to be hiding something, has meant a drop in the use of hard drugs.

Prisoners who fear HIV infection have even been known to tell staff if they think someone is taking drugs. But the clampdown pushes more inmates into withdrawal symptoms. There is no methadone to use as a substitute for heroin. The only facilities for junkies going 'cold turkey' are a locked observation cell, bare apart from a mattress on the floor, and counselling from a social worker.

Despite the decline in drug use, Aids is a growing worry for senior medical officer Dr Neil Smith. Prisoners are not tested for HIV so no one knows how many are infected and carriers mix freely with their fellow inmates. "Glasgow will go the same way as Edinburgh in a few years so it's essential to educate staff and inmates about the risks and the precautions they should take. We also have to teach them not to shun people infected with the HIV virus." To this end, he has been showing a Home Office film to prisoners. Far more sexually explicit than any other government Aids material – and therefore infinitely more effective – it features scenes of homosexual lovers, both male and female, an illustration of how to put on a condom, and advice from HIV-infected prisoners. "We've had a good response from most inmates," says Dr Smith.

He has worked in the prison service since 1976 – he joined because it offered a better wage than general practice. But he now finds himself frustrated with the cramped and old-fashioned hospital housed in a warren of wards and corridors. Illness, he points out, is often worsened by basic bad health. "A lot of the people we treat have very primitive lifestyles outside Barlinnie. They drink and smoke to excess, they don't eat healthily. That means many are very vulnerable to illness and need a great deal of care."

"The main change I've noticed over the years is that prisoners are more demanding," he says. "They know their rights, they are constantly testing the limits. They want their own clothing, their own music, canteen food. I think it's a good and healthy attitude."

If Dr Smith and his medical team have an arduous job caring for the bodies of Barlinnie's inmates, the task facing the men who look after their souls is no less daunting. Part-time Church of Scotland and Roman Catholic chaplains are available for counselling, and there are services on Sundays and at festivals. New prisoners receive a card giving details. On it there is a quotation from the New Testament, "And Jesus said when I was in prison you visited me." One inmate added "and so did Beltrami", a reference to Glasgow's most famous lawyer, a Barlinnie celebrity.

The prison's barn-sized ecumenical church looks perfectly ordinary – until you notice the section that's been fenced off at the back. This is for prisoners – mainly sex offenders – on 'protection' from their fellow inmates. They are segregated at their own request because they fear what may happen to them. Father Frank Gallagher, the RC chaplain, is a familiar face to many of the men, as he also serves the parish of St Margaret Mary's in the city's Castlemilk council estate. Working in prison appealed to him because he wanted to help the poor. "Let's face it, it's poor people who are in here. But no matter how poor you are, you don't have to live in spiritual poverty," he says.

About 50 men attend the Catholic service every week, and many ask for private sessions with the chaplains. Father Gallagher tries to give them a sense of hope and a view of another way of life. "Sometimes you do see people for whom prison is very spiritual. They go away and change their lives completely." Sandy Roper, the Church of Scotland minister, agrees. "It's amazing the number of people who ask to see me and who want real guidance on becoming more Christian. Some are full of remorse." But he adds, "There's a very big difference between remorse and repentance."

Father Gallagher is saddened by the huge number of confused and mentally disturbed people he sees in Barlinnie, as well as those addicted to drink or drugs. "It keeps a few off the streets, but apart from that I can't see why many of them are here at all."

David Crawford, head of Barlinnie's social work team, leads a staff of 14 tackling the problems that concern so many of the prison's professionals. But with an average of 12,000 admissions each year, it's hard to give any real help. "Barlinnie's biggest problem is its size. The very short sentences men serve mean they're in and out before we've had time to see them more than once."

Many social workers view prison work as a move up the career ladder, away from child-care which dominates the job outside. However, in prison they find themselves dealing increasingly with the perpetrators of sexual crimes against children, as more of these cases come to light. Crawford and his team do their best to be positive. "We try to affect their outlook and behaviour. It's only in the long-term that we'll know if our work is successful." Child sex offenders often face terrible problems when they are freed. "They've lost their own families, and there is a tendency to go out and find another one, so the whole situation can be recreated. We have to try and work against that before they are discharged."

Crawford estimates up to 60 per cent of the prisoners are in Barlinnie for alcohol-related offences. The huge problem of alcohol addiction is combatted by just one visit every week by Charlie Canavan from the Glasgow Council on Alcohol, though there are hopes the service will be extended.

Canavan, a pensioner who used to work full-time for the GCA, allows me to watch a counselling session with an English prisoner. He asks 25-year-old Gerry about his drinking habits, nodding silently as the prisoner explains he has been drinking regularly since he was 15. His girlfriend drinks and takes drugs, he says, and he can't stop once he starts. Often he gets into pub fights, spurred on by fits of uncontrollable jealousy about his girlfriend. Canavan asks him to consider whether any of his problems are related to drink, and suggests controlling his habit might be a good idea. However Gerry is more concerned about arranging a transfer to a prison in England. Sighing, Canavan gives him the address of the Alcohol Council in his home town.

"I try and make the men see the connection between their drinking and the mess their lives are in," he explains. "It's surprising the number who've never thought about this." Unfortunately, lack of personnel means he can't find out how many follow up his sessions by contacting outside agencies.

Unemployment and poverty undoubtedly bring many of the prisoners to Barlinnie. Poverty also inspired most of the older officers to join the service in search of a secure career. Jim McMahon is one of them. He came to Barlinnie 30 years ago to escape the slums of St George's Cross in Glasgow's city centre. He wanted a job with a better future than his post at a ships' chandlers. "The staff quarters were far better than the house we'd been living in, and the pension was excellent," he explains. "I had no qualifications, and I had very few choices."

McMahon's first memories of Barlinnie are of a very disciplined place with a carefully regulated routine that rarely wavered. He has also seen it in the worst days, when almost all discipline had broken down. Now, he thinks, the balance is good. "At the time of the riot, morale was at rock bottom and it was a frightening place to work.

Now I doubt if there's a prison in Scotland with better staff morale. There was a rapport missing before that has been recreated thanks to Alan Walker's leadership. His policy is that there's nothing to hide at Barlinnie, and he lets his staff know they're appreciated."

If McMahon represents the old guard of Barlinnie staff, then Audrey Mooney is a good example of the new blood joining the service. The pair share an office with two other assistant governors – unsurprisingly, office space is limited. Mooney wanted to be a prison officer when she was at school. "It sounds very pious but I saw it as a way to help people. I've always felt, 'There but for the grace of God go I'."

She is not the only woman in senior management at Barlinnie. She says men respond well to her and often treat her with more respect than they would a male officer. "It's a man's world, but that can work to my advantage. They won't argue with me, whereas they would with a man."

Although the officers are happy working under the new regime, many still do not admit to outsiders what they do for a living. "I tell people I'm a civil servant, which is true," says Bob Luke, who was a psychiatric nurse before the higher wages attracted him to prison work. "You never know when people will be sensitive about prisons. Maybe they've been inside, or have a relative here." Families of inmates often do a similar covering up act – many children think the imposing Glasgow building they visit each week is an oil rig.

It's now 4pm and the prisoners are returning to their cells after a day spent in the kitchens or one of the prison's various workshops. At five o'clock they'll eat and by 9.30pm everyone's in their cells, ready to be locked up for the night.

For most, the stay in Barlinnie is short, unpleasant but not unbearable. There are always candidates for the suicide surveillance cells, but the vast majority serve their sentences without incident. "Once you're used to it, it's not bad," says one inmate who has spent most of his life in Barlinnie on a succession of short sentences. "It's only when they lock you up at night that the realisation hits you, you're not a free man."

Discharge is almost as impersonal as the reception process. Social workers try hard to prepare prisoners for freedom, but it is almost impossible to find them either jobs or homes. David Crawford sometimes advises the homeless to stay in Glasgow. "At least there is some provision for them there. In Ayrshire and Lanarkshire there is next to nothing," he says.

The mentally confused are among the saddest cases. "Often they go into the worst end of the accommodation market, sleazy bed and breakfast hotels. Or they just sleep rough. It's a disgrace that there's no provision for them," says Crawford. "Barlinnie is being used as the classic Victorian asylum."

But not everyone welcomes the thud of the prison gates closing behind them. One man, suffering from paranoia, had served his sentence quietly and without complaint. On the day of his release he tried to hand back his discharge papers, and begged to be allowed to stay in his cell. "Let me stay here for the rest of my life," he pleaded. "In here, I'm safe. I'm scared of the rest of the world."

September 17, 1990

Discordant notes

Neville Garden

The other night I attended a concert in the Usher Hall in Edinburgh. But if I had shut my eyes, I could well have been at the Royal Infirmary in a ward devoted to respiratory diseases. Maybe even the ear, nose and throat department.

Every time the orchestra began to woo me with a particularly lovely phrase, somebody coughed. Not a subdued, muffled or apologetic cough – but a full-blown explosion whose ferocity might well have put a mortar bomb to shame. In every corner of the hall, the bronchitic saboteurs were at work. One woman, in the row behind me, coughed once a minute with clockwork regularity. I know because I was so distracted from the music that I actually timed her.

Now, everyone gets colds, especially at this time of the year. Everyone coughs as a result – and no one at a concert minds the odd cough, carefully muted by a handkerchief and ministered to by gently sucked pastilles. But an 'odd cough' is a very different thing from a fusillade guaranteed to drown out a fortissimo chord from the brass section. The question has to be asked: Do people with persistent coughs ever stop to wonder whether they will be a nuisance? Do they ever say to themselves: "Perhaps I'd better stay at home tonight?"

Nor are the coughers, the sneezers and the snufflers the only people who can turn a rewarding evening of music into a nightmare.

Every bit as bad are the *Conductors*. Not the ones on the platform: the ones who sit next to you and saw the air with their right hands. Usually out of time with the music. Really bad cases hold a pencil like a mini baton.

The *Vocalists* sing along with the music, so softly as to be almost inaudible, but not quite. They are invariably tone deaf, so are singing in a different key from the orchestra. They never know the melody with complete accuracy.

The *Kickers* have their feet resting on the back of your seat and exert rythmic pressure on it in time to the music. The effect on you can be something akin to sitting on a rocking horse, since you are pitched forward and back all evening.

The *Sleepers* pretend to be listening with their eyes shut but are actually dead to the world. Quite often they emit soft, hissing sounds: at their worst they snore and look hurt when wakened. They are more prevalent than might be imagined.

The *Readers* follow the score of the work being performed. (I even saw one with a pencil-light torch.) The constant turning of pages is vastly irritating to the majority of listeners: and one always has the feeling that the offenders can't actually read a score but merely follow the tunes.

The *Rustlers* are more likely to be encountered in the theatre than the concert hall. They nurse boxes of chocolates on their knees and dip noisily into them at regular intervals. The trouble is, if you turn round and say "Sssshh..." to them, you make more noise than they do.

The *Dodgers* are always directly in front of you and move their heads irregularly, always from side to side as if attempting to thwart a sniper somewhere in the building. They make it impossible for you to focus solidly on the platform or stage.

The *Clappers* burst into applause almost before the last chord has died away. Sometimes even before it has done so. They seem anxious to show the world they know when a work has ended. I have never yet heard the final bars of the first act of Puccini's *Madam Butterfly* in a live performance. These nit-wits always begin their cheering and yelling the second the curtain begins to fall – instead of waiting to hear what composer, conductor and orchestra have so carefully arranged for them.

But all these musical menaces pale into insignificance, in my book, when confronted by the *Experts*. These are the ones who give us the benefit of their wisdom – either in whispers during a performance, or very loudly in the bar during the interval. "Oh, my dear – it's not a patch on Glyndebourne. They just haven't a clue!" Or: "It's not bad, I suppose. But you really should have heard Karajan do it at Salzburg in '81. That was something else."

There is only one consolation when dealing with these people.

They are quite easy to nail to the mast. I once extolled to one genius the qualities of Carl Nielsen's Seventh Symphony, which I claimed to have heard at an early Edinburgh Festival. He agreed that it had been superb. Since Nielsen wrote only six symphonies, I felt I had won a tiny, private victory.

No one is perfect. My wife tells me that if I am unhappy about a conductor's interpretation, I emit tiny, soft sighs – which she finds intensely irritating. As Sir Thomas Beecham, questioned about making records, once said: "There is nothing to equal the excitement of a live performance in the concert hall – even if you do have to put up with an audience!"

November 12, 1989

The new morality

Joyce McMillan

I saw Lech Walesa once; not in London last week, but in Paris in 1981 when he was still riding the first wave of Solidarity success, and the glamour surrounding his stand against the Brezhnev empire was tremendous. There was a bright red and white awning over a pleasure cruiser on the Seine, a sudden crowd, placards in a strange language; then a coach gleaming to a halt, and in the doorway a blunt, familiar figure, pipe in hand, waving and smiling.

I couldn't help noticing, though, that the demonstrators with the placards weren't the usual students and trade unionists; most were middle-aged emigres, many of them women in smart coats and furs. And instead of applauding and cheering Walesa they were fighting to get close to him. I began to catch a whiff of something unfamiliar and unpleasant. It was the odour of religious fervour – Walesa's devout Catholicism was already well-known – combined with the smell of money; even then, I found it sickly.

Yet it seems to me that that smell is something we'll have to get used to as the new Europe takes shape. All across the East, the churches – Catholic and Orthodox – have been a focus of anti-communist feeling during the long decades of Marxist-Leninist materialism. Now, as Eastern Europe opens itself to the West, their entrenched hatred of communism naturally casts them as allies of capitalism; and the old alliance of authoritarian religion and right-wing politics has room to flex its muscles again.

Hence the spectacle of Western economic liberals – like the Adam Smith Institute gurus who recently held a series of seminars in Warsaw – happily making common cause with traditional religious movements, whose attitudes on moral and family issues should make their freedom-loving hair stand on end.

But then it's becoming apparent, as the decade ends, that many of Britain's free-market ideologues are not liberals at all, except in the narrowest economic sense. Last weekend the *Sunday Times* (whose immensely wealthy proprietor Rupert Murdoch recently announced his conversion to Christianity) ran a controversial piece, by American academic Charles Murray, on the growth of the British 'underclass', a group characterised, he argues, by a set of attitudes – a high illegitimacy rate, unwillingness to work, family breakdown – that mark them as alienated from 'normal' society and its values in a way that the 'decent' poor are not.

But what was revealing and shocking was not so much the article itself, as the *Sunday Times*' editorial response to it, which seemed to take its cue straight from the new current of right-wing moralism drifting across Europe. For after several paragraphs berating the British churches for "peddling politics" when they should have been "preaching family values", the paper abruptly suggested that what was needed to prevent the further growth of the underclass was a return to the days when unemployment and illegitimacy carried a social stigma. Social stigma, it argued, "is an essential ingredient of social order, and must…be restored".

Now, apart from the sheer practical absurdity of this suggestion – I suppose the idea is that the church should start re-training people in how to cold-shoulder fallen women and taunt fatherless children – there are two aspects of it that chill the blood. The first is the bare-faced moral hypocrisy of it, for there is clearly no intention that any social stigma should attach to the private lives of playboy newspaper editors or much-married millionaires; as usual, it is the poor bloody infantry of moral rearmament – the poor, and particularly poor women – who have to deliver on society's moral posturings. And the second is the shameful social amnesia it betrays, as if everyone had simply forgotten why people found those rigid moral codes unacceptable in the first place.

The problem in staging a fightback against this kind of reactionary nonsense is that the forces of real liberalism in Britain – those who are proud of the personal freedoms men and women have won this century, and who can envisage a future that combines that freedom with social responsibility – have become complacent, have forgotten just how ugly an authoritarian moral climate can be. When religious intolerance reared its head in the Salman Rushdie case, the liberal establishment took a while to rediscover the vocabulary in which such judgmental arrogance must be fought; when reactionary Anglo-Catholicism tries to claim the Church of England for its own, the liberal bishops – who are quite right to place Christ's Church unequivocally on the side of the poor – hardly seem able to defend themselves.

But if liberals do not begin to find a voice again, and to make common cause with their allies in western Europe, then we could find ourselves facing a tide of religious reaction – fuelled by the strength of the liberated Eastern churches – that would make recent battles over abortion legislation and gay rights look like a tea-party. As for those seduced by the idea that today's poor are feckless and undeserving, they should remember that the Victorians – who knew a thing or two about underclasses – had a popular song about it. "It's the same the whole world over," it goes. "It's the poor what gets the blame. It's the rich what gets the pleasure; ain't it all a bloomin' shame?" On reflection, I don't think I could have put it better myself.

December 3, 1989

Scotland 2050

Rob Edwards

Imagine the scene: May, 2050, and you are spread over the burning sands of Morar on the West Coast soaking up the sun, sipping freshly-squeezed juice from the orange trees of Arisaig and contemplating another lazy dip in the refreshingly cool waters of the Sound of Sleat.

Inland, you can glimpse a wheat field swaying gently, but no trees. Out to sea what were once fishing boats are plying a busy trade sailing tourists along the coast. For the most part it is quiet: there are few cars and fewer seabirds. You lie dreaming vaguely about the past, present and future.

Paradise? Maybe. But only for a while. If you sun yourself too long you will suffer. If you are, in the words of the leaked United Nations report on the impact of climate change, one of the "fair-skinned Caucasians in high altitude zones", you will probably contract skin cancer.

You are plagued by swarms of bees and wasps. In the evenings the dense clouds of blood-sucking midges seem even denser and more unbearable than when you were a child. Large numbers of cleggs, black flies and mosquitoes all regularly join the hunt for your veins. As if that was not enough, you have diarrhoea from a gut infection.

The Arisaig orange grove is alternately infested with pests, and loaded with pesticides. The seabirds have been silenced for the same reason the local fishing industry has faded away: the fish on which they both depend have moved on in search of sustenance elsewhere.

Some local farmers, always experimenting with new, traditionally-southern crops, are doing all right for themselves. If they can control disease, they can harvest bumper crops of apples, pears, damsons and raspberries. Their potatoes, however, diseased by blight, constantly fail.

In other respects the local economy is booming. Increasing numbers of migrants from southern Europe, where most crops have failed, are attempting to settle in the Highlands, along with many others from the south of England fleeing a series of recent malaria epidemics.

Further north there has been a radiation scare after an extraordinarily fierce April storm destroyed the sea defences around the European nuclear waste dump near Thurso. The huge underground cavern containing many tonnes of highly radioactive waste is still flooded with seawater. Electricity generation from the Atomic Energy Authority's massive new wave-power station situated offshore has again been disrupted by freak wave conditions.

Elsewhere around the coast, low-lying towns and villages have been flooded and abandoned. The Firths of the Forth, Tay, Moray, Dornoch, Clyde and Solway have changed beyond recognition, forcing industries, residents and wildlife to move. In Edinburgh, housing schemes have been permitted on Arthur's Seat, the Braid Hills and the Pentlands in response to pressure from developers.

All around the coast, communities are complaining that their sewage keeps returning to the shore with the tides. In Inverness, work is almost complete on the third rail bridge over the Ness to replace the one that was washed away in the record floods a couple of years ago. At Kyle of Lochalsh, engineers are on the point of abandoning prolonged attempts to secure the Skye tunnel to the seabed after unusual sea currents dislodged it.

In the Western Isles, Orkney and Shetland, islanders are struggling to survive in an increasingly unpredictable and often extremely harsh climate. The 20 or so remaining residents of Foula, west of Shetland, and Fair Isle, between Shetland and Orkney, have made a heart-rending decision to evacuate. The wind turbines that used to provide them power have been blown down.

Ski facilities on Cairn Gorm, at Glencoe and at Glenshee have long since been replaced by huge open-air mountain biking arenas. Birds like the ptarmigan, snow bunting and dotterel that used to roam the high peaks have become extinct, along with a wide range of alpine flowers.

Red squirrels, pine martens, crossbills and their rare Scots pine habitat are disappearing. All salmon and trout fishing has been banned to try and protect their fast declining populations. The forestry industry and its beloved blanket conifer plantations are both dying.

Every night on the satellite news there are terrible tales of mass starvation, huge migrations, and war in Africa and India. Many of the ten million refugees from the flooded river deltas of Bangladesh, Egypt and Vietnam are still homeless. America, under its Radical Party president, Fay Fonda, is facing a major social and economic crisis because of declining grain harvests.

In England and Wales, the fourth post-Thatcherite regime is considering new hardline immigration controls and mandatory birth control to reduce the population. Southern European governments are fighting to preserve order as people take to the streets to object to the introduction of food rationing.

In Moscow, the capital of the Central Slavonian republic, the Liberal leadership is drawing up a new list of the forbidden zones – places so polluted or so short of resources that people are denied access to them.

In Scotland, the First Secretary of the Assembly, Green Party leader Joanna Spaven, is struggling with new transport and energy controls which have made her unpopular with the minority 'deep green' wing of her party. They want to see a total ban on non-essential traffic and the complete outlawing of any form of combustion.

Back on the burning beach of Morar, you sit up, take off your extra-protective sunglasses and rub your temples. You feel suddenly very tired and slightly sick. Paradise has been lost. You stand up, walk into the sea and start swimming west.

May 27, 1990

Poetic justice

Kenneth Roy

On the day that anti-poll tax demonstrators threw custard pies in Nottingham, clashed with mounted police in Bristol, and besieged the Town Hall in Birmingham, I met the Scottish poet Douglas Dunn in a peaceful book-lined study overlooking the Tay. "You don't see the sun setting from this house," he said, "you see it rising. Almost enough to make me an optimist."

"Almost?"

"Optimism is stupid. But I'm not a pessimist, either. Pessimism is a disease, and I'm not diseased. Yet."

The room contained a double bed (unmade), a sofa and chairs, a superb working library, and a big desk with a photo-copier and typewriter (but no word processor, apparently) where the distracted writer can sit and admire the view across to Broughty Ferry. The river glistened in the first pale sunshine of Spring: it was no day for pessimism.

But in a few weeks, the room with a view may look quite different. Although he has refrained from tossing a custard pie, Douglas Dunn has refused to pay the poll tax, has no intention of paying, and now awaits a visit from Gray Scott & Co., Sheriff Officers, Dundee, who have been instructed by Fife Regional Council to enforce the collection of £320 (plus a penalty of £32). In the books of Gray Scott & Co., he has become an awkward, 13-digit case.

No. 0162963020005 relaxed in one of the chairs he may not possess for much longer, lit the mildest of cigarettes ("Norman MacCaig calls it an expensive form of breathing") and enlightened me on the legal implications of civil disobedience.

"What do you think will happen?"

"The municipal psychology is that they've got to collect the money at any cost. A warrant sale, I expect. But they're not allowed to take your bed or your children's clothes. And since books are the tools of my trade, I don't think they'll be allowed to touch my books, either."

"What if they do?"

"Let them try," he exploded, "and they'll face five foot six of diminutive wrath!"

As the Militant mob and the Tory voters of Devon unite in common cause south of the border, each pursuing their separate brand of narrow self-interest, there is something nicely symbolic about the emergence of a poet as the most articulate opponent of the tax north of the border. For in Scotland, the argument has always appeared to be driven at least as much by offended principles of fairness as by the depth of the hurt to individual pockets.

Next week, the tone of an increasingly violent debate will be improved when Douglas Dunn's reasoned denunciation of the poll tax is published in Counterblasts – a series of pamphlets by leading British writers of the left, challenging the orthodoxies of the Thatcher era.

But why a poet? And why this particular poet?

"Something's gone in our literature – that Orwellian capacity to discuss topical issues and current affairs. You're supposed to do that with the left hand, while the right hand goes on writing stories and plays and poems. But it should be done with the same hand. You're alive, you're living in a certain place at a certain time. To dissociate poetry from everyday life weakens literature."

So Dunn decided to abandon fiction for a while, and become a political commentator-cum-investigative journalist. One of his first discoveries was that there is nothing new about poll taxes. In an emergency measure to settle a debt with the Army, the Crown raised such a tax as long ago as 1641 – though unlike Margaret Thatcher, Charles I graduated it according to people's ability to pay. (A duke was charged £100, an esquire £10.) The present poll tax, he believes, also has something of an emergency feel about it. Its immediate aim – disastrously misconceived, as it now turns out – was to appease a minority of voters disenchanted with the rates. But behind the bungled expedient, he detects the ideological hand of Margaret Thatcher's 'New Conservatism'.

"The poll tax is another step in the dismantling of restraints on free enterprise – an attempt to get rid of the power contained in the local councils. This government isn't just interested in cutting public expenditure. It wants to change the whole fabric of British society. That's the function of the poll tax, but I don't think people have quite realised it yet."

"This New Conservatism you loathe so much. How does it differ from the old?"

"What's happening with the poll tax in England is exposing the difference. Old-fashioned Conservatism – the sort you associated with people like Macmillan and Heath – was liberal, had a capacity for elegance and clarity, and wasn't ruthless. New Conservatism simply imitates American values. It's a businessman's party."

However, the people who have sustained the government in power for 11 years are not businessmen, but the English working-class and lower middle-class. Douglas Dunn acknowledged that he did not fully understand this phenomenon. But since the jingoism of the

Falklands war he had wondered whether there might be an uncomfortably close link between the National Front and the English psyche.

"Are you saying that you dislike them as a race?"

"Some of my best friends are English. No, what I dislike is what this government has encouraged them to believe. The encouragement of cruel self-interest."

"Why is it cruel?"

"Because it is poverty-producing as well as wealth-producing. Because it tells people not to contribute to the welfare of others."

For several years, Dunn worked as a university librarian in Hull. There he developed a close friendship with a poet who made no secret of his admiration for Margaret Thatcher. I was curious to know how he and Philip Larkin had managed to hit it off.

"We argued about politics once or twice, but then agreed to differ. Mostly we talked about jazz or gossiped about people we knew."

"What was it Larkin liked about Mrs Thatcher?"

"Philip 'adored' her – his word. He associated her with some very old-fashioned standard. An almost domestic rectitude. Balancing your books personally as well as publicly. I think he was wrong. But maybe that's part of the appeal Mrs Thatcher has for many people."

"It's all part of her emphasis on self-reliance."

"That's just government rhetoric," he said derisively.

Later in the conversation, as he recalled his childhood in the Renfrewshire village of Inchinnan ("They built Erskine New Town over my childhood – but I can hardly complain about that"), the phrase self-reliance cropped up again. But this time, it was Douglas Dunn who raised it.

"My father had a great belief in education. I could read from the time I was four, and it was my father who taught me. Like so many Scots men of his generation, he had a quality that I might call self-reliance. But I won't, in case you start accusing me of supporting Mrs Thatcher."

"When is self-reliance a virtue?"

"When it's the kind of working-class initiative that makes you want to study, to fulfil your life in the best way you can. Whereas Mrs Thatcher's self-reliance is just a cover-up for dismantling public services."

Invited to describe his father's character, Douglas Dunn said he would do so through an anecdote. "He worked in the India Tyres factory. Eventually, he had quite a lot of responsibility. But if he had to go anywhere in the factory wearing a suit, he always wore a boiler suit on top. I'm a bit like that myself."

"Signifying what?"

"Loyalty," he said softly.

"To what?"

He said he didn't know, and gave an alternative answer about the nature of Scottish politics and culture. When I persisted in asking about his parents, his face reddened. "I find it embarrassing having to describe them," he said. "Not because I didn't love them, but it seems like stepping beyond natural reticence." So we dropped the subject; and the uneasy mood was lifted by the timely entrance of a young musketeer brandishing a plastic sword.

"I'm D'Artagnan," he declared.

"He's only three and speaks better than I do," said the young musketeer's father.

Douglas Dunn has been married twice. His first wife, Lesley Wallace, senior keeper at Hull Art Gallery, died of cancer. Afterwards, he spent a year drinking hard, travelling obsessively and feeling scarcely human; then, after a long interval, produced an intensely moving collection of poems, Elegies, inspired by the experience of grief. It was Whitbread Book of the Year in 1985.

"As a writer, the experience made me more spiritual. Someone described me as close to a mystic in some poems. I don't relish that, because I don't think I am. But it gave me a greater sense of poetry as something almost sacred. Something that people share."

"So you don't believe in writing just for yourself?"

"I've always believed in writing – not for 'the public', I've no idea who they are – but for other people. When you write only for yourself, all sorts of obscurity and self-indulgence creep in...the great curse of the modern arts."

He has been "an inveterate scribbler" for as long as he can remember. In his early teens he wrote his first novel, a "very bad" parody of Buchan, in a school jotter. He has kept the jotter, but many years later junked another attempt at a novel. Satisfied now that he will never be a novelist, he intends to concentrate on short stories and poems – when he is not reviewing books for the *Glasgow Herald*, lecturing at St Andrews University, compiling Faber's anthology of 20th-century Scottish verse ("that'll make me a few enemies"), lambasting the prime minister, or playing with D'Artagnan.

"When you were young, what did you want to say in your poems?"

"I've no idea. I don't think any young poet knows. I don't think Keats knew what he wanted to say, and he died before he could say it. His poems are almost like a substitute for having something to say. They're just wonderful poems."

Of Scottish writers, he has a particular admiration for Burns –

because of his directness, his willingness to declare himself, and his artistry in verse: "I resent the way he is represented as a ploughman, when he is such a sophisticated literary artist."

"So you don't approve of the January blow-out?"

"I'm all in favour of a blow-out. Any excuse will do. But I've been to one Burns Supper, and I'm no' goin' back!"

When I asked him if there were living Scottish writers he liked, he reeled off more than a dozen names, with Tom Leonard and James Kelman first. What did they have in common? A conspicuous absence of the tight-lipped, he thought.

"And you're not tight-lipped?"

"What I aim to be is sane, but passionate with it. That's what any poet has to be."

We returned finally to questions of the spiritual (his word). How did he define spirituality? An interest in life beyond our own, he said.

"Are you a believer?"

"No, I'm a poet."

"You can be a believer too, can't you?"

"There have been some."

"But you aren't one of them?"

"I believe in certain spiritual things. But I don't believe in organised Christianity."

"What about God?"

"I use that word in poems from time to time."

"Yes, but do you believe in God?"

"To the Christian, He's the first resort. To the poet, the last. That's the difference between a poet and a Christian."

D'Artagnan was back, accompanied by a warlike young friend naked from the waist down. Enough of God, the poll tax, and the conspicuous lack of the tight-lipped: it was 1 o'clock and time for a pint in the Bell Rock Inn.

The poet has a large, unkempt garden, with comforting weeds more than a year high. As we set off for the pub, he noticed a household brush in the middle of the wilderness and couldn't think how it got there. My own, unvoiced suspicion is that one of the young musketeers put it there. By the time the Sheriff's men arrive, I expect all three musketeers to be on duty, waving their plastic swords in a fairly intimidating fashion. If Gray Scott & Co. have any sense, they will leave the poet's books well alone.

March 11, 1990

The worm turns

Joanna Blythman

Imagine you were sitting in a very fancy restaurant tucking into an expensive duck mousse salad and you came across some little hard bits of something in amongst the raddichio and endive. You taste it, assuming that it is an interesting garnish of chicken only to discover that it is tightly screwed-up tissue hanky. What would you do? Throw up? Complain? Demand that amends be made?

I pose this question not to overstate the case, but simply because it is a true story. The recipient, in this case, of the scrunched-up Kleenex was none other than Tom Jaine, editor of the *Good Food Guide*. Not someone, you might assume, who would be slow to pull a restaurant up by its socks. So how did this unsavoury event draw to a close?

The dish was sent back to the kitchen for the chef to see, the meal continued, no apology, the bill arrived with no deduction, the unhappy editor paid up and left. Amazed? Perhaps this isn't so astonishing when you appreciate that Mr Jaine like many Brits confesses that he "hates to complain". "I'm the sort of person who can't face rows. I'd rather just go."

We aren't all temperamentally unsuited to complaining, of course. There are those who come into the category of what Jaine, who has run restaurants in the past, refers to as "stunning complainers, who simply adore venting their spleen", who can try the patience of even the most modest and accommodating management. But equally well there is the person of normal ego, and I include myself here, who goes out to eat to have a nice time and enjoy good food, and who pays with their own hard-earned cash.

Speaking as someone who is a seasoned eater-outer, and fairly confident in a restaurant setting, I find myself complaining or querying more than most. Empirical experience shows that establishments which don't respond well to a gentle and tactfully-put complaint are in the minority.

Here's a recent example. After two excellent courses I am served a dessert where the pastry is undercooked and therefore paste-like and unpleasant. Decision time. Keep quiet and feel secretly disappointed, or point it out? I take the latter course, the cook arrives to explain why the pastry is like that, not necessarily admitting fault, but interested in my remarks, instantly offering a substitute. The replacement dish is better, no charge is made for the first, I go home happy and prepared to recommend the place despite small imperfections. For any forward thinking establishment, such an outcome is infinitely more desirable than a disgruntled customer, badmouthing you to all and sundry.

"Complaints keep restaurateurs on their toes," says Jaine. "Complaints really dig deep, and generally the customer who makes the most fuss gets the best attention."

So what about going a step further. When should you expect not to be charged for a mistake? Quite recently, I ate in a restaurant which presented a diabolically over-grilled slice of haddock (or possibly cod), described on the menu as turbot. My companion and recipient of this miserable fish happened to be a caterer who knows fish like the back of his hand, and so had detected that in Scotland Yard parlance, "the anatomy of the corpse was not consistent with that of a turbot". We queried it, the chef held firm. What conclusion then, is the aforementioned chef a villain or a plonker? Fortunately we didn't have to reach a verdict because the manager stepped in with offers of amends.

"Complaining has its part," says Jaine, "but it is important to marry external reality to your subjective impression. If you are going to take the tack that you can't pay for it, it depends on how heinous the mistakes are on the line between truly bad and not very good – overcooked fish is one example. You may simply get the 'most of our customers do like it this way, so get stuffed' reaction and have a tricky time proving your point. You may think that Britain's taste is execrable, but that won't help you to make your case. Focusing on the contractual aspects of the meal is usually a stronger position – was it served on time, with reasonable politeness and was the food as described on the menu?"

"The main incentive for complaining is to bring about some short term practical effect on your meal," says Jaine. So if, for example, you ordered avocado salad with asparagus and basil hollandaise because you were attracted by the sauce, but you are served avocado with a cold herb mayonnaise, you do have an alternative. Point out that the dish is not what you ordered and ask for the real thing or another dish, or sit and eat it (and say that it's very nice anyway) like the average wimpy Brit. After all, a complaint is likely to result in some immediate improvement – a substitute course, a price reduction, at very least an apology.

There are, of course, apologies and apologies, as this final and magnificently ghastly real life horror story illustrates. A diner in a very upper crust restaurant is munching her way through a sumptuous halibut steak, only to be greeted by a horrible little worm, still wriggling. Shock horror! Open mouths all round, waitress gags and removes, no further mention is made. At the end of the meal the bill arrives which shows that the full charge has been applied. On the back of the bill is a handwritten note from the chef/proprietor as follows: "A 'nematode' is a common occurrence in fresh fish, and quite a harmless phenomenon. Its presence is nevertheless regretted."

April 22, 1990

A woman's work

James Naughtie

One of the great tricks in politics is persuading yourself and others that everything has changed when everything is staying, stubbornly, the same. Malcolm Rifkind and Margaret Thatcher, in their different ways, have done it in the last few days and nobody should underestimate the achievement: they were not lining the streets of Aberdeen to cheer the prime minister, but she has won herself more time from her party which is what she needs above all.

You may well wonder how it has been done. Inflation is bad and getting worse and the economic outlook is as grey and gloomy as the North Sea at Aberdeen yesterday. England and Wales are going to take a long time to learn to love the poll tax. The regional election results, north and south of the border, were very bad for the Tories. There are European problems ahead. Yet inside the party some of the tension has gone. It proves, updating the adage, that a day or two is a long time in politics, and that the whole business is often a matter of illusion.

Look at the regional election results. In Grampian, where Mrs Thatcher stood yesterday, the Tories' position compared with eight years ago, say, is disastrous. In Strathclyde, for all the roof tax pandemonium, Labour suffered not a scratch at the hands of the Conservatives, and hardly any more from the SNP. One senior party figure was saying in Aberdeen that he simply could not understand how it was that the party had not tumbled to the truth about its position.

Rifkind, however, like Kenneth Baker in the south, has managed by sleight of hand to use the elections to lift the atmosphere of gloom that had enveloped the government. Ministers this week have been smiling a little more easily and the fever in the Commons has subsided. This may all seem mysterious, given the happenings in the outside world, until you realise that it has got nothing to do with events and everything to do with the need for relief from the horrors of the last few months. Baker, as Peter Pan, says that if you try to believe it for long enough it will eventually become true, and so it has.

Mrs Thatcher spoke yesterday about the drive towards the fourth term in the same way as she has spoken about all the challenges that have faced her. "A woman's work is never done," she said in a classic Thatcherite phrase. It draws together the characteristic of which she is proudest – her determination – and the fact that she is different from all other prime ministers, something we are reminded of by her sex. So we are invited to believe that nothing has changed, it is the same prime minister who has triumphed before who will triumph again, and the jitters have been banished from the land. That, however, cannot be done by one speech whatever those who cheered her yesterday may believe.

Mrs Thatcher's future will be decided instead by how she deals with the issues that first produced the crisis. If by the time of the party conference in October there is no sign of a drop in interest rates, nor in the underlying rate of inflation, the gloom will descend again like a curtain.

Under these economic troubles lie what may yet prove to be the most dangerous iceberg of all. It is quite clear in Scotland, and increasingly in the south too, that there are many people who believe – almost as a matter of principle – that the prime minister has been prime minister for too long.

It gets more difficult with the passage of the years to find the same sense of urgency and excitement. An obvious tiredness starts to creep in. So yesterday there was no freshness about the call to arms. This party is battered by unpopularity in much of Scotland and recovery seems a distant hope. "Tomorrow will be ours," said Mrs Thatcher yesterday, but there is a long night to come before tomorrow.

It is natural that ministers should now be claiming that the Heseltine bubble is exploded and Labour's high tide is slipping back. They will not, however, forget the last few months: so grateful are they for the respite from crisis, thanks to the electoral blips of Wandsworth and Westminster, that they can now talk rather frankly and perhaps unwisely about the darkest days that are just behind them.

That is an experience which has left scars that won't easily heal, and having realised how close the government came to some kind of internal collapse this year it is rather easier now to believe that it could happen again. So two beliefs are struggling for supremacy in the minds of the party. One says that it is obvious the crisis is over, the other says that having happened once the crisis can easily come again.

At this conference, a psychological mood has been successfully engineered – despite the bizarre intervention of Bill Walker in his effort to promote Michael Forsyth which did little but embarrass him – and for the moment everyone is prepared to believe that the storm has gone away. They know, however, that the government is not back where it was before the troubles began last autumn.

No cabinet can go through what this one has experienced and then erase the memory from its mind. Mrs Thatcher is as aware of that as any of the ministers who sit around her and who are watching her so closely.

The Aberdeen speech was a typical piece of defiance, and it was what the party needed. It will not, however, solve the difficulties. Mrs Thatcher knew as she left the platform yesterday that rhetoric can change an atmosphere, but not the world.

May 13, 1990

A pow-wow of Helmuts

Alan Taylor

This is the flat season, the off season, the low season, when horses don't jump, footballers migrate to Benidorm and hoteliers thank God for conferences. In the streets of the windy city, kilted guides force-march posses of neuro-surgeons and toy salesmen up and down the Old Town, skirting scaffolding wrapped in Axminster carpet, the feet of their zimmers trapped between cobblestones as a double-decker capsizes towards them. This is the part of the conference that the programme has left blank. You are free to do the sights.

Cheesed-off talking about air traffic control or potato research, not to mention immunology and coal science, these fellow travellers happily sign on for an hour's serious walking and talking. As the guide launches into his spiel about John Knox and monstrous regiments, splinter groups tarry at Crawford's window drooling over macaroni pies. They resume the tour reluctantly. I followed a group the other day from the castle to the palace, ducking into doorways and pubs when I thought they might be on to me. From their accents most were American though some were German; tanned, beefy and bored. Each wore a nameplate, presumably to save time on introductions. It is a boon to the town's winos who can now accost the Eugenes and Helmuts on first name terms; familiarity brews bottles of Carlsberg Special.

Conference-goers are the contemporary world's displaced, a tribe to rival the Vandals and Goths, swooping into town aboard blunder buses, armed with plastic and confidence and the weariness of those who have heard it all before. They know the smart cities blindfold; conferences are never held in black holes, always in *bijou* locations where gift shops abound and they know a croissant from a slice of sweating toast.

Every profession has its annual trip to a watering hole, even the Cremation Society which has a jolly time in Bournemouth worrying about vandals fishing in ornamental ponds and fussing over the merits of makes of incinerators. (I know this because I am an avid reader of the 'trade' magazine, *Pharos*, which keeps me up on the British way of death.)

In another incarnation I was a pretty assiduous conference-goer myself; consequently few know so much about the fading seaside resorts of England as I do. Loitering in the reception area as the delegates check in, it is impossible to guess which profession they represent. There is a festive air, suits are eschewed, Reeboks replace high-heels, power-dressing is out, country casual in. There is the bonhomie of backslapping and the tweeking of bra straps, though not much pecking of cheeks. The luggage is no giveaway: pristine Antler suitcases, squash and badminton rackets, golf clubs, air rifles, even a saddle – the horse, presumably, was still in its box. This particular gathering was the Police Federation's annual pow-wow but it could just as easily have been a fusion of nuclear scientists or a welding of civil engineers.

The real veterans of the conference scene are academics. In a year rent with vacations the air lanes are clogged with eggheads heading for the sun. Campus followers of Messrs Bradbury and Lodge will be familiar with the scenario: the sherry reception, subliminal chat-up and oneupmanship, the footnoted pillow-talk.

Something happens to people when they are divorced from their humdrum existence. There is the opportunity to be someone you always wanted to be but dare not among friends. Suddenly, a man who has been trussed in corduroy for 20 years sports a stetson and cowboy boots, his accent is honeyed and he chews Slim Panatellas as if he was Clint Eastwood. He has a new past and a rosy future, a repartee rehearsed in front of a hotel mirror and an aftershave as potent as nerve gas. When you see him making his way towards you, you know the time has come to hear what the funny man in the kilt and the clipper-board has to say about this terribly fascinating place.

May 13, 1990

In search of the hard man

Ajay Close

Monday night in the Gorbals, half a mile and a million light years from the Merchant City. The bar is a curious mix of Curry House imperial and Carnaby Street. Red and gold flocked wallpaper, ultraviolet strip lighting turning the barmaid's T-shirt blue, a jokey sign above the optics announcing *yirfaesiskrewdup*. Several hundredweight of amplifying equipment crowds a postage stamp stage, menacingly biding its time. The mirrorball on the ceiling is spinning in anticipation, freckling the handful of punters with silent stars.

It's an average crowd. Old men who've been nursing their pints since opening time, a couple using contiguity instead of conversation, an ex-safeblower, and one of those relentlessly gregarious Glasgow barflies who gives you his life story in the first five minutes.

The retired safecracker is Paddy Meehan, a veteran of the Glasgow underworld who achieved unenviable fame by serving seven years for a murder he did not commit in the 1970s. Chain-smoking his cigarettes down to the filter, he reels off a roll-call of the great Glasgow hard men: Paddy Slowie, Peter Williamson, Dan Cronin, Billy Fullerton, Benny Davidson. All dead, he says sadly.

A born storyteller, Paddy works his way through the canon. Dan Cronin, co-founder of the Beehive gang, once challenged a man to come outside and fight for a penny wager. Paddy Slowie only used a weapon once in his life: when he was attacked by a man wielding a hatchet, he seized the axe and struck his assailant with the blunt end. Benny Davidson was sentenced to four years by a judge who told him: "You go off on a Sunday morning to have a stand-up fight the way other men go off to have a round of golf." John Currie, 6ft 2in and the last of the old school still living, fought a gypsy scrap-dealer by the banks of the Clyde where the tradition was that the victor walked the suspension bridge and the vanquished swam the river. Big John beat his opponent and remarked later: "I had to win – I couldn't swim."

Most of the hard men were criminals; but this was incidental. The

Glasgow hard man was a hero, nemesis of the liberty takers, custodian of a code of decency in an uncivilised world.

"The hard man was very popular in his own area. The violence was never random: it was the cock of the walk syndrome. A lot of them had very high moral standards. Normally they would never ever bother an innocent person and the only thing they ever got out of it was ego," he says.

The rules were known. An enemy in the company of an acquaintance was safe from challenge – until the mutual friend departed. You sprang to the defence of anyone in your company, even against your own brother. A guest in another's house never raised his voice whatever the provocation; but once outside, the gloves were off and the proper form of retribution was the 'square go', a stand-up fight using only fists, hands and feet.

The 'square go' is central to the sentimental aura surrounding the hard man, and yet weapons were always a feature of Glasgow violence. The gangs fought with anything which came to hand; way back in the 1920s the Billy Boys favoured hatchets, swords and sharpened bicycle chains. And still Paddy laments the passing of a golden age.

"Maybe they'd resort to weapons in situations; OK, you'd get a razor slashing, but unless it was something domestic and a chap stabbed his wife or girlfriend, you never heard of someone stabbing someone, and very rarely you heard of someone shooting somebody. The image of the hard man changed around the early 1960s," he says gloomily. "Today the hard man is more likely to be a psycopath, a headbanger."

There have to be easier quests than tracking down the Glasgow hard man. Everyone knows a hard man but you won't find anybody admitting to being one. Men like Paddy will tell you the species is extinct, yet the epithet is still in general currency across the city, from senior common rooms and expensive restaurants to smoke-filled pubs on the more notorious housing schemes. I'm reminded of the child's nonsense rhyme:

As I was going up the stair
I met a man who wasn't there
He wasn't there again today
Oh how I wish he'd go away.

A mile across the city centre, in an anonymous municipal office in George Street, sits the man responsible for putting the smile on the City of Culture. Harry Diamond is a poacher turned gamekeeper, and truly repentant of his sins. As a crime reporter in the late 1940s – he still has the snapshot of himself in trenchcoat and trilby, dowt hanging from the corner of his mouth – he did his bit to underline the image of the city that he now spends his days as public relations officer working to erase.

Down south every Glaswegian is a hard man; nice boys from Bearsden will tell you that a Glasgow accent is the best protection you can have if you run into trouble on the mean streets of London. There's an honourable tradition of Scots in England – men like Jimmy Reid, Arsenal manager George Graham and the recently departed editor of *The Times*, Charlie Wilson – doing very nicely out of playing up to the image, or not talking it down; Glasgow is synonymous with danger.

It was hype, Diamond says now. Too many newspapers in one city, and too many reporters too lazy to look further than their own doorstep. Yes, the razors and the gangs existed, but the gulf between Glasgow and other industrial conurbations has always been overstated.

But it was not just the grubby hacks of the national press who had a stake in the Glasgow hard man. Glaswegians have always been ready to give the image a helping hand. When the high-kicking crooner Frankie Vaughan went up to Easterhouse in 1968 to declare a weapons amnesty and put an end to gang warfare, the kids were rifling their ma's cutlery drawers and their da's toolboxes for something to hand in.

Every city has its roughnecks: men who can, as the curious phrase has it, handle themselves. What distinguishes the Glasgow strain is what they fought about. While the East Londoners or Mancunians waged warfare in the cause of organised crime, the Glasgow hard man often joined the battle for less tangible gain; and a whole romance sprang up around this difference, exercising a fascination far beyond the sub-cultures of adolescent boys and petty criminals who worship at the shrine of physical violence in other cities.

Even Diamond, spokesman for the new city of style, is susceptible to this romance. "When you use the phrase hard man in isolation, it means a thug who would cut your throat for a cigarette. I would define the Glasgow hard man as someone who's very quick to defend himself and what he considers his rights, his wee bit of territory, his integrity. I refuse to think of the hard man as a guy who roams the streets bashing people, that's not a hard man – that's an idiot. The hard man is the man who's been forced by circumstance to defend his entire way of life and his philosophy. He hasn't had the chance to be educated to the standard where he can tear two strips off someone in a few well chosen words so he has to resort to the only way he can," he says.

"The Glasgow hard man could be very human and generous. A couple stopped my father in the street one night and were very menacing, asking him for money and cigarettes. He said: 'I haven't got any left, and if I had any money I wouldn't be walking the street,' and these two hard men actually gave him half a crown to get home."

In a pub in upwardly mobile Partick, Dr Sean Damer, sociologist, Glasgowphile and – at least in the gentle precincts of Glasgow University – reputed to be something of a hard man, chooses a seat with his back to the wall and explains the unique combination of factors which in the 19th century led to the evolution of the Glasgow hard man. Three waves of immigrants, from the Lowlands, Highlands and Ireland, each with a fighting tradition; fierce competition for jobs; sectarian oppression; and the habit of escaping appallingly overcrowded homes and brutalising physical work through drink, at the pub.

Damer, who spent a year in Govan's Wine Alley housing scheme, has met his fair share of hard men and is not pleased to be included in the category. The 'respectable' prototype can still be found, he says, but the Glasgow hard man has other faces: the bankrobber class of professionally violent criminal; the semi-professional who, as a stick man, used to protect the street corner bookies and may now be found providing muscle for the moneylenders; and the psychopath.

"The incidence of the square go involving the first type of hard man has always been inflated and thoroughly romanticised, but they did exist. Every tenement neighbourhood, every kind of scheme of the poorer variety, would have its 'respectable' hard men. There might not be one up your stair but there'd be one up your street and there might be several. Many of them did resemble something which William McIlvanney is trying to capture in his novels – decent blokes – although not all of them were," he says.

"But what's happened over the past couple of decades is that the number of the second, third and fourth types has increased exponentially. These guys don't deal in the square go, they deal in hurting people. Glasgow is swimming with hoods and they're bastards: they break people's legs and burn people's houses and terrorise kids. You can smell the fear around them."

An upmarket Italian restaurant on Great Western Road. Starched napery and Pavarotti. William McIlvanney lights another cigarette and rolls his eyes at that old question. As creator of the *The Big Man* (coming soon to a cinema near you), chronicler of the Glasgow underworld in *Laidlaw*, and – bookish sources whisper, dry-mouthed with excitement – something of a literary hard man himself, he has been pilloried as principal myth-maker to the breed.

He writes about violence because it's there, he shrugs, because it was and is an integral part of working class life. "If you have people who stand up on their own collateral – they've got nothing else – they develop a physical pride. I'm not saying that this was a great benign ethic but, given the shittiness of most industrial lives, this was less malign than most ethics.

"It's a kind of democratic machismo. Not 'I can murder you', but 'Don't aggress on my territory'. A really hard man from London once said to me: 'This place is full of amateurs'. Cockneys are very smart-arsed, it's 'you're a hick and I'm not'. The key to being a Glaswegian is 'you don't know any better than me'. It's a leveller."

A collector of classic hard man stories, he relates one about a student teacher called outside after singing a beery duet with a woman in a Gallowgate pub. He was rescued by a total stranger who appeared with a hammer and told the over-protective husband to leave the boy alone. "There *were* people prepared to go into situations that weren't really theirs. It's that Robin Hood quality of being prepared to cave someone's head in for what they thought was a good cause."

But where is this hard man today? He shifts slightly in his seat. "If it does exist now I would think it only exists in people of an older generation. That kind of approach to life was pretty dependent on roots and a sense of shared values and I don't think that's nearly as strong now. I've met men who purport to carry that set of rules within them but I don't see it in action."

The problem with democratic machismo is that it disenfranchises 50% of the population. In a comfortable council house in Knightswood, over buckets of tea and tattie scones, the playwright Aileen Ritchie considers the problematic sexual fascination exercised by the Glasgow hard man. It's an issue she addressed in her first play, *Can Ye Sew Cushions*, and her latest work, *Will Ye Dance At My Wedding?*, in which one of the characters gets involved with a hard man who turns out to be married.

"It's that thing about courting danger. She's attracted to the glamour and the whole sense of exhilaration and power that living against the rules gives her. The closer to the edge of things you get, the stronger sense of life there is about it. That goes for violence as well," she says.

Ritchie is not immune to the appeal herself, however clear-sighted she may be about its often disastrous consequences. The hard man's shell is brittle, and his sociopathic preoccupation with his own image all too easily slips into the need to prove himself at the expense of another. The women's refuges of Scotland are full of residents with cause to rue the allure of the Glasgow hard man. We nod in proper feminist agreement, then, simultaneously, give way to guilty laughter.

Her starting point in *Can Ye Sew Cushions* was a desire to put a female perspective on McArthur and Long's *No Mean City*, the most famous of the canon of novels dealing with the Glasgow hard man. Two years ago David Hayman, now artistic director of 7:84, also tackled *No Mean City*, directing a stage adaptation in Glasgow. His aim was to deal a death blow to the image of the hard man; instead, he was reviled for glamourising and sensationalising the violence.

As he is now busy directing the touring production *Nae Problem*, my first attempts to speak to him are filtered through other members of 7:84. The message comes back that he is not interested in talking about being a hard man. Intrigued, I reply that nothing was further from my mind – until he raised the possibility.

When we finally speak, he explains apologetically that he has been dogged by the tag since playing that most famous of hard men, Jimmy Boyle, in the film *A Sense of Freedom* – but he assures me he has never hit anyone in his life.

Although 7:84's *No Mean City* was misconstrued by many of the middle classes who came to see it, he believes he did get through to the working class audiences who came in record numbers. "I tried to take that dreadfully gratuitous book and look at why it's important to us. We were trying to deflate the whole image of the hard man and say they're just a bunch of gorillas, we've no real need of them, and it's ridiculous that we still glorify them," he explains.

But part of that exorcism involves acknowledging that the hard man is there, like a recessive gene, in the make-up of many Glaswegians. "I probably wouldn't have been able to embody the spirit of Jimmy Boyle without releasing something inside myself that was dormant. I had the same background as Jimmy and I suppose even though I work in a middle class profession it would have been very easy for me to go off on another road. At the end of the day I turn round and say 'that's my culture, that has to be within me'."

Eight miles from the city centre, Drumchapel – the desert with windows – is well outside the cultural capital's exclusion zone. Even against the washed-out sky, the concrete is colourless. More than half the adults and nine out of 10 teenagers are out of work. If the moneylender holds your 'Monday book', you don't even get your income support.

If the Glasgow hard man still exists, surely it is here he will be found. The pubs are furnished much like pubs anywhere: mock-deco mirrors, cod-Edwardian lampshades and other manifestations of contemporary *retro*. But what *really* smacks of the past is the people. One bar is crammed with men, most of them standing up; the only female face is the barmaid's. Sitting at tables in the other room are the women who have asked their men's permission before coming out, and a sprinkling of couples still sufficiently in love to brave no man's land together.

Old attitudes die hard in Drumchapel, but the tradition which lives on is that of the razor gangs, not the square go. In pubs which change their names constantly in a futile bid to escape their reputations, the catalogue of weapons unfolds: baseball bats, clubs, chair legs, hammers, glasses, and every conceivable sort of blade from the malkie, or meat cleaver, to the Stanley knife and paper scalpel.

Glasgow is the city of chibbing, where a man marks his opponent's face with a blade, leaving a graffito of scar tissue to announce 'I was here'. The 'mars bar' is so common on the scheme it barely rates a mention among an individual's distinguishing marks. One man recalls a trip to Derry and remarks wonderingly that no-one in the dance halls had chib marks on their faces.

Drugs are the most routinely cited explanation for the decline of the traditional Glasgow hard man. Their influence has distorted accepted values and upped the ante on violence, ushering in the sinister forces of organised crime. But drugs won't do as a scapegoat here. The Drum is not overrun with heroin. The most popular poisons, after the bevvy, are hash and sulph. Temazepam (£3.50 a tablet) is getting steadily more common, but there's still no comparison with Haghill, known with gallows wit as Tems Valley.

Frank, a big man with the sort of moustache which means one thing in Glasgow and something very different in San Francisco, tells me that the square go died out in the 1960s, now the violence is just 'evilness'. But the women round the table widen the discussion to the culture of hardness, still very much alive: its cripplingly narrow definitions of manhood, the emotional inarticulacy and terror of ridicule. Frank grows increasingly restless. He has no time for this talk of how men must soften up, learn to go shopping with their wives, collect their weans from school. If a man is insulted he *should* fight his corner. "No one likes to be called a poof or a clown or a bastard," he protests. Shortly afterwards, he walks away from the conversation.

Violence in the Drum is rarely about profit. The issues are wounded vanity, slighted status, liberties taken. The line can be crossed with terrifying ease. There are stories of fights started by the accidental spilling of a pint or the theft of a cigarette, murders triggered by brothers who took offence because someone called their sister a cow or criticised the shape of her nose. Honour is appeased by giving someone 'a doing', but that in turn tips the balance of power, leading to 'comeback'. And so it goes on. A mild mannered man with glasses bears a pale mauve line 5in long down his cheek, the result of a bloody and unforgiving revenger's tragedy which has already lasted 15 years.

Leaving Drumchapel, it strikes me that I've been on a fool's errand. You don't have to go looking for the Glasgow hard man, he's there all the time: in the Gorbals pub, the municipal office, the Knightswood council house, the yuppie pub in Partick and the ritzy restaurant in Great Western Road. He's a myth Glaswegians carry in their cultural chromosomes. Maybe he did – does – exist, but the idea has also cloaked every kind of vicious and pointless violence in the city.

Something Damer the sociologist said comes back to me: "The point isn't whether it's literal or not. A myth isn't a mere fantasy, it's part of how a society sees itself – it has real force. They don't disappear in history after the circumstances which gave birth to them have passed on. Myths stick."

March 25, 1990

Trial at Titwood (1)

Robert Philip

Two Scotland on Sunday sports writers went to the same cricket match on the same afternoon, but returned with strikingly different impressions of their experience. First, Robert Philip.

They tell me it was 87° in Barbados on Tuesday. At Tamarind Cove, the turquoise waters of the Caribbean lapped on to sand as white as snow. Some swam, a few windsurfed, most were content to slump in the shade of a coconut palm, rum punch to hand. The sugar cane rustled gently in the tropical breeze.

At Titwood, it pissed down. The temperature reached a 'high' of 54°, the smell of wet barathea blazers filled the dank air, and a few eccentrics tried to stage a cricket match. Even more risible, a group of us turned up to watch.

Gordon Greenidge was there and Gordon Greenidge should know

better...he was born in Barbados.

For reasons best known to his accountant, G.G. has chosen to live in Greenock and is therefore eligible to represent Scotland's national cricket team (as a boy, he had probably wanted to be an admiral in the Swiss navy). To a man raised with the sun on his back and the calypso in his soul, the prospect was gey dreich. The rain pattered down on the clubhouse window, the scoreboard stood petrified in the gloom like a giant tombstone, across the road a new Safeway supermarket was being noisily erected on a site once occupied by Crossmyloof ice rink.

If one of the world's most accomplished batsmen can bring himself to leave an island paradise where the sun shines 3,000 hours a year to risk catching pneumonia in what is fondly referred to as the "Scottish cricket season", have I been too quick to ridicule? "You can't dislike something you've never tried," witter the white flannel brigade. Oh yeah? What about folk dancing, tripe, do-it-yourself evening classes?

"A village green in summer," goes the rhapsody, "the sound of leather on willow, birdsong, 'Good shot, sir', real ale and clotted cream." Utter tosh. A few second-division football nations apart, no one plays it (certainly not the Brazilians, or the Italians who are sports crazy), nothing ever happens and the only excitement generated is when those wise in such matters occasionally intone: "That bugger turned a bit."

Malcolm Forsyth, a doughty stalwart for the Ardrossan Second XI, admitted cricket has an image problem. "I think it's still perceived as being an unsuitable game for real men. It's not exactly considered a contact sport, is it? Actually, it's a lot meaner than you think. All sorts of skulduggery goes on: stupid appeals against the light, people wasting time by pretending to tie their bootlaces and all that sort of thing." The cads.

Nicholas Duncan of Douglas Academy in Milngavie and Keith MacDonald of Airdrie Academy were due to sit their Higher and O Level French the following morning. Both are enthusiastic players and keen students of the game, but young master Duncan was forced to concede: "It's a great way to unwind during exams...I mean, there's not much to get terribly excited about is there?"

Perhaps an umpire can put me wise, shed some light on cricket's nuances, explain why Titwood is a sporting theatre to rank with Wimbledon, St Andrews, Firhill. "Actually, I love coming to Scotland," enthused TCCB umpire Kevin Lyons. At last, the secret of cricket's fascination was to be unfolded. "The way the weather is up here, I always have time to catch up on my paperwork, letters, bills etc. I also bring a lot of books."

After five hours of intermittent rain (during which time not a single ball had been bowled), a perfect round hole in the cloud appeared, the sun's rays played across our faces, beers were ordered in readiness for the start. Then came the announcement: "Ladies and gentlemen, the tea interval will now be taken."

As a firm believer in the three-hour lunch, it came as a surprise to learn cricketers are expected to stuff down four courses, wine and brandy in a mere 40 minutes. "It's just tea and scones for lunch, usually," said the man from Ardrossan. What is served at tea seemed the obvious question. "Tea and scones," came the equally obvious reply.

My gaze returned to an elderly gentleman perched on a shooting stick. Surreptitiously, he looked at his watch for the umpteenth time that afternoon. "Wife can't stand the game so it gets me out the house. Don't think much of it myself, really, but the bar stays open all afternoon. Who's supposed to be playing?"

I was glad to learn I am not alone. A BBC survey shows cricket trails eighth in television popularity, far behind the big three – football, tennis and athletics – and only just ahead of ice skating and gymnastics. Play finally began, the great man was out for one. We retired to a welcoming watering-hole.

"Where have you been?" inquired the waitress as the cork made a satisfying plop. "Cricket." "Who won?" she asked. "Who cares?"

May 13, 1990

Trial at Titwood (2)

Neil Drysdale

October is a funny kind of month, according to Denis Norden. "For the really keen cricket fan, it's when you discover your wife left you in May." Cricket, like life, sex or anything else worthwhile, does not always rise to the occasion.

But even at its most uninspiring – and our visit to Titwood on Tuesday, for the most part, fell into that category – the game offers compensations to explain its remarkable appeal for so many disciples throughout the world. That includes Scotland, which, given this country's meteorological conditions and general suspicion of anything invented by the English, might appear one of the most unlikely bastions of cricket.

Yet, the unmistakable conclusion to be drawn from all the developments which have occurred north of the border during the last decade is that the sport currently enjoys both a groundswell of popularity and an increasingly high profile which would have been unthinkable in the stagnant pre-1980s period. This season's Benson & Hedges campaign certainly bears that out. From the recruitment of West Indian Gordon Greenidge to the establishment by the Scottish Cricket Union of a daily Cricketcall service, a long-overdue but welcome wave of professionalism has swept through the domestic scene.

Whereas in the bad old days, the SCU's approach to media and public relations was about on a par with their rugby counterparts – "Cricketcall, old boy? Sorry, that's an ex-directory number" – SCU official Mike Stanger, of Michael Kelly Associates, now disseminates information with the air of a kindly grandfather. Indeed, the bullish attitude of all the officials gives you the distinct impression they are no longer embarrassed about spreading the gospel in Scotland. Nor should they be: with only a few reservations, cricket remains a marvellous way of life, and one with a greater grip on reality than many other sporting pursuits.

Unlike soccer, its administrators acted immediately to tackle sporadic problems with crowd trouble. Unlike rugby, the misguided souls who joined Mike Gatting's rebel tour of South Africa earlier this year have been unceremoniously booted out of the Test arena.

No one is trying to pretend that cricket boasts unceasing entertainment. But then, as frequent visitors to Easter Road these last two seasons can testify, football hardly offers any guarantee of excitement. Gloriously unaffected by the blight of violence and hooliganism which continues to shame that game's authorities, Glasgow punters mingled with visiting supporters from Nottingham and blazered members of the professional classes last week outside a relentlessly busy beer tent, swapping stories, with good humour the prevailing factor throughout.

This, despite the frustration of staring at an empty cricket pitch for a little matter of six hours, and the untimely dismissal of Greenidge, the man most of the crowd had come to watch, when play eventually began.

You need only compare that with the unlikely scenario of Leeds United or Chelsea, for instance, arranging a pre-season friendly with any Premier Division club and the almost inevitable mayhem their delightful supporters would wreak, to understand why many parents in England have swapped a Saturday on the terraces for a few hours underneath a spreading chestnut tree on the village green.

Not perhaps a purveyor of quickfire thrills and spills, cricket nevertheless possesses ample charms for those prepared to open eyes and minds. There are, of course, none so blind as those who will not see, but not even the loss of his sight was an obstacle to the great Yorkshire all-rounder Wilfred Rhodes's lifetime passion for the game. Sitting with a friend at a match one afternoon, he remarked that one of the pacemen was pitching the ball too short. "But how can you possibly tell?" asked his incredulous companion, to which Rhodes slowly replied: "By the sound of the bat. The ball keeps hitting the splice, which means the bowler can't possibly be hitting a full enough length."

On such observations does the beauty of cricket rest, the constant changing of tactics, the one-to-one battle between individuals which rages within the context of a team sport, the narrow dividing line between death and glory.

I suppose there will always be those for whom such delights are hidden, who will take refuge in cheap gibes and cries of "boring" in an attempt to justify their position. As Frank Bruno would say: "That's life, Harry, that's cricket." When the prophet points at the moon, the fool looks at the finger.

May 13, 1990

Ghost ride

Alan Taylor

Those who do not like to dig too deep for derivations claim that Burntisland got its name from the small island in the town's harbour, inhabited by fishermen whose homes were destroyed by fire. The cynical visitor arriving by rail, however, has an alternative etymology thrust upon him. Outside the deserted station, its ticket office bleakly boarded, is a dockyard, home to a hulk of floating scrap-metal from Scandinavia. At the station's entrance, the British Rail sign is singed at the edges, as if it has been torched by a half-hearted arsonist. The building next door is derelict. Round the corner, opposite the Smuggler's Inn, is a wasteland where any old iron turns ochre in the afternoon sun.

The impression is of a town being cremated: ashes to ashes, rust to rust.

It is the height of summer. At two o'clock in the high street, you could play a set of tennis without being disturbed by traffic. Bunting flaps in the breeze. In a shop window, a poster proclaims forthcoming attractions: a meeting of the Burntisland Badger's Club, a Strongest Pub Tournament, the Grand Exemption Dog Show. Contain your excitement. There are a couple of amusement arcades, fish and chip shops and Chinese takeaways, a shop selling cheap china souvenirs and enamel doorplates, but little else to indicate that Burntisland was once a humming holiday resort.

According to Samuel Lewis, author of a 19th-century gazeteer of Scotland, "From the favourable situation of the place, and the facilities of bathing which this part of the coast affords, the town is much frequented during the summer months." He also noted: "A fair is held on the tenth of July."

Its modern manifestation is to be found at the north end of the town on the verdant links. The first caravans arrive at the end of May. "When I see them coming I know that summer's here," says Caroline Anderson, who has a fancy goods shop and electrical business in the town. For her and other diehards, the romance of the fair is still palpable: the sickly smell of hamburgers and onions, toffee apples glued to gums, candy floss, the tattooed hunks who birl the waltzers and chat up the girls. It's a recipe guaranteed to bring on Saturday night fever. Without all this, aficionados say, it would be a ghost town. "If they close the fair down, they might as well close Burntisland," Anderson reflects sadly.

From May till late August, the fair expands and contracts as the show people come and go. At its height during the Glasgow Fair fortnight at the end of July, explains David Gordon, Kirkcaldy District's Site Superintendent, the fair swells to accommodate over a hundred attractions. Before and after this period, however, local resident Malcolm Malarky describes it as "a bit tatty, nothing but a ragbag of stalls and antiquated rides".

Three and a half years ago, Malarky bought a house on Kinghorn Road which runs parallel to the links. Though he was not from Burntisland, he was aware that there was a fair during the summer on the links. What he was not prepared for was the length of its stay. He was appalled and angry at the nuisance it created. "In my sitting room," he declares, "I could tick off numbers on a bingo card. I could organise a disco in my back garden from music playing a hundred yards away."

Others were similarly incensed and together they formed the Burntisland Links Action Group, which is campaigning to curtail the fair. "During the heatwave early in May," says Malarky, "you couldn't move for coach parties and Sunday school picnics." Now the fair has come, he feels that a different crowd is attracted to the town.

The show people have heard it all before. There are slim pickings to be had this afternoon from a party of school children and a group of teenagers messing about. In any case, few of the rides are open; Abba's greatest hits have expired, and even the bingo caller has taken a break.

Cadona, Taylor, Lovett, the familiar fairground dynasties are all here, their names framed in coloured bulbs on their sideshows. A father and son bolt together an ancient carousel, while a solitary dodgem sparks an untrammelled circuit. Mr Cadona dozes in the sun outside his huge caravan, a shining Mercedes parked at his side.

Ninety-three-year-old Nellie Strand stands by her daughter-in-law's rifle range refuting allegations that the guns are bent. She has just arrived from her home in the north of England. Like most show people, she winters in town and takes to the road in summer. A pot of parsley grows outside her small caravan. Inside, a plethora of bags await unpacking.

She has been coming to Burntisland most of her life. "I got my ears pierced here," she says, wincing at the memory. What age was she then? "Four years old." 1901. Then, the fair was hectic, but didn't last nearly as long. Her husband was among those responsible for extending it – it wasn't worth all the effort of travelling, setting up and taking down stalls for just three or four days.

"It's a hard life," she says. But she and the others wouldn't have it any other way. A hermetic community, inter-marrying and self-dependent, they follow well-defined routes. "We're in the same place at the same time every year," explains her daughter-in-law Alexis Strand. At the end of August they head for Falkirk, then Hamilton, then Glasgow. She is quick to point out they are not travellers or gypsies, but show people, members of the 8,000-strong Showman's Guild of Great Britain, established in 1889, 'to govern and superintend the interests of the showmen'.

Glenda and Arthur Hancock have a bingo stall. While he's away picking up a Viking boat for Burntisland community council's gala day – an indication of how integrated the show people are in the life of the town – she scrubs dirt from counters.

Like other regulars, she has noticed the fair is less busy these days. "There are very few bus trips," she says. "There's not much in the town now that they've closed the swimming pool." She is aware of hostility from local residents, but, like other show people, is reluctant to be drawn into any mud-slinging. She believes the complaints come from recent incomers. Malcolm Malarky, however, denies this: "I don't feel it is an incomer's problem. We have people in our pressure group who have lived in Burntisland all their lives."

"You'd think," says Alexis Strand, gesticulating towards the substantial villas on Kinghorn Road, "that if you had enough money to buy a house over there, you'd have the brains to know about what happens on the links."

Deeper into the fair, Mandy Gamble presides over a darts stall and the ski jump. Conciliation, not confrontation, is her philosophy, born of long hours encouraging day-trippers to throw darts at playing cards in the hope of winning a goldfish. Her caravan is a palace, spotless and spacious, with fitted carpets, a stacked hi-fi, microwave, flushing loo and electricity. The Gambles have a three-year-old daughter who, when she reaches school age, will go to one primary in winter, another in summer. On a sunny day in the fresh air, it seems an attractive proposition; who would want to live any other way?

The answer is not far off. In the high street, Burntislanders have awoken from their siesta. In the cramped supermarket, opinion about the fair is divided: if your business relies on the custom of the show people, you're for it; if not, you're against. At a local estate agents', the secretary says bluntly, "I hate it". There is no record that house prices in Kinghorn Road and its environs are affected by the presence of the fair, but they try to sell them in spring and autumn, just in case. When did Malcolm Malarky buy his? "In November."

Ironically, the local library has chosen now to celebrate the fair with an exhibition. A painting by Andrew Young, entitled *A Scottish Fair,* and dated June 25, 1910, illuminates the changes that have taken place since Nellie Strand had her ears pierced. Even allowing for artistic licence, it was a hubbub of activity, a marketplace as well as a funfair. Rents from the stall-holders, then and now, are paid into the town's Common Good Fund. The dodgems alone profit Burntislanders to the tune of £130-£140 per week throughout the summer, reckons David Gordon.

The exhibition concludes: "The fair is without doubt an established and important part of the town's life." Malcolm Malarky, for one, would disagree. He avoids it like the plague. He visits just once a year, the day before it departs, "to buy goldfish for the pond I inherited with my garden".

July 15, 1990

Lucky breaks

Roddy Forsyth

Whenever he was thinking about promoting one of his generals, Napoleon is supposed to have asked: "Is he lucky?" For some reason, this piece of information has a habit of turning up in newspaper articles and last week it actually appeared three times in various previews of the World Cup. But what is the point of the story?

If the French had had the sense to ask Napoleon what kind of luck he enjoyed, he would have been back in Corsica in short order. For one thing, he was notoriously constipated and by the time he invaded Egypt he was suffering from haemorrhoids; in fact, he endured a particularly bad dose of the River Niles on the day of his unsuccessful engagement with the Duke of Wellington. No wonder he had an obsession with the throne of France.

For a man who killed so many people he made a remarkably poor job of his own end. After he surrendered for the first time, but before he was shipped off to Elba, he swallowed a vial of poison, which only succeeded in giving him an embarrassing attack of violent hiccups. Eventually, it was probably a combination of arsenic poisoning, cancer and a perforated ulcer which did the job. Not exactly a life full of laughs, you will agree.

Incidentally, before they buried Napoleon, they removed a particular item of his anatomy and mummified it. It was last seen at an auction sale a few years ago and now Bob Geldof is trying to track it down to add to his collection of relics, which includes Winston Churchill's last cigar. Just so long as Bob knows which is which when he wakes up in the middle of the night, gasping for a smoke at any price.

Where were we? Oh yes, luck. Well, of course, your luck is what you make it, as we are so often told, which must have been a great comfort to the Japanese couple who found that their house had abruptly evaporated, along with the rest of Hiroshima, one sunny morning in 1945. Not surprisingly, they piled what little they had left into a pram and set off to stay with the wife's mother, who happened to live in Nagasaki, which they reached in time for the next big event.

As far as is known, they are the only people to have survived two atomic attacks and they are known in Japan as the world's luckiest couple, which does seem to be stretching the point, rather. At least they were more fortunate than the gentleman known as Lucky Mick Malloy, who very nearly established himself in 1933 as one of life's true indestructibles.

Malloy was a drunken New York Irishman chosen by a speak-easy gang to be the victim of a murderous fraud. They took out policies on his life with three insurance companies, then gave him free credit at the bar in the hope that he would drink himself to death. After a while they slipped him a glass of antifreeze, but Malloy asked for five refills before passing out. He drank antifreeze for a week, followed by turpentine, horse liniment and rat poison.

He ate rotten oysters in wood alcohol and decayed sardines laced with carpet tacks and survived being thrown drunk into a snow drift, as well as being run over twice at 45mph by a hit-man in a taxi. Eventually, the gang connected Malloy's mouth to a gas cooker via a rubber tube and succeeded at last, only to be caught and sentenced to the electric chair. The ringleader remarked: "It was just our luck to pick Lucky. We thought he was called that because he had no luck at all. He was the luckiest guy on God's earth till we thought of the gas stove."

If only our footballers were as hardy as Malloy. Still, we go to Italy this week, having excluded France from the World Cup. And as Andy Roxburgh said on Tuesday: "Thirty million Frenchmen would think themselves lucky to be in our place." Quite right too, just so long as we don't lose to Costa Rica. After all, we wouldn't want the amiable Andy to be conserved for posterity as part of Mr Geldof's curious collection.

June 3, 1990

War games

William Paul

Niccolo Machiavelli, the 16th century Italian statesman whose name is synonymous with ruthlessness and cunning, would have greatly appreciated the 20th century goings-on in his native country last week. The World Cup, an emotional firestorm of agony and ecstasy, is the crucible in which national prestige and self-esteem can glow red hot or crumble to ashes in the space of 90 minutes. It has everything to do with image and status and honour and that is why it is imperative to win or, at the very least, lose with dignity.

Even those with no interest in the sport, or a reactionary hatred of it, acknowledge that when the majority choose to invest their sense of collective identity in what happens on and around the pitch, it is the whole nation, not just a representative squad, that lines up to play each match. The population shares equally in the risks and rewards, and since the delight of every winner implies the despair of a loser, it makes the venture a very dangerous game indeed.

"Learn from the fox and the lion," advised Machiavelli, one of the first thinkers to turn his mind to the psychological consequences of winning and losing. "Because the lion does not defend himself against traps, and the fox does not defend himself against wolves. So one has to be a fox in order to recognise traps, and a lion to frighten off wolves."

Ancient wisdom updated and refined by the 'Indomitable Lions' of Cameroon, who were cunning enough to beat 1986 champions Argentina in the tournament's opening match while having two men sent off for ruthless tackles. The West Africans then sprang the same trap for Romania on Thursday and are now assured of playing in the second round against all pre-tournament predictions.

"Africans do not consider themselves as outsiders in football terms," said Christopher Lobe, a sports journalist with Cameroon television. "It is wrong. It is an imperialist view and it is absurd that the UK should be accorded possible places for four constituent countries when there are 43 independent countries in Africa and we can only get two. What African teams have done so far shows that we deserve more."

Lobe, nursing a celebratory hangover in the Cameroon capital Yaounde for most of last week, has a persuasive argument. The World Cup finals are the clearing in the woods where the wolf pack of nations fight to establish the contemporary international hierarchy of dominance and subservience. Cameroon – unbeaten in the 1986 championships – are a warning that the old order centred on Europe and South America is changing. Argentina is the pack leader, Italy and Brazil running close behind, but other unfancied teams from unfashionable areas like Egypt in Africa and Costa Rica in Central America refuse to accept the status allocated to them.

Hunter Davies, author of *The Glory Game*, has taken four weeks off work to do nothing but watch football. "It is sad really that football should be so important to people," he said yesterday, taking a break from cutting the grass before the Brazil-Costa Rica match. "But it is nice to see the small countries doing so well. It would never happen if it were armies fighting it out. The people I really feel sorry for in this World Cup are the players who have so much pressure on them."

Meanwhile Scotland, an ever-present but ever-ineffective threat to the big names, take what pride can be squeezed from a record of qualifying for the finals five times in a row and tend to view the avoidance of outright humiliation as the principal objective. We have fond memories of Denis Law with his jersey outside his shorts and Jim Baxter playing keepie-up at Wembley; they may be fading into the distance but they still inspire pride and satisfaction. Cameos of brilliant moments in the past are the scraps on which Scotland and other eternal also-rans feed their national psyches.

National stereotypes still prevail. Brazil has the Samba-style, Italy the passion, West Germany the organisation, Argentina the volatility and England the frustrated ambition but it may not be long before emergent nations begin to create their own league table of appropriate adjectives.

The idea of organised sport as a ritual display of aggression which serves as a substitute for war begs the question of whether the aggression exists of its own accord or whether it is created by the organisation of the sport. Jonathan Spencer, a social anthropologist at the London School of Economics, believes there is some credibility in the safety valve theory, pointing to sectarian tensions in Glasgow which are focused on the Old Firm Rangers-Celtic rivalry while the same divisions in Northern Ireland have become heavily politicised.

"What goes on in football is almost like a pantomime," Spencer said. "It is an identity you wear while the game or the tournament lasts. It may be a commentary on current events but it is unlikely to have real political influence. When it is over everybody goes home."

England played Argentina in Mexico in 1986 amid dire predictions of what would happen following the Falklands conflict. In the end, nothing much happened except that England were beaten and out of the cup. An exception to prove the rule was the infamous 'football war' in 1969 when El Salvador invaded Honduras after riots at World Cup qualifying matches between the two neighbouring countries. Thousands were killed in four days of fighting, but the underlying cause of the outbreak was attributed to a long history of mutual antagonism. Football just got caught in the middle.

All competitive sport is a struggle for superiority and football is the biggest sport of all for most of the world. That is why the World Cup is so popular and so important. Three months ago, Scotland's Grand Slam rugby team briefly eclipsed their footballing counterparts after winning the five nations' championship with style and panache, but yesterday's defeat by the All Blacks in the first test match at Dunedin was somewhat downgraded in the national consciousness as Scots braced themselves for last night's Sweden game. "Courageous in defeat," said the New Zealand commentator ominously.

Desmond Morris, author of *The Naked Ape* and *Manwatching*, went to football matches to study players and fans and saw the echoes of a much more ancient form of society. "I found that soccer gives people a chance to be a member of a tribe," he explained. Wallace Mercer, the owner of Hearts, has condemned opposition to his proposed takeover of city rivals Hibs as tribalism, but if his dream of Edinburgh United does become reality, its commercial success depends on creating a new tribe with a new sense of identity.

Politicians – tribal chiefs – have little choice but to identify with the fortunes of the national team. Margaret Thatcher, brazenly overcoming ignorance about anything to do with football, has shown face at Hampden and Wembley in the hope of gaining popularity. Carlos Menem, president of Argentina, went further than most when he borrowed the No. 5 shirt to play in an exhibition game. He is now regarded as something of a jinx after the shock defeat by Cameroon, which did not help the morale of a country that has seen its currency devalued by 700,000% in the last five years. Beating Romania helped a little, just a little.

In Holland last week, more than six million hugely confident people watched *Oranje* scramble to a 1-1 draw with Egypt and the recriminations began immediately. "Within a few days the nation became a nervous wreck," said Ruud Verdonck, a newspaper columnist. "It happens in countries where people have forgotten it is only soccer. You can win, draw, or lose. We Dutch forgot the last two options."

The English, long ago winners in 1966, had to swallow their ageing pride when the Republic of Ireland held them to a predictable draw. Scotland's loss to Costa Rica was yet another blow to the world-weary Tartan Army that has been in general retreat since Ally MacLeod promised the earth in 1978 and, for some reason, all Scots believed him. There was no hype this time, no orgy of optimism, and the fact that defeat should still come as a surprise remains surprising in itself. The pragmatic are pleased that Scotland are likely to return home soon. It means they can enjoy the football without the emotional torment of actually taking part.

Not that winners are ever likely to have much sympathy for losers. Blaring car horns and flag waving supporters took to the streets of Yaounde after both Cameroon victories so far, mimicking identical sights and sounds in Italian cities after their national team, the *Azurris*, had performed as expected. It was the same in Cairo, where a cabinet meeting on foreign policy has been postponed because it clashed with today's game against the Irish, who regard their earlier draw with England as a moral victory, confirming manager Jack Charlton's reputation as the most popular Englishman in Ireland and prompting a "nod and a wink" from the Gardai that Sunday licensing restrictions will be relaxed today.

In San Jose, Costa Rica, the Sir Laurence Olivier Theatre was packed with VIPs to watch the Scotland game. The goal was greeted with a delirious ovation and President Rafael Angel Calderon, sitting with an open telephone line to Italy to thank the players for their efforts win or lose, waved sympathetically to the five Scots in the audience. He was too hoarse to speak. Outside, afterwards, the cacophony of blaring horns was deafening.

For these teams, anything else that is achieved in Italy will be a bonus and perversely the pressure now begins to build up on them, particularly on Cameroon as the most high-profile giant-killers. "They were not expected to do well and had a fairly cavalier attitude," said sports psychologist Graham Jones at Loughborough University. "Now expectations have been heightened and they are expected to win. The attitude will be totally different."

Ben Williams is a chartered psychologist who makes his living by explaining how managers can be moulded into high-achieving teams. Last week, as the World Cup was starting, he returned to his Edinburgh base from Milan, where an electronics company had hired him to present a course on leadership skills. Football is no different from any other endeavour, according to Williams, and basic psychological principles can be used to create a degree of success.

In America, experiments have shown that there is little difference between the performances of teams who train together physically and practise moves and teams who just sit around together talking about what they are going to do and watching videos of what is required. The formation of an intangible team spirit is as important as the technical demands of the game, Williams insists. It makes people transcend their individuality and consider the best interests of the team ahead of self. It breeds commitment. It makes the boys prepared to die for the jersey. And in that context, players having a few drinks together after Scotland's defeat by Costa Rica was a positive team-building response.

The world's fascination for football does not extend to small corners such as New Zealand, where rugby is king, or to the most powerful country in the world, the United States, which has rather curiously won the right to host the World Cup in four years time. The current American team, making an appearance in the finals for the first time in 40 years, were almost entirely ignored by their countrymen when they crashed 1-5 against Czechoslovakia. No problem for the national psyche there.

The average American did not particularly care either when the team rallied to an honourable single goal defeat against Italy. In fact, on the subject of soccer, NBC news devoted more time to an item on the enforced celibacy of the current Italian team compared to 1938 when the players were escorted to brothels as a means of relieving tension.

"Soccer doesn't have a US audience," said David D'Arcy, a sports journalist for National Public Radio. "The real audience is among immigrants but each one is rooting for their individual country of origin. The reason soccer has never been successful is the lack of a big television contract. When the World Cup is hosted here it will bring more attention to the game, but it still won't come anywhere close to making it as popular as other sports."

America's indifference to the fatal attraction of football is in direct contrast to its obsession with other sports like basketball, grid-iron football, and baseball. The season's climax for baseball, by way of example, is billed as the World Series although it is exclusively a domestic affair. Such insularity makes it a small world indeed for baseball players but it at least ensures that, whatever the result, American supremacy will be confirmed. Machiavelli could not have arranged it better.

June 17, 1990

The King and I

Ajay Close

Take an Englishman, an Irishman and a Scotswoman; an establishment conspiracy to get rid of a local heroine; a battle for the soul of a city waged by the workers against the Thatcherite marketing men; a power-struggle among the political movers and shakers; and in the background, the dark shadow of the property developers.

No wonder *Elspeth* is the hottest show in town. With a soundtrack by Andrew Lloyd Webber it could transfer to London's West End.

Of course there are some philistines who claim that it's much ado about nothing: you can't base a blockbuster around a middle-ranking local government employee who fails to get her promotion...They don't know Glasgow.

A few programme notes for those who haven't yet bought tickets: Glasgow District Council announces that it is reorganising its museums hierarchy to create a new post of keeper of social history. It is widely assumed that this will be filled by Elspeth King, the Fife-born curator of the hugely popular People's Palace, on Glasgow Green.

The city's English director of museums and art galleries, Julian Spalding, advertises the post, to protests that King is effectively being forced to apply for her own job. Interviews are conducted by a panel of four council officers which appoints Mark O'Neill, an Irishman who has run Springburn Museum in Glasgow for the past five years. Uproar.

King appeals against the decision within the council, claiming sex discrimination, and lets it be known she may go to an industrial tribunal. Twenty-five councillors sign a motion calling on their 35 colleagues in the city's Labour group to review the appointment. But, in a neat procedural sidestep, council leader Pat Lally refuses to allow any discussion of the issue on the grounds that King's appeal, to be heard next Friday, has rendered it sub judice.

King is forbidden to speak to the press but her supporters put her case in the *Glasgow Herald*, whose letters pages since the affair began read like a Who's Who of the city. Last Friday's paper carries a protest signed by 64 assorted prize-winning novelists, comedians, poets and pop stars including James Kelman, Billy Connolly, Spike Milligan and the ubiquitous Pat Kane.

Ordinary Glaswegians are as outraged as the glitterati. A defence campaign meeting is packed to the doors with snowy-haired trades unionists, leather-jacket revolutionaries and gallus Glesca women who have emptied their grannies' attics for the People's Palace collection. They are asked to put pressure on their local Labour councillors to get the extra six signatures needed to review O'Neill's appointment. A list of those who have not yet signed is helpfully provided; 100 people picket the City Chambers.

What happens after the interval is anyone's guess.

While it is no fun for the two main participants – both King and O'Neill are under considerable personal strain – it has to be said that the furore over the keepership of social history has all the ingredients of a classic Glasgow stramash, the city's favourite sport.

Over the past two weeks the story has rarely been off the front page of the *Glasgow Herald*, which has abandoned all pretence of simply reporting the affair and emerged as a major – and, until a baffling volte-face yesterday, highly partisan – player, fanning the story for all it was worth, and more. Ravenscraig, where 770 livelihoods, not one person's non-promotion, are at stake, had a fraction of the column inches devoted to it last week. But then Ravenscraig lacks the sheer showbiz potential of the Elspeth King affair.

There are the goodies and baddies indispensable to popular entertainment. On the side of the angels: a champion of working-class culture whose intrepid forays into condemned tenements to salvage precious remnants of Glasgow's past have made her a heroine in the city. In the opposite corner: the combined forces of the English cultural establishment, the Pavarotti-pushing PR men, the efficient political machine which runs Glasgow District Council and the property developers who want to concrete over Glasgow Green.

Cue conspiracy theory number one.

To her supporters, the evidence is overwhelming. King is a maverick in the kow-towing world of local government, who has regularly criticised council cultural policy, and opposes its proposals to build a tourism and leisure development on Glasgow Green. She enjoys what amounts to a personal power base in the city, and does not make a habit of dressing prettily and smiling for her political masters. Her criticism of the £3.5m Glasgow's Glasgow exhibition under the arches of Central Station is thought to have been the last straw.

According to the Euro-MP Janey Buchan a rumour that she was to be removed and replaced by O'Neill was circulating four months ago.

As the *Glasgow Herald* put it: "Elspeth King is a coal-miner's daughter with a first-class honours degree. She is a woman. She is a Scot. She is the wrong class, the wrong sex, and she does not toe the Establishment line. That is why she did not get the job."

All grist to the mill of regulars at the Scotia Bar, favourite watering hole of the Glasgow radicals who object to the city's reincarnation as a citadel of pricey international high culture.

The 'whose culture is it anyway?' debate (also known as The People versus Pat Lally) has been raging throughout the city and within the Labour group itself since the laundering of Glasgow's image began in the early 1980s.

Among the loudest voices are the Movement for A Socialist Scotland (and its founder member James Young, professor of history at Stirling University); the Friends of the People's Palace; Glasgow For People, which is campaigning against development on Glasgow Green; and Workers City, a group which arose out of the publication of an anthology of Glasgow writing two years ago and has campaigned against the Year of Culture, most recently decrying the sanitising of local history represented by Glasgow's Glasgow.

These groups share a belief that Glasgow's socialist history is being rewritten and working-class culture systematically suppressed to make the city more appealing to the yuppies (shorthand for the middle-class/nefarious commercial interests/old-fashioned political fixers/anyone who isn't Scottish). This view is endorsed by a number of Labour councillors who complain that political debate is being stifled within the Labour group, with crucial policy decisions on 1990 events being railroaded through.

There is a plausible case to be made for much of this, but the problem with hanging issues of this size on one woman's shoulders is that it's difficult to achieve a perfect fit. The victimisation of Elspeth scenario ignores such messy possibilities as a bad decision being taken in good faith or indeed the right decision pleasing the politicians for the wrong reasons.

There are a number of inconvenient details. First, the question of just what the 'conspirators' could hope to achieve. Despite a widespread misapprehension that she has lost her job, King is still curator of the People's Palace. To assume that she could be forced out at some later date or simply gagged from criticising the new Glasgow ignores what makes her a thorn in the flesh in the first place: her fighting spirit.

The panel of officers which failed to appoint King 'because she's a woman and a Scot' turns out to have comprised an Englishman, an Irishman and two Scotswomen, one of them the council's equality officer. Spalding, cast as the councillors' stooge in the selling of Glasgow, also refuses to stick to the script: last year he actually tried to scrap the Glasgow's Glasgow exhibition.

Finally, there's the man who did get the job. Surely Mark O'Neill, as preferred candidate of the forces of darkness, should be a sharp-suited, middle-class opera buff, snug in the pockets of the City Chambers politburo. Central Casting has slipped up here. The curator of Springburn Museum is a bearded, bespectacled figure, with something of the perpetual student about the shapeless greatcoat and six inches of shirt cuff extending below the sleeves of his jumper. If this is the face of the new, slickly-packaged City of Culture, Saatchi's should sue.

He's not Scottish, but he isn't English either. His criticism of the 'cultural commissars'' lack of confidence in the city, leading them to invest in international culture before the local variety, is not the talk of a man trying to sweep working-class tradition under the carpet. His mother was a hospital cleaner, his father was unemployed for most of his childhood.

He and King are much more evenly matched than her supporters claim. She has been called one of the three best curators of social history in the world, but he gets his share of invitations to address prestigious overseas conferences. Last year Springburn, which he set up from scratch five years ago, won the National Heritage Museum of the Year award and was described as the only real community museum in Britain.

However well-loved the People's Palace may be, it could be even better. A bigger budget would help, but O'Neill's backers claim he has the ideas and administrative skills to take it further. The jury is still out on this, as it will be another five weeks before he starts his new job – assuming the King camp doesn't manage to reverse his appointment.

Cue conspiracy theory number two. A handful of King's friends are increasingly uneasy that their campaign is being hijacked by a faction whose principal interest is in replacing Pat Lally with a left-wing council leadership less sympathetic to the private sector. The tip of a white flag has now appeared above the parapet, with suggestions that she might be persuaded to withdraw her appeal against the keepership decision if offered a face-saving upgrading of her current post.

As the showbiz cliché has it, this one will run and run.

June 10, 1990

Dying for a smoke

Jeremy Watson

Friday lunchtime at Fat Larry's bar and Tam McGuire and his wife Ellen are settling down with their fags and booze. Between gulps of his hauf an' hauf and draws on his roll-up, he attributes his heart attack and Ellen's five to smoking.

"The doctors asked me what I thought had caused it and I said the cigarettes. I tried to stop but soon after I came out of the hospital there was a Rangers-Celtic game. I had to have one," said Tam, 59. "And as my pal was having a drink I joined in." Ellen, who suffered her first attack ten years ago at the age of 51, was last in hospital four weeks ago. "I would love to stop, I really would," she said, admitting she was back to 20 a day.

Fat Larry's, next door to Ricky's Fish and Chicken Bar, lies on the boundary between Airdrie and Coatbridge, one of the most economically-depressed areas of Scotland's central belt. Last week the Monklands district that embraces both industrial towns was confirmed as the country's leader in the heart attack league.

In a survey of 22 districts covering two-thirds of the Scots population, researchers at Dundee University found that twice as many people die from heart disease in Monklands as in Eastwood, a middle-class dormitory suburb of Glasgow. Although levels of cholesterol in the blood were similarly high, more than half of the population smoked in Monklands compared to 29 per cent in Eastwood. As the researchers pointed out, cholesterol becomes a bigger health problem if a person also smokes.

The area also fared badly when rates of exercise and eating habits were studied. Although not the worst district in the league table – this dubious accolade went to North Glasgow – there was a marked lack of fresh fruit and vegetables in many people's diets.

Doctors working in Monklands insist that many of these factors are symptomatic of life in an area which also scores highly on any scale of deprivation. Heavy smoking and drinking have always been prevalent and are now exacerbated by the effects of unemployment as traditional industries such as steelmaking have gone into decline.

"This is an area of high unemployment which may itself lead to smoking and an unsatisfactory diet," said Dr Christine Rodger, the consultant cardiologist at Monklands General Hospital. "Deprivation in years gone by may also have predisposed the area to coronary heart disease. Small birth-weights and bad nutrition may now be coming through in this way."

Monklands is characteristic of a wider Scottish malaise that has put the country at the top of the world league for heart disease. More than 18,000 Scots die every year from heart attacks. Cholesterol levels are universally higher than in England as is the rate of smoking. Monklands has been an internationally-recognised blackspot since the World Health Organisation decided six years ago to mount a research project in Airdrie and Coatbridge, when it emerged that a third of all deaths were caused by heart disease.

Some attitudes also die hard. When Lanarkshire Health Board commissioned research into lifestyles last year, it had to be abandoned because so few people were willing to fill in the questionnaires. Although there has been a mushrooming of health clubs, they have been of the muscle-bound variety. "It is anerobic rather than aerobic exercise," said Dr James Ferguson, the board's chief medical officer. "Weightlifting rather than jogging, which may not be the best form of exercise."

In spite of the district's appalling record, Rodger detects hope for the future in the people who attend her clinics. "Ten years ago it was common for them to say they were smokers. Now it is unusual for them to admit it. Most of them say they have stopped or are stopping."

Next year Rodger will chair a new working party being set up by Lanarkshire Health Board to tackle the heart disease problem. The aim will be to find out what is already available in GPs' surgeries – blood pressure screening, blood fat screening, anti-smoking and nutrition clinics – and then correct deficiencies and spread good practice. Spending more money getting the health education message across was not necessarily the best way, said Rodger. "I think people have got the message. It is often whether they can afford to do anything about it."

For many people, heart attacks come as the first public health warning that their lifestyle is self-destructive. One was John Smith, the shadow Chancellor of the Exchequer. Smith, 51, suffered a heart attack just over a year ago. His front-bench duties had committed him to a punishing work schedule in which the desirable goals of a healthy diet and plenty of exercise had to take second place.

In the first three months following the attack, he shed a surplus two and a half stones with a rigorous diet and decided to take to the hills as regularly as possible. He set himself a target of climbing 30 Munros by the anniversary of his illness and is now determined to do 40 by the end of the year. "I wanted to do this before, but the heart attack gave me the stimulus to do it," said a fitter Smith last week.

He is firmly behind calls for a much tougher campaign to reduce Britain's heart disease statistics. "In the United States campaigning has worked to the extent that the rates are falling. If that happens here then you would not need to spend as much of the country's money into putting it right. As a potential chancellor in charge of health spending that is obviously of interest to me."

December 17, 1989

Brigadoon revisited

Kenneth Roy

"Well, Sir John," I began, "as all the world knows, you come from Auchtermuchty." Fleet Street's legendary Scot gave me a withering look. "Only you know that," he answered venomously. "The rest of the world knows I come from Glasgow."

A year later, I am still haunted by this disastrous lapse. My plea in mitigation is that John Junor has written so much in praise of Auchtermuchty that I came to believe he must be a native of the burgh. Is the old curmudgeon not known as the Sage of Auchtermuchty, for heaven's sake?

Jean Rook suggested in her memoirs that the village was a product of Junor's imagination. Sometimes it feels like that. "I was looking for a sort of Brigadoon for my column," Sir John explained. "A village which would contrast the old normality – decency, old-fashioned virtues – against the ugliness of the outside world."

"What patronising rubbish," I thought, while failing miserably to utter the words. Ever since, I have been waiting for an opportunity to prove him wrong, to demonstrate that Auchtermuchty is as wicked as Ecclefechan and twice as ugly. Last week, when I heard that the Auchtermuchty Galaxy Twirlers were about to give their annual exhibition, I realised the time had come.

My first stop was the parish church. Here was a simple test of the Junor theory. If it was open, he was right. If it was shut against the vandals, he was wrong. This round went to Junor as soon as a friendly old door creaked ajar. I scanned the visitors book for JJ/Sage/Old Curmudgeon, but found no evidence that he had been there.

In the pulpit, I detected a first hint of the ugliness of the outside world. For here was the dreadful New English Bible with its Sunday newspaper prose. Genesis 1: "In the beginning, when God created the universe, the earth was formless and desolate." It was only when I rummaged among the communion cups in the vestry that I found the King James version. Genesis 1: "In the beginning, God created the heaven and the earth. And the earth was without form, and void; and darkness was upon the face of the deep." Not even Sir John could have written a passage of such peerless beauty; yet the Muchty faithful appear to believe that it is capable of improvement.

Junor scored an easy victory in the Royal Hotel. People looked up when I entered and welcomed me cordially. "Anyone using bad language will be refused service," said a sign above the bar. The background muzak was a tape of Scottish jigs. The only symptoms of the outside world were fairly minor: a fruit machine, a snooker table, a beer garden, and a lunchtime menu which included "Death by Chocolate Gateau, 95p" not, alas, a dish I was able to offer Sir John.

"The time's goin' awfu' slow the day," said a patron. The Sage of Auchtermuchty would have been delighted to hear it. For him, this is a place where time stands still.

The Forest Hills Hotel with its "bistro" and "conference suite" gave me renewed hope. Elsewhere, I noted a Sky satellite dish and a boarded-up window with the word "penis" scrawled on it; good, good. But I could have done without all those sweet little cottages with names like "Shrang-ri-la" and all those smiling faces outside them; and I regret to report that the telephone box was in perfect working order.

Although a number of scantily-clad girls were loitering at a street corner, I must admit that it was very hot and that their ghetto-blaster was modest in size and volume. In fact, the only cheery aspect of the town for me was the disgusting condition of the public lavatories. Thanks to Phil fae Gauldry and the Sex Pistols.

Just as I was leaving, the Junor camp delivered the final blow. Dick and Liz appeared from nowhere and accused me of being a columnist from *Scotland on Sunday*. They were deplorably friendly, wished to say that the 10th Auchtermuchty Festival (including the annual fiddling and diddling contest) was about to start and assured me Muchty had a community spirit second to none.

"Yes, yes," I growled, exasperated by all this goodness, "but what about Junor?" Dick said they invited him to the festival every year. And every year he sent back a charming note explaining that he was just about to leave: for the South of France.

August 5, 1990

The surplus sex

Sue Innes

Find the young men, they said. Find out about them, their habits, their thoughts, their lives…It was an – let's say interesting? – assignment. Our interest, you understand, is purely professional. To do with demographics, and the word sex is to be understood as in 'ratio' not as in 'act'. Though that, ultimately, has to be what it is about.

In a demographic change which has attracted curiously little attention, there is now a surplus of men over women in Britain at all ages below the forties (where the sex ratio is roughly equal, with a preponderance of women beginning at 49). It is a situation which is unprecedented. Never before has there been a surplus of men over women at 'marriageable age', which is, after all, when it really matters.

In Scotland, there are 37,416 more single men than women between 18 and 23; one in seven of that age group is notionally spare. This is the age at which long-term relationships are being established and work choices made; it is also the age group of the most troublesome members of the manic-depressive tartan army, the age at which men are seen as causing most havoc.

Before male readers head off for Caracas – the destination of two lads in *Gregory's Girl* where there were supposedly ten women for every man – those figures deserve qualification (in any case there are actually 613 more men than women in Venezuela). The main reason the disparity of single people is so great in that age band is that women tend to marry men older than themselves and, on average, women are still marrying younger than men. But on age alone, there are still 12,657 surplus Scottish men aged 18-23. That is 5% of men in their age group, a smaller proportion than those who are actually single but not inconsiderable – particularly if you are one of them. It means a largeish group of chaps who, unless there is a rapid turn to polyandry, are not going to find a partner.

One immediate result is that 'the bachelor' is about to hit popular culture in a new, updated version; like Sindy's man Paul he comes complete with things to buy appropriate to his lifestyle. Single chaps, after all, have more money.

Yet bachelor is a curiously dated word, suggesting the 1930s, white bags and natty straw hats (which have also made a reappearance). As the trend continues into the next century can we expect a generation of down-market Bertie Woosters or uncles in cardis? Or ageing thrash metal fans unwilling to part with their studs and leathers?

As bachelor turns from word to marketing concept, it may need redefining. While in tabloidese it means 'is-he-gay-then?', it none the less implies an element of choice, of eligibility. Just as the term 'bachelor girl' enjoyed a brief heyday for women who enjoyed being single, so 'spinster' is being used for men perforce on the shelf. Essentially sexist, language is.

This new bachelor is fashion conscious: the self-absorbed male models may be prophetic. Expect the reappearance of movies with a loner hero – and no babies. They live in cities, and according to one survey, they have chapped lips and eat hamburgers. He sees himself as sexy (how poignant); the image of man as desirable, as object of attraction, that has spread from homosexuality across marketing for a whole age group – sexy in Levis, sleek and muscled in high-cut underpants, naked in after-shave – is a deeply significant shift.

They kill themselves intentionally: the suicide rate is highest among single men; not quite so intentionally: in car and bike crashes which are the biggest causes of death for young men; and even less intentionally by dying of Aids. They are almost three times as likely to be unemployed as women of their age.

And they tell market researchers they are pretty decent sorts of chaps really. Mintel, in their study of Men 2000 last year, found that most men want most of all to be seen as sensitive and understanding, with loyal and trustworthy a close second and witty and entertaining next.

The new bachelor spends a lot of time in the pub and smokes too much. And as yet, by and large, he doesn't know he is the new bachelor but assumes there is a wife somewhere over the horizon.

So if you see this man in the pub in sexy underwear and chapped lips, cracking jokes and looking sensitive but loyal, he could be a spare man. But we offer no guarantees since the mechanisms by which mass statistics impinge on individual lives are far from automatic. Lindsay Paterson, as a statistician working in the social sciences, is cautious about moving from aggregate statistics to individual behaviour; statistical significance depends very much on context, he emphasises. "You are talking about 0.7% of the population after all. Would you notice them walking down Princes Street? – I doubt it."

It depends what you're looking for. Lindsay is a bachelor. Carol on the other hand is a young woman of 19. Did she know, I wondered, that there were more men than women in her age group? "Of course you know," she said, a touch witheringly. "You know from school. And you see them." She listed in detail where the spare men hang out.

In fact Carol was unusual. Most people I asked were not aware of any disparity between the sexes in their age group; most guessed there were more women than men.

It must matter most where girls meet boys and boys perhaps don't meet girls. With an appropriately-aged friend as native guide I went on a tour of pubs and clubs; with no eye but to journalistic endeavour, I accosted young men at parties. How easy was it to meet the opposite sex, I wondered? (While they wondered why I was wondering.)

For Jim, Brian and I'm-no-tellin-you-my-name (all 19) it was hard. They had taken up a stance at the edge of the dance floor, clutching half-pints and watching the few couples and groups of girls dancing to Erasure. They wore Top Shop versions of the gangster look which somehow served to emphasise their skinny, undoubtedly callow quality. Jim had a large raffish gold earring in one ear; I.n.t.y.m.n., a patchwork print waistcoat. Would they move in on those girls dancing? "It's pretty hard," said Jim, wriggling. "It's easier after you've had a few drinks," opined Brian, in common with all the other men I talked to. All three said they were looking for someone to go steady with, and their replies were so fervent I believed them.

Talking to the girls, it was hard not to feel the boys hadn't a hope.

They were vivacious and apparently confident; well-dressed courtesy of Chelsea Girl in wide trousers or leopard leggings, off-the-shoulder T-shirts; with well-tended curls, sleek bobs.

Diane and Rose were both 18, but looked older. "We're out to enjoy ourselves. We can't be bothered wi' men," Rose said defiantly. "You get the odd moron coming up wanting to dance," said Diane indignantly. Well, yes, if you wanted to 'pull' someone it would be easy, they said. "But," Rose says in a rush, "half of them are all do'nuts, you know, plebs. If you wanted to get off with someone nice it would be hard." She revised her opinion: "Very hard."

Talking to students, talking to car mechanics, talking to hairdressers, secretaries and engineers, the impression remains the same. Barring a few flash young men who say girls throw themselves at their feet, young women feel that it is infinitely easier to go out and find a man than vice versa. Kelly (a shop assistant) thinks you would have to be wearing chador to fail to score on a Saturday night. Wander twice round the floor of this club and you'll have a choice of 20 fellas, she says with certainty. That's if you're not too fussy of course. "There's plenty of men, there just aren't any *viable* men," said Valerie (a student) with some scorn.

Perched on the edge of the balcony in the pub, the better to scan the action, she and her three friends wore black and white, red gashes of lipstick. Well yes, there were plenty of men – but. "They just stand on the edge of the dance floor and don't *do* anything," she said despairingly. "They don't dance, they just stand there looking at you." "And the nice ones just stand about and think they're cool," said her friend.

"Well, you go out with your mates," Pete said. "Either you'll go to a club or you'll just go on a pub crawl. Yes, with the possibility of picking up." But it wasn't often you did, he said. "I don't know, I think I'm becoming more defeatist now I'm older"...(he's 22)..."I don't know. Sometimes I think, what am I doing sitting in this bar all night with all these blokes getting drunk – I'm blowing all my opportunities."

Despite their apparent freedom to make the first move, many men expressed apathy, some the fear of rejection. Playing the field, I realised, is often a euphemism for going out with your mates, getting drunk and going home again. It was also striking the degree to which they saw relationships as about settling down and working hard to pay for a mortgage. Promiscuity was less than ideal but a steady relationship meant "staying in and watching videos". How they felt about being single seemed to depend a lot on whether their friends were too; both men and women said they'd like a long-term relationship, but not yet.

An ongoing study of 16-19 year olds (using Kirkcaldy as its Scottish sample) suggests that finding a partner is high priority. When you ask young people who they spend most time with, even at age 16 both boys and girls say it is with a partner. Settling down "is generally taken for granted as something that will happen," says researcher Lynne Jamieson, "though they don't generally want it to happen soon." The survey also indicates that finding a partner is at least as important for boys as for girls, she said.

This point is emphasised by Professor Leo Hendry, who is studying young people's lifestyles in Aberdeen. "We've found that girls have very much moved away from the idea that life is about getting a boyfriend and getting married. They are equally ambitious in career terms. They like young men and having a good time – but a small network of close friends is more the kind of scene than one boyfriend. I don't think that young men are changing as quickly. Boys very much take it for granted that somewhere along the line as well as a career they're going to have a wife."

It would be tempting to see differences in young men and women's attitudes as an expression of demographic reality. But when you try to understand what is behind it then the young men's lack of sexual confidence and fear of rejection is clearly important, and that was true 20 years ago.

Young men go to the bingo now, which certainly didn't happen a few years ago. Could that be an instinctive response to demographic realities? Or just that the unwritten rules are loosening up? In neo-hippie, independent clubs there's a change which anyone over 25 or so finds striking: it is now acceptable for men who are not gay to dance together. A rational response to demographic trends perhaps, but it is equally if not more about the loosening of sex roles.

In a different, distinctly cool club, after dancing to Happy Mondays, Bob, unemployed and all in black, and Russell, who looked more like Shelley with wild hair and dopey gaze but was unexpectedly an engineer, drooped in elegant melancholy at the edge of the dance floor. "Well, dunno really. We always come on Fridays," said Bob. "I don't have a girlfriend. But then I blame myself for that, it's not that I don't ever meet anyone. No, it doesn't much matter really." Simon, unemployed and upper-middle class, in layered T-shirts under a short jacket, said loftily that it wasn't so much pairing up any more, just groups of friends some of whom you might sleep with. You came for the music, the scene, not to score.

It was all so mellow I was convinced – until I went into the cloakroom. The girls were jostling at the mirror for room and paying minute attention to make up, contriving an elaborately uncontrived look, just as at any mirror in any club on any Saturday night. What's all that for then?

It is not surprising if young people do not notice the demographic trends of which they are part: no one links their own lives with statistics, and in any case it is a fluid time especially in terms of relationships. They may notice when they're 30, 35. What is curious is how little discussion this demographic change has generated. Yet it raises questions for a number of areas: for education, for health, for people who work with young people at risk. A change in the sex ratio could have implications for employment patterns which have remained gender-segregated. It also suggests that equal opportunities policies will need to be reinforced. That young men have been economically and educationally dominant when they were not numerically so hardly bodes well for when they are.

As women have changed – and they have done so dramatically in the past 20 years – men have been left, or chosen to stay, behind. Perhaps numbers will do what exhortation couldn't. Could it be that demographics is a feminist issue?

What will it mean for girls? More pressure to marry? An erosion of the determination to have both a brilliant career *and* a fella?

What discussion of it there is divides into two main hypotheses: either men will become nicer or they'll be nastier. That they will adapt their behaviour to what women want; or that without the power of sex, love and related cheap thrills to soothe the rampant male breast, there will be an increase in aggressive behaviour.

Many people argue that a surplus of young men will lead to an increase in random aggression. This seems to rest on common sense and observation in any city centre on Fridays and Saturdays where you see them hanging out, roaming the streets in packs, horsing around, peeing against walls, kicking each other's heids in. Court figures show that more than half the offences proved in Scottish courts are committed by men between 16 and 30. Yet they are contested as inaccurate and prejudiced by some criminologists. All such statistics betray is self-fulfilling prophecy, they say; because young single men are seen as troublemakers, the police pay more attention to them. Recent research shows that young men are also the main victims of crime.

That's all fairly academic for Rab the bouncer. In his club, the numbers are manipulated to keep a 60/40 female to male ratio. "If there are a lot of women, the guys won't be looking for fights. There's more to bouncing than meets the eye – you need a wee bit of psychology in this job." Then "Sorry lads", putting his arm across the door. "The secret of avoiding bother is a tight door. Groups of more than three men are trouble."

Yet exploring even the issue of violence and loutishness, a new image of young man emerges – not so much beast but beastie, of the timid cowering sort. Bravado and aggression are increasingly explained as a response to the confusion brought by changing sex roles and as a cover for insecurity, sexual anxiety.

Author and sex educator Carol Lee describes the issue as a 'time bomb'. "As a society we just do not know how to handle young male sexuality." She is particularly worried by hardening attitudes of misunderstanding and hostility to girls, which are dangerous but avoidable. "We know how to behave with adolescent girls, we are protective of them. With boys we view them as a potential aggressor – but not as a potential father, a potential lover. We get what we invest in."

When women were seen as surplus in the last century, they were shipped off to the colonies to effective sexual and domestic slavery. Barring Caracas, will we be more sympathetic to our spare men?

But the whole notion of 'spare men' in itself demands unpicking. Do we really see people only for pairing? It is relatively recently that we have put such a high degree of emphasis on the couple to the exclusion of all other emotional bonds, on the nuclear family to the exclusion of all other domestic groups. Before the mid-1950s, large numbers of single men and women were quite usual in Scotland.

David is 18; he has a neck of a remarkable thickness, a nervous guffaw and a philosophic bent. Is he looking for a girlfriend? "If it happens it happens. If it disnae, it disnae."

June 17, 1990

GoGo and BoBo are missing

Robert Philip

Like the twin towers of Wembley, the view up the 18th towards the last green at St Andrews, or the sight of your £1 each-way hope rounding Tattenham Corner three lengths clear on Derby Day, the Centre Court can take your breath away.

It seems huge, too big for a single tennis court, surely; room for 13,000 people with picnic hampers, the umpire's chair which has stood there for 70 years, the old clock, forever nudging the stroke of two in the mind's eye, the Royal Box where the Duke and Duchess of Kent were to be found last week, and the Gloucesters, and Charles Dance, Susan Hampshire and Kate Adie. Fergie and Di are coming on Tuesday.

But for all its pomp and circumstance, Wimbledon is a circus, and just like Billy Smart's, the clowns and sideshows are frequently more interesting than the acts in the big tent. Thus, while arguments rage as to the source of Mr Dance's suntan (Barbados or Boots'), the true thrill-seeker sallies forth to the 15 outside courts.

Wednesday was a typical day on Court 8, offering the varied delights of a women's doubles featuring the third-seeded Soviet pair Savchenko and Zvereva, a men's singles involving the gentle skills of Ramesh Krishnan, and a men's doubles with GoGo and BoBo (Andres Gomez and Slobodan Zivojinovic).

While a motley assemblage, armed with Tupperware survival packs of blackening banana sandwiches and warm cans of Tizer, took up position on the uncompromisingly hard park benches at courtside, those wise in the ways of Wimbledon headed for an unmarked door under the stands of number two court. Through this door and up a narrow spiral staircase can be found one of the All England Club's most delightful secrets – a tiny balcony providing unobstructed views of courts 6-8 with the 15th-century church spire on Wimbledon Hill shimmering among the beechwoods in the distance.

As Australian Darren Cahill and Dutchman Paul Haarhuis were launching the first in a whole series of missiles at one another across the way, on Court 8, Natalia Zvereva was being buzzed by a bee which appeared intent on spearing her bum. Zvereva, known as the Minx from Minsk, loves an audience and her contortions were both wondrous and numerous before the offending pest was swiped into oblivion.

The richly-talented Soviets had less trouble with their opponents Barbara Romana and Eva Sviglerova, the Italian-Czechoslovak partnership winning a mere two games before it was sporting handshakes all round...

On Court 7, meanwhile, Haarhuis had just won the opening set against Cahill, now being closely observed by Australian Davis Cup captain Neale Fraser, who beat Rod Laver to become Wimbledon champion in 1960.

Sweden's Niclas Kroon came as something of a disappointment to the watchers on Court 8. Obviously fond of his beer, Kroon is more likely to be mistaken for Jocky Wilson than Bjorn Borg. Nor does Krishnan, son of 1960 and 1961 semi-finalist Ramanathan Krishnan, resemble a sporting god; short and delicate, he serves like a schoolgirl, seldom moves at anything quicker than a trot, and caresses every ball with deceptive tenderness. "He's like his father," said Fraser, as Cahill levelled at one set all below and Krishnan left Kroon flat-footed with an audaciously angled volley. "I played him in the semis here in 1960. Sometimes he made me look like a complete dingbat."

At that, Krishnan jnr struck the sweetest of forehands which landed a millimetre beyond the baseline. He studied the strings of his racquet with a rather hurt expression. "More emotional, though," said Fraser drily. "His father would never have done that."

It was not to be India's day. Kroon won in four sets and punched the air in triumph, and Krishnan set off to pack for the return flight to Madras.

Perhaps he bumped into GoGo and BoBo at Heathrow, because they never showed up on Court 8. The official reason was an injury to Gomez, but rumour suggests otherwise...did anyone else spot BoBo (a ringer for Christopher Reeves' *Superman*) among the Yugoslav fans in Florence last night during the World Cup game with Argentina?

P.S. When last seen, four hours on, Haarhuis was serving for the match at 5-4 in the fifth...

July 1, 1990

Now for the rumba

Kenneth Roy

A correspondent to *The Times* wrote that the only activities he ruled out absolutely were incest and the Highland fling. My own list of personal aversions is considerably longer. I doubt that I shall ever drive a car, grow a beard, wear a kilt, use a portable telephone, join a club, spend a second night in Mallaig or read a modern Scottish novel to the end.

Above all, I shall die content having avoided any active participation in ballroom dancing. For some reason, this blameless pastime fills me with gloom and horror; so much so that I would rather write the authorised biography of Esther Rantzen than attempt to earn the approval of Angela Rippon by becoming the Closed British Senior Latin American Champion. But that does not prevent me from being a closet addict of *Come Dancing* (BBC1), which entered its fifth decade last Monday at the suitably furtive hour of 11.30pm.

Angela, defiant in one of her comic dowager creations, looked more than ever like a refugee from the hockey club dinner-dance. Can this be the woman who once lent such gravitas to the reading of the news and impressed the nation with her pronunciation of the name Mugabe? "This is the world's longest-running TV series," she announced, "and we've given it a bit of a facelift." Co-presenter Charles Nove had been refurbished for a start. He was sporting a white jacket and spotted bow tie, but had discarded his green-rimmed specs.

"And now," said Angela, "for the sensuous rumba." That is the first lie about ballroom dancing. Despite the best efforts of lighting genius Ron Minty and Angela's inventive commentary, there is nothing sensuous about the rumba as it is performed by Linda and Warren, Melanie and Darren. The boys move as if they are in the initial stages of rigor mortis; the girls stare at the ceiling and think of Congleton. "They graced the floor in Leningrad," said Angela. "Now they're partners off the floor as well as on." This says more about the aphrodisiac qualities of Leningrad than it does about ballroom dancing.

For a genuinely sensuous experience, look no further than the World Cup (most channels, most days). The most passionate kissers are the Italian players, who may require water hoses if they win the championship. Such an excess of loose, uncontrolled emotion makes one long for Central Park, Cowdenbeath, on a wet Saturday in November. Well, almost.

Meanwhile, we have Jimmy Hill and Desmond Lynam to endure for yet another week. Hill is a lost cause, but Lynam – normally so laconic and hard to impress – has allowed himself to become just another England fan with a microphone. Too many hot studio nights in the company of footballers have reduced him to the same gibbering level. "Waddle's done pretty good," he said on Tuesday, celebrating the victory over Belgium.

The commentaries are not only debased in their vocabulary, but unapologetically partisan. "We" are the English, never mind that the BBC also serves Scotland, Wales and Northern Ireland, and the only matches that matter are played between 'the lads' and 'them'. The recent Glasgow debate over Elspeth King's non-appointment has revealed an ugly streak of racism in Scots who ought to know better – but it is a racism fed by the smug, uncritical nationalism of the Lynams and Hills, the little Englanders for whom 'getting a result' seems to be the only point of the experience.

At its worst, *World Cup Grandstand* (BBC1) has been unbelievably myopic. On the night that 250 English 'fans' were deported from Italy for their thuggish behaviour, the studio pundits chewed the fat for half an hour before the kick-off. Yet the only World Cup news that really counted was not discussed: not so much as mentioned. Perhaps it was considered too embarrassing for what Lynam called "England's big night", or perhaps the BBC's sports department clings to the illusion that it is possible to keep football separate from life.

I caught my only glimpse of the tennis in a Kirkcaldy pub. It is always a relief when another Wimbledon comes round and Dan Maskell is still alive. But once he goes, they should call it a day and spare us the annual ordeal of all those grunting adolescents.

July 1, 1990

Tartan special

Joyce McMillan

Yesterday, the left-nationalist establishment of Scotland gathered in a field near Stirling, under the auspices of the STUC, to celebrate something called A Day for Scotland. I couldn't be there, and for once I wasn't sorry. The truth is that my faith in the future of this country – in what MacDiarmid once called "Scotland's hidden pooers" – has taken a terrible beating over the past four weeks; and it was the football that did it.

In the absence of a serious political focus for our sense of nationhood, football really matters in Scotland. I remember, for example, the precise moment when I realised that the present constitutional arrangements in Britain were driving Scotsmen slightly mad. It was during the World Cup final of 1966 when I watched one of my uncles – a man who had spent the best part of his youth fighting the Axis powers up through Italy – suffering emotional agony because England were about to take the trophy rather than West Germany. Over the years, I came to understand that this blind preference for almost anybody over our nearest neighbours was somehow bound up with our little-brother status in the United Kingdom, and I began to hope that we could, as a nation, fight our way out of such a psychological and political dead-end.

In the 1980s, there came a generation of writers and artists with a vision of Scotland that seemed capable of taking us out of old imperial Britain and into Europe, without compromising our identity. Suddenly, the relationship with England seemed to matter less. Scots were no longer going via London; we were forming independent links with the cities of America, Europe, the world. Even the Tartan Army seemed to sense the new atmosphere; they stopped ripping up the Wembley turf and began to behave like ambassadors.

And then came this year's World Cup, bringing with it – out of the blue – the most blatant outburst of anti-English feeling I can remember. It wasn't so much that the Scots failed to support the English, as that they shouted for any tinpot dictatorship whose football team happened to be lined up against Bobby Robson's men; and eventually the tide of bile spilled over into the Scottish press.

I suppose the occasional outburst of unreason can be expected from popular papers like the *Daily Record*, but last weekend *The Scotsman* and *Observer Scotland* also ran smug and unrepentant expressions of football Anglophobia by senior journalists who should have known better; one columnist even put his infantile resentments down to the nationalist "zeitgeist". As for the SNP, it covered itself with shame by sending a telegram to the Cameroon team, commiserating with them on their defeat by an "obviously" inferior side.

And so, reluctantly, I have learned a thing or two about the Scottish "zeitgeist" of 1990. I have learned that for a huge proportion of Scots, the emotions of Scottish nationalism and Anglophobia are still hopelessly intertwined, and that the widespread tolerance of anti-English feeling alienates me from a movement that I want and need to support. I know why the sourness and hatred exists. It is the dark mirror-image of English cultural arrogance and, more profoundly, of insidious assumptions about status that have distorted Scottish life ever since the Union.

But whatever the source of the anti-English passion, it's of no use to Scotland now. At worst, it gives the nationalist movement a poisoned strength that can only lead to racism and chauvinism; at best, a burning hatred for Jimmy Hill is a poor substitute for a positive vision of Scotland reborn as a modern, inventive and enlightened social democracy in Europe.

In fact, things have changed since 1979, and the potential exists for a crucial shift in our relationship with England. The idea of Britain has grown steadily weaker, and this week's sad outburst by Nicholas Ridley against the fact of German economic power only indicates the depth of the post-imperial identity crisis now faced by the English themselves. But we Scots, it seems, are not very interested in that, nor in the complex truth about our own role in the British imperial adventure. We prefer the simple image of ourselves as the wee, poverty-stricken victim of the Union, the one who wuz robbed.

Believe it or not, there are reformers in England – like Hugo Young, writing this week in *The Guardian* – who are looking to Scotland to lead a constitutional revolt in Britain, should the next election result in a fourth Tory victory on a minority vote. But I hope they will not hold their breath. For if the Tories win, I have a sinking feeling that the Scots will do nothing. We will settle down happily to another five years of blaming the English for everything and taking responsibility for nothing. We will sing through our noses the popular anthem, *Flower of Scotland,* never pausing to think how clearly – in its obsession with the English, its belligerent tone and its strange circular structure – it reflects the emotional pattern of our impotent nationalism.

And when asked to do something concrete – gather outside St Andrew's House, say, to tell Michael Forsyth his time is up – we'll snort "bloody politicians", and settle down at the telly with cans of Tartan Special to support whoever is playing against England. When it comes to expressing nationalist feeling, it's certainly the easiest and most futile of options; but for the time being, it's the one Scotland seems to prefer.

July 15, 1990

The trial of John Buchan

Trevor Royle

Fifty years to the day of John Buchan's death, Trevor Royle borrowed the novelist's heroic style to recount his (imaginary) trial for alleged racism.

Sir Edward Leithen awoke with a high heart. Gone was the misery of the past months when each new morning had brought the familiar sweats and tightness of breath which had left him fevered and liverish. Instead, he felt singularly light-headed and the world, which had seemed rather futile, was now brisk and alluring. A cold bath had put him back in sorts but the immediate cause of buoyant spirits was the breakfast tray which his man Cruddock had prepared for him. On the table in his smoking room were homemade scones, russet pancakes, hot buttered toast, two boiled eggs and coffee as made by one who had learned the art in France.

Idly Leithen scanned the newspapers. There was unrest again in the Balkans and the Near East. Perhaps his old chum Sandy Arbuthnot was already at work there, in disguise no doubt, stopping the region from plunging into further nationalist beastliness. He smiled at the thought: it struck him that Azerbaijan was just the sort of place that might stop a man from yawning. And here were two editors jawing about night clubs and gals and all that sort of rot. Once upon a time, in his green days, Leithen had laid about a chap with a champagne bottle in Rapachini's restaurant in Soho, but that was after he had drunk too many whiskes-and-sodas. Nowadays his life was calm and sedentary with long hours in the courts and at his desk, for Sir Edward had made a big name for himself at the English Bar.

The pleasing reverie was interrupted by his man Cruddock. "Remember you are in court today, sir," he coughed politely. "The John Buchan case."

"I had not forgotten," Leithen answered softly. A frown masked his aquiline features; the moment of reckoning had finally come.

"Will you get him off, sir?"

"Depend upon it. His enemies have powerful evidence, but they have forgotten that what seems good evidence on paper is often feeble enough in court."

"I hope you are right, sir," said Cruddock as he cleared the table. "Our lives depend upon it."

Leithen took a taxi from his rooms in Down Street for the days were long past when he could walk any Highland ghillie off the hill. It was a beastly business, this charge of racism and anti-Semitism but, for Buchan's sake, it was one that had to be faced. Leithen glanced at his papers. The judge was a fair man – he had been in his house at school as the small Etonian shield on his watch-chain testified – but his adversary, the prosecutor, was of a different kidney. He had a dancing light in his eyes, a restless intelligence which was at once attractive and most disquieting. Leithen frowned as the prosecutor addressed the court: here was a man who had spent his days in dusty legal files when the world was chock-full of more amusing things.

"My Lord," he began, "I shall prove that, not only in his novels, John Buchan was guilty of prejudice against non-white people, that his characters used racist sentiments to describe Jews and Africans and that, in so doing, he helped to perpetuate racism in this country."

There was a murmur of dissent from the public galleries. "These are ugly charges, I know," the prosecutor continued, "but they can be proved by reference to the books and by calling on the characters to answer their use of phrases like 'fat Jew,' or 'blue-black dago' or 'sullen dark-skinned people'. My case will rest on the written word, for, after all, did not Mr Buchan himself admit that: 'Frankness in literature is an admirable thing, if, as at various times in our history, it keeps step with social habit; but when it strives to advance beyond it, it becomes a disagreeable pose.' I submit that Mr Buchan adopted that 'disagreeable pose' when he came to write about other races."

Leithen then rose to address the court. "Indeed," he began politely, "but did not John Buchan say in the same passage of his autobiography that modern critics were owlishly earnest and wholly humourless who had a limitless contempt for whatever did not conform to their creed of the moment? Did he not also say that they were like debauchees turned flagellant?"

Laughter greeted Leithen's grim little comment. "No, my Lord, it is my intention to prove that as far as John Buchan, Lord Tweedsmuir, was concerned fiction was fiction and reality was reality. In his day-to-day life he pursued a course of blameless support for the Jewish people and, as we shall see, he became something af a grandee in the Children of Zion. How could a man of honour abuse that trust? As his son William has written so perceptively: 'One hint from any of his Jewish friends that he was doing them a disservice would have been quite enough to change his mind. Yet no such hint ever came.' I shall show that Buchan the public man was one thing, Buchan the writer another."

The first witness was Sir Richard Hannay, the South African mining engineer who had fallen into such enjoyable adventures in *The Thirty-Nine Steps, Greenmantle, Mr Standfast, The Three Hostages,* and *The Island of Sheep.* A mixture of Nestor and Odysseus, he was fluent in a dozen languages. A master of disguise who knew the veldt like the back of his hand, he had picked up the disconcerting Mashona trick of flinging a hunting knife into the air and catching it with his teeth. During the Great War he had been a general and had saved the Allies from defeat on several notable occasions.

"General Sir Richard Hannay, you are what might be described as a civilised English gentleman," the prosecutor began. "Your social position is secure, you have an estate at Fosse in Oxfordshire and you are not without wealth?"

"I'm what you might call a sportsman," answered Hannay modestly.

"Indeed. Was it sporting of you, Sir Richard, to describe yourself as 'a nigger driver' in *Greenmantle?*"

"Well, I have been that in my time!"

The prosecutor ignored the remark and turned to face the court.

"In a manner of speaking, no doubt. But was it gentlemanly to describe a jazz group in *The Three Hostages* in this way – 'a nigger band, looking like monkeys in uniforms, pounded out some kind of barbarous jingle'? Does that not show a severe limitation of the imagination?"

Hannay coughed and inspected his highly polished brogues. "The world knows full well that I don't care for music except pipes or the regimental band."

"Very well," continued the prosecutor, none too pleasantly. "Let us turn to our friends the Jews. In *The Thirty-Nine Steps* you approve when Franklin P. Scudder, the murdered American agent, says: 'The Jew is everywhere, but you have to go far down the backstairs to find him…if you're on the biggest kind of job and are bound to get to the real boss, 10 to one you are brought up against a little white-faced Jew in a bath-chair with an eye like a rattlesnake.'"

Hannay interrupted angrily. "Steady on, Scudder was being inconsistent. I replied that his Jew-anarchists seemed to have got left behind a little. Anyway, Sir Walter Bullivant proved that Scudder was biased against Jews."

The prosecutor smiled at this outburst. "But in the self-same novel did not you remark that 'when a Jew shoots himself in the City and there is an inquest, the newspapers usually report that the deceased was 'well-nourished'?" Is that not gratuitously distasteful?"

For his part Sir Edward found Hannay an uneasy witness. He seemed nervous and out of sorts, as if he were worried about getting too soft in his old age. It was easy to prove that, being a South African, words like 'nigger' and 'kaffir' fell easily from his lips. They were descriptive, not prescriptive. But it was the anti-Semitic remarks that stuck in the court's gullet. Hanney had been too fond of equating 'Jew' with 'vulgar wealth' and no one in court really believed Leithen's claim that the witness had been 'jawing in the manner of the times'. He was not helped when Hannay started talking about 'a sportsman called Nietzsche'.

After luncheon – which Leithen took in his club with Charles Lamancha – the prosecutor got his teeth into the case. He proved that the word 'nigger' appeared no less than three times in *Prester John* and that one of the white characters had said that the difference between him and a black man was 'the gift of responsibility'. Leithen retorted by claiming that the novel was really on the side of John Laputa who although 'black as my hat…might have sat for the figure of a Crusader'. He raised the ghost of a laugh when he added that if 'nigger' were to be condemned then Mr Joseph Conrad would have to find a new title for the *Narcissus*.

Then came the other witnesses. There was a stir when the prosecutor called the Princess Saskia, once a great émigré beauty, who was now living again in Russia, having been granted a pardon by the authorities. In *Huntingtower* she and Dickson McCunn, the Glasgow grocer, had foiled a Bolshevik plot, hatched, she claimed, by 'the Jews'. Then, to Sir Edward's discomfort, Mrs Lamington was called. With a shudder he remembered that in *The Dancing Floor* she had no sooner glimpsed the exquisite Koré Arabin than she asked: "What a remarkable girl. Is she a little mad, or only foreign?" The old dear had even had the nerve to suggest that Leithen had fallen for the gal and that there had been 'an affair of the heart'. Nonsense, thought Leithen. Like Buchan's Sir Walter Scott he regarded women "very much as a toast to be drunk after King and Constitution".

The final witness was John Buchan himself. He had lost nothing of the dignity and decorum that Leithen remembered. "Contained, positive, swift-moving," William Buchan had written of his father, "he had no private demeanour that sharply differed from his public one, except that, in private, he would allow himself the luxury of reverie and the pleasure of a joke."

"Lord Tweedsmuir," the prosecutor began expansively.

He was quickly interrupted. "John Buchan will do. It's my name as a writer and it is as a writer that I should be tried." He spoke with a gentle soothing Scots, like the speech of a Border shepherd.

"John Buchan, then," continued the prosecutor. "You are one of the best known British writers of the 20th century. You have written around 100 books including a sizeable number of novels which might be described as bestsellers. *The Thirty-Nine Steps* alone has never been out of print and it has been made into three very different films. It has sold millions of copies in many languages and yet your erstwhile friend Hugh MacDiarmid claimed that your work as a novelist 'disappears entirely in the light of European assessment'."

"He also hailed me as Dean of the Faculty of Contemporary Scottish Letters," Buchan retorted with no little pride.

Ignoring him, the prosecutor changed tack. "Forget about the plaudits," he sneered. "I have evidence that writers like Graham Greene, Philip Toynbee, T.E. Lawrence and Virginia Woolf were all made uncomfortable by your self-complacent snobbery. Moreover, they found your anti-Semitism repugnant and irresponsible. Let me take you back to your service with Lord Milner in South Africa. In your letters home you wrote disparagingly about the Jews who had made their pile after speculating in gold. You didn't like them?"

"No. I found many of them vulgar, but I also wrote that for every fellow 'in large checks, diamonds and a pink satin tie, you will find 50 quietly dressed well-mannered gentlemen'."

"Is it important to be a gentleman, to have breeding?"

"I have said as much in my 'shockers'. My heroes are what might be called men of the totem – keen, courageous and fond of a cold plunge before breakfast."

"And guilty of racism like Richard Hannay, Mr Buchan? I put it to you that you allowed him to utter disgraceful comments about fat Jews and black niggers and that in so doing he was reflecting your general attitudes."

The prosecutor paused before summing up his case. "Hannay's references to Jews, invariably sneering, have that self-congratulatory tone used by people who think they have something agreeable to say to their audience. I believe that you were doing the same thing to your readers, and that your assumption of their approval was misplaced. Naive or innocent you might consider yourself today, but neither can be held up as an excuse in law. On that count alone you are guilty."

Leithen rose to question the defendant. From long practice in cross-examination he was used to reading faces, and in Buchan he saw a puzzled man.

"I said that I would concentrate on the man himself," he began, "but there are things which have to be said about the books. In spite of what my learned friend has shown, some of Buchan's Jewish characters have been drawn sympathetically. For example, Adela Victor in *The Three Hostages* is a decent type – she married that French aristocrat we used to call Turpin. Funny chap. And in *The African Colony* Mr Buchan speaks warmly of Jews, calling them 'men of mental vigour, so eagerly receptive to new ideas'." Leithen paused. "But to the man...John Buchan, you and I have known one another longer than we may care to admit, ever since *The Power-House*, in fact. You have not always been a writer, though?"

Buchan smiled in response. "In my time I have been a journalist, a publisher, a barrister, a soldier, a Member of Parliament and an imperial servant. Latterly I was Governor-General of Canada."

"You have also done your share of good works?"

"Some."

Buchan's modesty prompted Leithen to add, "Especially for the people of Israel?"

"I was a friend of Chaim Weizmann, who was largely responsible for the Balfour Declaration of 1917 – you'll recall that the British government promised the creation of Palestine as a Jewish homeland? Well, in my time I chaired the parliamentary Pro-Palestine Committee and I pride myself that I was one of the first British writers to speak out against Hitler in 1934. For centuries the treatment of the Jews has been a stain on the gentile people. In any case, as a child in my father's manse I sensed the power of Israel in the Scottish psalms. Yes, Sir Edward, I consider myself a friend of Zionism. I like to think of myself as a friend of Zionism."

"And this was recognised by your friends?"

"It was," said Buchan quietly. "The Board of Deputies of British Jews were kind enough to inscribe my name in the Golden Book of the Jewish National Fund. A singular honour, I have been told."

Sir Edward relaxed for the first time since breakfast. He felt the same elation that he had experienced all those years ago after winning the mile at Eton and on the day that he had been elected to Pop. "Just so," he said, almost inaudibly, "just so. I have nothing more to add, only these sentiments which John Buchan expressed in the year before our country was plunged into war with Nazi Germany: 'Our creed was not based on antagonism to any other people. It was humanitarian and international; we believed that we were laying the basis of a federation of the world.' And with those wise words, I rest my case."

Like wraiths the characters departed the stage and the court slowly cleared. Readers, you are the jury, the verdict is yours. Is John Buchan guilty of the charges brought against him?

February 11, 1990

Sink or swim?

Derek Bateman

The Economist got it wrong. When the London-based periodical broke with convention and publicly gave its backing to independence, it said Scotland was not yet a nation. In delivering his ground-breaking view from the south, the author of the leading article made the mistake that no home-based Scot would permit by confusing nationhood with statehood.

It is a crucial error since it goes to the heart of the present Scottish condition, the dichotomy that Scotland is by every benchmark an identifiable nation but one which surrendered its independent sovereignty and statehood in favour of merger with another.

We are already a nation, a pre-packaged state-in-waiting. The recreation of an independent Scotland involves no rejection of ethnic groups as in America or Romania and no redrawing of artificial borders as in the GDR. There is no confusion over who is a Scot, no doubting the historical claim to sovereignty and no question over where the frontier lies.

Expressed more emotively the Scots are a people who invited their overbearing neighbour to take command of their levers of power and for more than 280 years have appalled themselves at their own sense of helplessness and injustice. In Sillars-speak it is summed up thus: "Either you exercise political power over yourself or somebody else exercises it over you."

No one from left or right in Scotland, interventionist or free marketeer, denies the historical claim. The argument against statehood is based primarily on the efficacy of independence – is it realistic to disengage from England? Would we be isolated? How much would it cost? The case for status quo is that the Union is working and it is this assumption that *The Economist* challenged, using Ravenscraig as its point of departure.

Scotland on Sunday has argued that resistance to self-government runs counter to Thatcherite philosophy as the government devolves power to parents, tenants and shareholders, obliging them to face the realities of their own decisions and inculcating a sense of responsibility and independence. Quite apart from the historical dimension, Mrs Thatcher's rejection of the mass demand for home rule is a monument to interventionism and a brake on enterprise.

Yet what brand of defeatism and self-denegration is it that continues to drive many Scots to believe they will fail where Denmark, Ireland and Luxembourg succeed? National psychoanalysis would deduce it was another symptom of the lopsided Union which forces us to argue from a position of relative weakness for the financial palliatives grudgingly conceded by an unsympathetic government (Labour or Conservative).

The Economist encapsulated it as "today's half-angry, half-embarrassed dependency status" and lent its name to a growing undercurrent in British politics which is prepared to think the unthinkable, that Scotland can be free.

Last week, Sir Russell Fairgrieve, a former chairman of the Scottish Tories, reiterated his strong belief that Scotland need not suffer from having its own government and for the first time used the language of the Nationalists in rejecting the 'Westminster crutch' in favour of Europe. Fairgrieve's opinions matter because not only is he a senior Tory, but he is an industrialist in his own right and a member of the Conservatives' influential Scottish Business Group. He represents a growing number who fear that failure to provide a safety valve through an assembly is forcing the political pressure to build up behind independence, the head of steam partly powered by English backbenchers contemptuous of Scottish aspirations.

In its campaign against public subsidy, which it associates most closely with the Scots, the English right-wing advocates cutting Scotland off from our London benefactor to let us sink or swim. This movement taken together with Alex Salmond's reawakening of the Scottish financial sector to the possibilities of independence and the publication of his budget calculations last year, and Fairgrieve's intervention, is beginning to shift the balance of the argument.

Voices are increasingly united on both sides of the border challenging the status quo and placing the onus on the Unionists to justify their case. *The Economist,* bible of the business community, has joined the chorus and bestowed on the nationalist argument the cachet of respectability.

The question to be addressed now is not 'Can Scotland do it?' It is 'Should Scotland do it?' As the Ravenscraig debacle and Malcolm Rifkind's doomed mediation has demonstrated, an independent government with powers of intervention is the only way to sustain an indigenous industrial base. Only economic decision-making in Scotland can balance the anti-competitive concentration of development in the over-subsidised south east.

If Thatcher had the courage of her free market convictions she would end the constitutional log jam with an elected assembly. With the explicit support of the influential *Economist* and presumably, some of the movers and shakers who read it, independence and a seat in the European council of ministers looks increasingly credible as the price Scotland exacts for her failure to do so.

June 3, 1990

Grandstand finish

Graham Spiers

He bowed out in style. Nothing else could be said of it. Playing to the galleries, shouting to hotel windows, fighting with his caddie, regaling the crowd. It was all there, a Vegas-type performance at St Andrews.

Goodbye Arnold Palmer. In three easy words, the Open Championship bade farewell to a man whose appearance 30 years ago caused such a stir in this same town. On Friday he took his curtain call, vowing as a player never to return. We shall have to wait and see, but this time it seems for real.

Palmer's presence on a golf course remains unrivalled. At 60, for sure, wear and tear are telling: his eye is not as sharp as it was, and his concentration, as he says, simply isn't there. Yet to see him before an audience is to experience his magic once more.

In the first two rounds he played alongside Gary Player and Rolf Muntz. What contrasts. Player, himself a legend, was studious at his game, mapping out yardages and becoming increasingly introspective. Muntz, the amateur, was overcome with nerves. Palmer, meanwhile, had enjoyment on his mind, clouting the ball, but letting his emotions run with it.

He's on the fifth, and picking out faces in the crowd. "Hey, how are you. I haven't seen you for a long time." Player goes through his swing, Muntz paces about. "Are you still living here?"

Nothing perturbs him. Going up the sixth, Greg Norman's name looms large on the leaderboard. "The one to beat," Arnie tells Player with a nod at the score. "Yeah," says Player, "the one to beat."

It continues apace, some wayward drives, erratic irons, a few awful putts. Yet in among them, a couple of Arnie gems, like a birdie putt at the 10th and a 20-footer at the 11th. The cheering applause nearly brought the scaffolding down.

And beside him, Tip. Tip, the most knobbly-kneed caddie on earth, Tip who carries the can and takes some flak as well. Way back on the fifth he's persuaded Arnie to change his iron – the resulting shot flew to within 10 feet of the pin. Next hole, however, Tip's advice proves flawed, another iron shot, this time flying 40 yards past. Arnie throws the club in disgust, his only flicker of rage.

To consummate their 30-year bond, the two men put on a cabaret on the 16th tee.

Arnie: "My driver please, Tip."
Tip: "But that's the wrong club."
Arnie (sharp): "What d'ya mean, it's wrong?"
Tip: "It just is."
Arnie (moving in): "Why, Tip...c'mon talk to me". He turns to the crowd. "See what I've had to suffer for 30 years?"
Tip: "There's rough on the left...it's a 2-iron you want."
Arnie: "Nonsense," before hitting his shot into the rough on the left. "You were right, Tip..."

Greg Norman, by this time finished and back in his Old Course suite, has seen the commotion on television and is waiting on his verandah overlooking the 17th fairway. "Keep going, old man," he shouts down to Arnie. "I'm catching you," shouts Arnie in mock determination. "The hell I am," he mutters under his breath.

Enough. This is a shameless piece of hero worship, Arnie-adoration of the highest level. Coming off the last, the weariness sets in, the crowd's applause once more ringing in his ears. "Phew, I'm getting old, I'm getting past this," says Arnie. The hell he is.

July 22, 1990

The last sleeper

William Paul

Eddie Straker settled down for an easy night as the last Paddy train prepared to pull out of Stranraer late on Friday.

He had four passengers to look after in the two sleeping cars designed to take 36. Another four had booked to board at Girvan and two more in Ayr. Apart from that the only other people on the four-coach train were three Celtic supporters in the seated carriage, over from Ireland for the Cup final at Hampden and relieved to find they would be able to get to Glasgow after all. If there was to be a murder on the Stranraer night express, there would not be very many suspects.

"But this train is going to London," said a Celtic fan with a green and white scarf knotted round his neck and a worried frown on his face.

"That's right but we have to go to Glasgow first."

"Isn't that the wrong direction?"

"We have to go north before we go south. It's the way it works."

Eddie sat in his cramped little compartment surrounded by little teapots and grinned. "This is an easy job, this is," he said. "I have been on the London to Edinburgh and London to Glasgow routes and they are always full. You never get a moment to yourself but here it is never like that. I have seen times when there has not been a single person except me and the driver."

A history like that would seem to justify British Rail's decision to save an estimated £200,000 a year by ending the Paddy service, so called because of its link to the ferries from Northern Ireland, but it has not always been so poorly patronised. As recently as the early 1980s, a 13-coach train was required to cater for demand and spare coaches had to be ready and waiting in the goods yard by the ferry terminal just in case.

"They were getting the passengers then," said leading railman Bill Mackay, making final checks before departure. "I don't know what has happened but we saw this coming, saw it coming from a long way. I suppose all good things must come to an end."

It might have something to do with the rise in fares and the increasing competition from the buses. A lot of people believe that a place like Stranraer simply did not fit in with the InterCity image and corporate strategy of fast links between major centres of population. Stranraer, unfortunately, was a frayed edge hanging from the central network of routes and one that any commercial, houseproud company would want to tidy by having it snipped off.

Appeals for a reprieve by local councillors and MPs to British Rail and to Transport Secretary Cecil Parkinson had no effect last week. The Paddy was doomed.

At Stranraer station, William Buckoke, a retired banker who has lived at New Luce near Stranraer since 1971, has been hugely irritated by the loss of a service he used regularly, about 20 times last year.

"InterCity says it makes a loss and so it must be closed," he explained as he loaded luggage on to the train for a holiday down south with his wife Isobel. "But they make no effort to advertise the service. People just don't know it exists and I suspect BR want it that way so they can say nobody uses it. You couldn't find it in the official timetable last year. It showed Dumfries as the end of the line which is like saying Canterbury is the end of the line for the Channel ports."

Isobel, chairman of the local community council, has sent letters of protest without success. "It makes you wonder about the future of the railway at Stranraer, not just this one train," she said. William interrupted. "I don't know how we will be getting back," he said. "Probably the sleeper to Glasgow and then another train down. You can probably get from London to Casablanca in the time it takes to get from there to New Luce."

Outside, on the deserted platform, there is no-one to read the new posters which trumpet "great news for ScotRail passengers in south-west Scotland". The amended timetable, coming into force tomorrow, promises improvements and extra travel opportunities. There is no mention of the demise of the Paddy and the nightly sleeper service to London. Passengers from the south-west will have to go 100 miles north to Glasgow two hours earlier to get a sleeper connection. It will not be guaranteed, of course. InterCity does not deign to wait for provincial services if they happen to be delayed.

The Paddy headed north to Glasgow on Friday night, leaving Stranraer exactly on time. At 1am there was much bumping and jarring as the diesel locomotive was uncoupled and the coaches joined to the overnight train coming south from Fort William. Eddie thinks coaches from Inverness will be added at Carstairs junction but is not sure and everybody is asleep by then.

The Paddy has been making the long roundabout trek to Glasgow before being able to head south since 1988. It used to run directly to London but even then had to take a 60-mile loop north through Kilmarnock. In the 1960s it ran even more directly eastwards to Dumfries but Dr Beeching put a stop to that in his own inimitable way by closing the line and ripping it up.

The Paddy, squeezed onto the front of the Fort William train and maybe the Inverness train as well, rolled into Euston Station for the last time exactly on schedule, 7.46am, yesterday morning.

Eddie had had a quiet night. None of his passengers had bothered him and the delivery of early morning tea to each person had taken only a matter of minutes. A few minutes more to retrieve the trays and wash up and he was one of the first onto the platform.

"That's it then," he said. "See you in Scotland next week. I'll be doing Fort William."

Tonight, meanwhile, Eddie is the attendant on the final run of the sleeper from Barrow-in-Furness to London. InterCity is closing down that route as well. Another frayed edge snipped off to keep the network neat and tidy.

May 13, 1990

Recipe for disaster

Derek Cooper

When I wrote my first food column for these pages one hundred Sundays ago, I had no idea what horrors were about to overwhelm us, and I'm not talking about British Food & Farming Year which was designed to draw attention to the heritage of agriculture and the wonders of our national larder.

It was a master stroke of unintended irony that 1989 was chosen to trumpet the great achievements of food and farming for it was the year that will go down in history as the one in which everyone realised that there were some terrible things going on behind the rural scenery.

For far too long, the dark mysteries of the way in which we produce our food had been kept out of the headlines. Food reformers, nutritionists, animal activists and the scientific community – academics, vets, researchers, drug and chemical corporations – knew exactly what was happening down on the farm but the public were either not aware or acted on the mistaken assumption that the government would not allow anything to occur which might in any way be a cause for alarm or anxiety.

Food & Farming Year was a centenary celebration of the Ministry of Agriculture and the 150th birthday of the Royal Agricultural Society. Schoolchildren were to be uplifted to the countryside in droves to watch farmers at work. There were to be exhibitions and shows of all kinds, thanksgiving services for Nature's bounty and the time-honoured skills of country folk, not to mention the food technologists, the biogeneticists and the battalions of chemists who have made our processed factory food an object of wonder to the rest of Europe.

Sadly, like an Exocet homing in irrevocably on a doomed ship, the missile which was to blow this expensively hyped year of myth and nostalgia to pieces had already been fired. It had impacted at the end of the previous year with the news that all was not well in the poultry sheds. All the antibiotics in the veterinary arsenal could not keep salmonella enteritidis at bay. The nation's eggs, lightly boiled, were potentially lethal for babies and grans.

As the festivities got into their somewhat inhibited stride, listeriosis hit the headlines. There was a frenzied rush away from herbs or coleslaw and the contents of supermarket cook-chill cabinets. Then we heard that dead sheep infected with scrapie were being fed to dairy herds. Diseased chickens, suspect eggs, BSE, milk secretly produced with artificial hormones, farm animals reared and slaughtered in unacceptably inhumane conditions – the news kept from the front pages for years gradually grew into a mounting indictment of our conventional methods of farming.

It was not only the way we treated our animals that shocked public opinion. We learnt that after 40 years of intensive crop production the land itself was poisoned with chemicals and our drinking water was in many areas irrevocably contaminated. The erosion of faith in the Ministry of Agriculture is now at an all-time low. "Rightly or wrongly," claimed the Consumers' Association at the end of June, "people no longer believe the ministry on food safety issues. In the long term, public confidence can only be restored by the establishment of a food agency independent of government and of industry."

That makes sense. The food and farming industry is geared not to safeguarding the health and nutrition of the nation but to maximising profits. The ministry is the natural defender of agribusiness, determined to protect its interests against all comers including, all too often, the consumer. Expanding production, cutting costs, increasing our share of the European market – these are the preoccupations of MAFF when it comes to food. The nutritional quality of that food is of secondary importance. Worried about your beef? Don't rock the boat says Mr Gummer, there's no evidence that it's not safe. It's all part of an EC plot to destroy our markets. British food, says his jingoistic sidekick David Maclean, is the best and safest in the world – don't worry.

The truth is less palatable. We now know that what's good for business is not necessarily good for the health and safety of the British people. Business looks for short-term profits. Want some cheap animal feed? How about these dead infected sheep – they'll make nice protein-rich pellets. Want to keep the price of chickens down? Pack them more closely in the cages and shoot them full of drugs. It may make economic sense but it has proved to be a recipe for disaster.

We desperately need an independent agency which will weigh up with great care the economic needs of the nation and the long-term health of our people. Such a body has been rejected out of hand by Mr Gummer who appears to have a blind and unshakable faith in the integrity of the private sector to serve the nation.

Labour have promised that if they are returned to power they will set up the kind of independent food standards agency which the consumer movement demands. Good for them. But I have a strong suspicion that if the Tories fought their way back they'd pretty soon get rid of it. After all, food is best left to enterprising businessmen who really know what's good for Britain. Mad cow disease? Never heard of it!

July 8, 1990

The Forsyth saga

Michael Fry

The Scottish Conservative factions seem intent on a fight to the death, with a partisan recklessness of which I used to think only socialists capable.

It comes as a genuine surprise to me to see how effective the left, represented by the Tory Reform Group, is proving in this latest phase of its campaign against Michael Forsyth. It looked like a bunch of has-beens with bankrupt ideas, inspired not so much by any coherent programme of reform, as by distilled hatred of our party chairman. But its ability to raise its profile just at the moment of his greatest embarrassment, on the departure of Douglas Young, has been a supremely smooth exercise in PR. It has been seen to rally about it many of the great and good in Scottish Conservatism, in an outspoken but quite explicit protest against the takeover of the party's apparatus by Forsyth's cold-hearted, wild-eyed fanatics. How much real support exists for either side among the membership is maybe open to question, since most Conservatives desire no more than a quiet life. But I dare say the TRG would, for the moment, come out tops in an opinion poll.

In attaining this prominence it has effectively obscured its own greatest weakness and exposed Forsyth's. Its greatest weakness is that it has nothing to offer Scotland, or the Tory party, that has not been tried and failed already. Few now recall that the TRG held a meeting some months ago at which it tried to elaborate policies. Even I, who take some interest in these matters, cannot remember a single thing proposed, except the selection of more women candidates – a certain vote-loser, in my view.

I suppose the TRG stalwarts want a return to the Youngerite consensus. But it was precisely that consensus which reduced us to 10 parliamentary seats. What would they do better the second time around? Still more subsidies? Still greater protection for Scottish vested interests? If so, we would be better winding our Tory party up and going over to Labour, which will always pursue these aims with greater enthusiasm. The only real way to be radical in a different way from Forsyth's is through finding the means to formulate policies in a specifically Scottish context, which eventually implies devolution. But, so far as I can see, devolution is still taboo inside the TRG.

Nevertheless, this mealy-mouthing and pussy-footing has been subtly covered up by the TRG's concentrating its fire, not on policies, but on personalities, on Forsyth's most vulnerable point. I do not mean to be taken as calling him a nasty young man. If I were of a more timorous disposition, I might be unnerved by his sinister appearance, but he has always been civil to me on the occasions when we have met. Nor can I claim that I, in his position, would have been much nicer to some of his victims. The chickens of Chester Street, the old guard running the central office before he arrived, were in almost every respect quite useless and thoroughly deserved a savaging.

But Forsyth evidently has encountered, or indeed caused, problems with personalities in his efforts to build up a replacement team, which now for a second time appears to be crashing. These shenanigans are very much *sub-rosa*, but from the outside his conduct has been marked by two motives. One is a desire for absolute ideological purity in those he selects. The other is an exteme impatience for results. If only the two were always politically compatible! But a pure ideology may be generated as much by sycophancy as by zeal. And sycophancy, while outwardly agreeable to politicians in a hurry, is not the best way to get results – socialism has taught us this.

So by contrast with Forsyth's sure touch in policy, in widening a radical agenda and getting things done, we have only a concatenation of failure in matters of personality. In politics unfortunately, both are indispensable for success.

In Forsyth the contrast is now so glaring that if he continues to get things wrong, and if his enemies show more of their recent skill and resource, his career could be wrecked.

Beneath the radical patina there may indeed be in Forsyth just an old-fashioned Calvinist, a typical scion of Montrose and St Andrews. In that case he is perhaps incorrigible. But, at the risk of appearing a patronising codger, I shall hope that his intolerance and impatience are the faults of an immature politician. In nearly all that he has attempted so far, Forsyth has been phenomenally successful, almost too much so. He has not learned many political tricks beyond the repertoire he acquired in the Federation of Conservative Students because he has not had to. But he will have to learn how to draw what he wants out of those who disagree with him.

For the rest of us, I believe we should accustom ourselves to the idea of Forsyth as the next Scottish Secretary. I do not think it would serve either Scotland's or his own interests if Malcolm Rifkind stayed at St Andrew's House beyond the general election. And no rival for the succession remotely matches Forsyth's qualities. I cannot vouch for what happened to him at Montrose and St Andrews, but an education which afterwards took him through the FCS, London PR and Westminster City Council certainly lacks something. He needs a sentimental education, if you like, which his colleagues can still give him and which he ought to have sense enough to accept.

August 5, 1990

Royal soap

Brian Groom

When a public figure is able to read his or her obituary over breakfast, it is normally because one of the august national daily papers has made an unfortunate boob. It happened a couple of years back to Rex Alston, the former cricket commentator (most famous quote at the microphone: "He's out and I've lost sixpence"). Reports of Rex's death were exaggerated.

For Queen Elizabeth, the Queen Mother, reading her own obituary has been a way of life for longer than many of us have been on the earth. More obituary-type prose has been written about her than about any other living human being. If *The Times* published the Queen Mother's obituary by mistake, I doubt if anyone would notice, so similar would it be to everything else that has gone before.

This summer has brought an outpouring of Royalspeak remarkable even by modern standards. It has been a summer of celebrations of her 90th birthday, culminating yesterday in The Big Day itself. She's probably still counting the cards: the last milestone 10 years ago brought 30,000 of them.

A computer study of the language used about the Queen Mother would probably reveal that the words which are normally most common, such as *and* or *the*, are outnumbered by words like *grace*, *charm*, *vitality*, or, increasingly, *durability*. What the lady herself thinks, we don't know, beyond the fact that she thought her 80th birthday tributes "very nice".

But what are we to make of a woman whose tastes range from the poetry of George Herbert to the novels of Barbara Cartland, or from the pictures of Wilson Steer and Augustus John to the comedy of Bernie Winters; who lives by a strong moral code, likes a gin and tonic and gets the racing results piped to Clarence House?

The curious thing about the oleaginous prose in which any writing about the Queen Mother is couched is that it isn't necessary. If anything, it does her a disservice. By any standards she is a figure of considerable historical importance to the 20th century monarchy. A little serious analysis of that would do neither her nor the rest of us any harm.

It's not so much that she "saved the monarchy", as so many of her biographers have it. I doubt that Britain was ready for the installation of a republic in 1936, though the abdication crisis was certainly more than an alarming wobble. As Edward VIII did the decent thing, the cabinet toyed with bypassing the Duke of York in favour of the younger Duke of Kent, whose past behaviour was at least as dodgy as that of the outgoing king and his American divorcee friend.

By choosing the Yorks, they not only weathered a crisis but gave the monarchy a new lease of life which has lasted more than half a century. The Royal Family had been a remote institution, respected but not greatly loved, rattling about formally in their 18 draughty palaces.

In its place came a new image, the royals as the happy family next door, supposedly like yours or mine, all comfy chairs and flowers and laughter and the patter of little princesses' feet. It was real enough for them, but for the nation it was a flattering ideal of how people would like to think of themselves. Arguably the wayward Duke of Windsor held up a more accurate mirror to a troubled century, but once the royal soap opera was under way there was no stopping it.

Though she hates people to say it, it was largely Elizabeth's doing. She gave her diffident and stammering husband the strength to rule. Biographers generally put it down to her background as an "aristocratic commoner", born into privilege without the stresses which royalty face. Possibly. Or perhaps it was just chance that gave her those rare qualities of determination, warmth and charm (there I go – how *do* you avoid those words?).

And so it went on, increasing the popularity of a previously outmoded institution through war, austerity and loss of Empire.

Behind the smiles, living up to the ideal involved a stern self-discipline. I wonder how much heartache would have been avoided had Princess Margaret been allowed to marry Peter Townsend – another divorcee, though himself the innocent party. Townsend remarked of the Queen Mother: "Beneath her graciousness, her gaiety and her unfailing thoughtfulness for others, she possessed a steely will."

That determination has given the Royal Family a role which will carry it into the 21st century though there are signs of strain. It was the first soap opera in an age which has become dominated by soap operas – and there is a strong streak of vicarious cruelty in people's enjoyment of such spectacles.

By the time the next century dawns, a new role will be needed. Prince Charles has already started to fashion one: royalty not just as a family role model, but as concerned public activists. It remains to be seen whether that idea continues to tap a vein of public sentiment, or whether ultimately it oversteps the boundaries of constitutional propriety.

August 5, 1990

Sex at the Festival

Peter Cudmore and Alan Taylor

Who knows what happened behind the closed doors of the Traverse Theatre in 1963. In the year sex began officially, at least according to Philip Larkin, everyone – so the story goes – wanted to "get off at the Traverse". "You'll be lucky," said an Edinburgh bus conductor. To the strains of Frank Sinatra's *Songs for Swinging Lovers*, those irrepressible Traversites Ricky Demarco and Jim Haynes pressed flesh in the sweaty space. Sex, said a suspiciously well-informed Edinburgh minister, was alive and well at the Edinburgh Festival.

But despite what the *Daily Record* had to say, recalls Ricky Demarco, there wasn't much sex at the Traverse, which in those days was situated in a former brothel in the Lawnmarket. However, everyone desperately wanted there to be.

"Now it's different. We're sated," says the sexagenarian gallery-owner, adding enigmatically: "It's become so commonplace you can't tell the difference between sex, bee-keeping and planting potatoes." Ignoring for the moment this odd conjunction, Demarco rattles off a favourite aphorism: "Art without sex is not art; religion without sex isn't religion."

Almost three decades on, the Traverse bar is the unsexiest joint in town. Hot chocolate, cheese rolls and theatre chat are the unlikely aphrodisiacs. Morag Ballantyne, the Traverse's PR, yawned when we tried to chat her up. "Permissiveness is a complete myth," she said. Jim Haynes, now lecturing on sexual politics in Paris, wasn't around. When we did catch up with him he said: "People are just too tired this year." If there's a faint whiff of the has-been about the Trav, where else is it happening? "Try the Assembly box-office," said Ballantyne helpfully.

Later. We'll try the Fringe Club first – surely something's

happening there? It echoes to the sound of Zimmer frames. Even the decorations look tired. The Assembly Rooms it is.

This needs some explanation. A week or so ago, Alex "Randy" Renton of *The Independent* revealed that he'd been offered sex for a review. Then he quoted a Fringe performer who said he had slept with just five people in his entire life (cue Patsy Cline), three of whom were box-office staff at the Assembly Rooms. Renton was obviously a man in the know, so we phoned *The Independent's* Festival flat. "Not here, in London," we were told. Run out of town, was the obvious thought. Not so, said "Randy" when we flushed him out in the London newsroom, where he was in the thick of the Gulf crisis. However, his expertise was not going to waste, having just penned a review of the revival of the nude review, *Let My People Come*. "I first came to the Festival in 1984 hoping to get laid," he said. "Actually, I didn't. We were staying at a girls' Catholic school in separate dormitories for each sex, so there was not much heterosexual sex going on." Nor was there much of the other kind, he suspected. "There's never much sex among the press," he said.

So far so bad. Still, there was always the Assembly Rooms. PR Jackie Westbrook said the box-office staff had enlarged "Randy" Renton's article. She wouldn't name names, in any case it was highly unlikely that the three girls referred to in *The Independent* would be employed there now. "There's a big turnover every year," she said, without a hint of innuendo. "There are 18 girls and five chaps in the box-office and the scandal diary they keep is bulging. Let's just say liaisons are being formed," said Westbrook. "A lot of flats are half-empty, others are double-full. It's all go down here."

Cheering as this news was, it was not getting us very far. Some people aren't interested in sex at all. One technician told us she gets an hour or two off at a time and it's feasible, but she's not going to risk getting back late and blowing her career.

We headed in the direction of the Bedlam, where we decided it was time to take action. We tapped a young woman on the shoulder and steeled ourselves.

"We're investigating...fun on the Fringe. Can we ask your name?" We can reveal exclusively that she was called Claudia, is from Bologna, studies in Florence and was indeed having fun. Thank God someone was. Whenever we mentioned sex, the talk turned to romance. Far from looking for sex, people raised papers to cover their face. A television producer claimed he had had two firm offers of sex but had turned them down flat. Why? "I'm married," he said, without a hint of shame. Another veteran Fringe-goer announced that he was getting married. This shocked his best friend, a poet:

"And as if that isn't bad enough," said the poet, "he tells me he is going to stay faithful."

This seems to be the way things are going. Every way you turn, the trend is towards fidelity, monogamy, ye Gods, marriage. A former editor of an Edinburgh-based magazine, now back in Edinburgh with a Fleet Street newspaper, claims that the Festival is more about romance than sex. "We have a photographer in the office now who has spent the last few days staring into the eyes of a woman." That, she implies, is as far as it is going to go.

August 26, 1990

Lockerbie: a year on

Keren David

The evening of 21 December, 1988 was typically quiet in the little Borders town of Lockerbie. Michael Aspel was about to surprise Harry Corbett on *This is Your Life*, and the bingo was due to kick off at the Rex Cinema in an hour. The 3,500 residents ate their suppers, washed the dishes, and wrapped Christmas presents.

At three minutes past seven, they heard a strange whistling wind, then a thunderous rumble that grew to a roar. The houses shook and rattled as a huge fireball lit the sky. An orange glow made the dark streets as light as day.

Sarah Campbell, a mature student at technical college, had just arrived at her sister's flat in the High Street, eagerly anticipating a night out at the bingo. "I was standing at the back door when I first heard the noise. It sounded like thunder, then I thought it was a train down at the station. When I looked up, I saw the plane explode, and the noise became about two million times louder. We went round to the front of the house and watched the engine flying apart and spinning down towards us."

Sarah started running. "My adrenalin must have been going. I went to see if my children were all right, then ran to my mother's house. I waited to see if there was anything I could do there, then I went to a friend's. When I came back into the town, the street was chock-a-block with traffic. I thought it was sightseers and I was shocked. Later, I realised they'd been diverted off the main road. I saw two guys just sitting and eating their dinners in a guest house, as though nothing had happened. And a woman came out of her house with a brush, swept up the debris on the path, then went inside again. I ran back to my sister's and we went to the bingo. There was nothing else for us to do."

The crowd sat soberly in the hall of the Rex Cinema that night, eyes fixed on their cards. A caller wept and had to run from the stage. The winners collected their prizes in silence.

Sarah left the bingo hall just after nine. By that time, ambulances lined the street and a helicopter hovered overhead. Makeshift lighting had been set up to illuminate the High Street. Dazed townsfolk wandered the streets. "It was just bedlam. I could hardly recognise the town," Sarah says.

The night of the disaster, many people wept with frustration, aware that family and friends from outside the town wanted to telephone but could not get through. Eleanor Hogg, Sarah's sister, recalls, "I've heard about people in London who tried for hours and hours to find out if their families were safe. That must have been terrible."

But Robert Riddet, chairman of the community council, comments, "At the time, we didn't think about the traumas our family were going through – we were so busy with our own small world, we forgot the world outside." Most homes in Lockerbie did not have telephone lines restored until well after Christmas, as police and rescue services needed all those available.

Just a few minutes, and the lives of the people of Lockerbie had changed. The world knows of the horror of Pan Am flight 103 and the explosion which killed 270 people. For many, Lockerbie became a symbol of human frailty, a reminder of the terrible truth that none of us are safe in our own homes. But life has moved on in the last year, and the townspeople have tackled the legacy of the disaster with remarkable courage.

'Before the disaster' is a time they remember wistfully. In those days outsiders knew the town only as a convenient stopping-off point on the A74 to and from Glasgow. "Sleepy" is the most popular word used by locals to describe the old Lockerbie, with "completely ordinary" coming a close second. Blank looks greet questions about the biggest happening in the town before December 21, 1988. The best offer is, "The Queen came to open the cheese factory in 1975."

Like any small town, everyday life was – and is – made up of events such as bingo sessions, school concerts and church services. The highlight of each year is the gala day celebrated on the second Saturday in June, with parades, marching bands and a party. Local farmers come in to market every week. The busiest time is autumn when lambs are sold.

Lockerbie is a town where people stay all their lives. House prices are low enough to allow children to buy homes next door to their parents – a semi costs about £25,000. Folk are often related. "You think twice before you gossip, just in case you're talking to the person's cousin by marriage," one local explains. "If you say, 'so-and-so's a friend of mine', you mean he is a cousin."

Robert Riddet, who has lived in the town for 15 years, still maintains, "I'm not a Lockerbie man." People say "Good day" to everyone in the street, and if it rains, you take in your neighbour's washing.

Locals are affronted at suggestions that their lifestyle is limited, however. With an ice rink, a squash club, a golf course and a bowling green, Lockerbie has better amenities than many towns twice its size. "It's quite a cosmopolitan place. We're not backward at all," asserts one resident.

They still laugh about the London reporter who got his Scottish stereotypes muddled and labelled the Borders town "a picturesque Highland village". Similarly, some people scoff at the journalists who described Lockerbie as close-knit. "There's social division here, just like everywhere else," they say. The town has grown in recent years, particularly with the influx of retired couples and 'white settlers' from England, Glasgow and Edinburgh attracted by the low property prices.

But the jet ignored social distinctions as it plummeted to earth. The cockpit landed in the tiny farming village of Tundergarth. A middle section containing 61 passengers crashed onto the terraces of the Rosebank council estate. And the worst damage on the ground was caused by a fuel-carrying wing, which gouged a huge crater among the owner-occupied houses of Sherwood Crescent.

Ronnie Hall lives in Park Place, the worst-affected street in the Rosebank estate. He moved to Lockerbie as a boy during the last war. "My father wanted to avoid the blitz, so we came here from Clydeside. Strangely enough our house there was never bombed." He was washing the dishes on December 21 when he heard the ominous rumble of the explosion. Seconds later a small piece of undercarriage crashed through the roof and sliced his wife's dressing table in half. Rubble and debris filled the bedroom destroying furniture and bedclothes. "There were feathers everywhere," Ronnie remembers.

However, he had smelled gas and was so busy getting his neighbours well away, he didn't discover the damage to his house until late that night. In fact, the confusion was such that he didn't realise a neighbouring house lay in ruins, filled with corpses. Ella

Ramsden who lived there had managed to climb out of the rubble almost uninjured.

The full horror of what had happened became apparent the next morning. The ground was strewn with passengers' belongings. Some were poignantly sad – like a Dutchman's identity card. Others were more bizarre. "There must have been hundreds of packets of darning needles just lying there. We think there was probably a trade consignment in the hold. It took ages to clear everything up. Somehow seeing the belongings was almost sadder than the sight of the bodies themselves. They seemed so pathetic, so exposed," comments one witness.

Most Rosebank residents were back home after a few days, even though the bodies still lay on the ground. The police could not move them until a full forensic check was carried out, and the first priority was to search the hills. Meanwhile, the casualties could easily be covered. Families spent days with curtains drawn, trying to block the grim sight.

"Christmas was dreadful," says Ronnie. The family bravely went out to dinner, but could hardly eat. "It was a non-event. My wife and daughters were in tears."

At least in Rosebank no local people died. Ella Ramsden's escape from her ruined home – clutching her budgie's cage – cheered her neighbours immensely. But in Sherwood Crescent the crater claimed the lives of 11 locals. Blazing aviation fuel set neighbouring houses alight – even the gardens burned under a thick pall of black smoke.

Father Patrick Keegans, priest to the 270-strong Catholic congregations of Lockerbie and Moffat, had lived in the town less than a year, and had hardly settled into his house at 1 Sherwood Crescent. His mother had arrived that evening for the Christmas holidays, and he planned to take her to visit his friends and neighbours Dora and Maurice Henry. However, she was tired from her journey, so he decided to let her rest before walking the 70 yards to the Henry's bungalow.

When Father Keegans heard the noise of the plane, his first thought was that a low-flying jet was about to hit his roof. "I just stood there. I thought I might be killed, and then I thought I might be badly injured. I wondered if I would be able to move. My mother was downstairs and I wondered how she was." He considered taking her to the Henry's for safety. The next day he discovered that the couple had been killed in the crater. Their bodies, their home and their possessions simply vanished.

He found his mother and together they stumbled out of the house. "I could see cars on fire on the main road. I thought a petrol tanker must have crashed. The garden was burning and I could see that No. 5 was in flames. The wind was blowing the fire towards us, so I knew we had to get away."

Firemen arriving at the crescent told him a jumbo had crashed. "We knew nothing about the crater. But once we were down in the town it became clearer what had happened. Thoughts of Maurice and Dora were going round in my mind. I went back to see if I could get into the crescent from the other side, but the flames and smoke prevented me. At the town hall everyone was talking, trying to form a picture of what had happened. There was a sense of excitement and confusion. The only way I can describe it is to say people were functioning on a completely different level."

Help flowed into the town. As police, army and rescue workers searched the hills, workmen strove to restore gas, electricity and telephone lines. Social workers set up a non-stop counselling service. Council staff worked round the clock to repair roads, water pipes and sewage services. Lockerbie Academy was commandeered as a control centre. Within hours the various groups – even representatives from the Jewish social services – were allocated office space. A suite of rooms was set aside for relatives expected from America.

As the specialists worked non-stop, some of the people of Lockerbie sat idle, desperate for jobs to do. "There was no work for us," explains Elma Pringle, whose home in Lambhill Terrace looked onto a hilly skyline strewn with wreckage and bodies. "All we could do was make coffee and snacks for the searchers. We opened the house to them, but we were still very frustrated. We wanted proper jobs, to be able to help."

Neil McIntosh, the chief executive of Dumfries and Galloway Regional Council, soon realised the community and their leaders needed a stronger role. A week after the disaster, a meeting was held in the Queen's Hotel. Everybody was represented, from the bowling club to the boy scouts. A committee was elected to make sure local people's views were not overlooked when important decisions were made. A newsletter was hastily produced – the first issue of *Community Update* appeared eight days after the disaster. It asked volunteers to contact a liaison office in the newly-opened library.

Home baking was among the first requests. "Even the older women could make a few cakes," says Elma Pringle. "It made them feel needed." Many of the police and rescue workers were too exhausted at the end of the day to eat a full meal and appreciated a choice of cakes and biscuits. The response was extraordinary. After four days, the third issue of *Community Update* reported that, because of the tremendous response, supplies were adequate for the time being.

Volunteers also started a laundry service, washing clothes for the emergency service workers. But from March they had a grimmer task. Every item of passengers' clothing is washed and ironed by local women before being sent to the relatives. A year on, the work is not yet finished as the police continue their detailed forensic examinations. A rota of women work eight hours a day. Elma Pringle is one of the volunteers. "The most upsetting thing is when a baby's clothes come through. All you can think is that these wee tots knew only happiness in their lives, they had no time for sadness. We were all especially sad the day the captain's hat arrived."

Alex McElroy was seconded from the region's education department to set up the office now known as Community Support, based above the Bank of Scotland in the town centre. With a small staff of council officers, he set about contacting all the agencies working in Lockerbie and co-ordinating them using local volunteers. Organisations like the Red Cross, the widow's organisation Cruse, the local health board and the Samaritans have all worked together.

Alex believes that the town's spirit of co-operation is so strong Community Support will be able to make a cautious withdrawal over the coming months. He admits to "amazement and admiration" for the skills and commitment shown by Lockerbie people working towards recovery. "The community's stoicism and strength is seeing them through. There is always someone on hand to talk to. Our role is not to tell people, 'This is how you should react,' but to listen to their needs."

Back copies of *Update* make heartening reading – they show the town making valiant efforts to get back to a normal routine as soon as possible. Items about keep-fit sessions, sheepdog trials and toddlers' groups soon began appearing amid information on memorial services and insurance claims.

Activities designed to shield the town's children from the sorrow of the first weeks were in the forefront. Games sessions were held in the scout hut every morning and afternoon during the Christmas holidays. Lockerbie was inundated with offers of free visits and treats for the children. "We went to the pantomime and an adventure playground in Carlisle," says Val Moloney, a volunteer involved in the project from the beginning.

"The kids were sombre in Lockerbie, but once they were out of the town they changed. When we came back, they became subdued again. You could feel the mood change as we drove in. Some were more affected than others. A lot of kids wouldn't sleep in their own beds." The problem was so bad that *Update* included a leaflet advising parents on how to deal with sleeplessness among children.

One mother was shocked by her eight-year-old daughter's behaviour the day after the disaster. "She went around singing, 'He jumped from an aeroplane at 30,000 feet' over and over. At first I told her to stop, then I realised that it was her way of coping."

The children went back to school, but the scout hut games sessions continued. Now Val Moloney and five other helpers run a weekly club for more than 60 primary-age children. Before the crash, a youth club for older children had been talked about, but it never got under way. It will start soon.

Adults also required help. Robert Riddet was affected for months after the event. "I had sleepless nights and wild dreams. In April we went on holiday and, at last, I slept soundly. But as soon as we came back to Lockerbie the problem returned. It's shattering, not feeling safe in your own home. If anything terrible happens away from home, you always have your own place as a refuge to return to. But we can never feel secure again." Like others in the town he still jumps at the slightest noise. The fast trains that speed through Lockerbie on the Glasgow to London line make him feel nervous. A banging door can also be frightening. But he won't consider moving. "That would be desertion." Even the swishing noise heralding the satellite weather reports on ITN reminds many of the sighing wind that preceded the explosion.

A huge burden fell on the town's three clergy in the week after the disaster. As well as providing counselling and spiritual guidance, they also had to conduct Christmas services and help plan the memorial service held on January 4. Father Keegans led a requiem mass on Boxing Day, and a few days later officiated at the funeral of Joanne Flanagan, one of the youngest local victims.

The church leaders were helped by a team of interdenominational clergy from outside. But the need for the local preachers was still great. "It would take hours to walk up the street, so many people wanted to talk. The whole place seemed traumatised," Father Keegans recalls.

Some people turned to the church for the comfort of ritual and a caring congregation. Others were wrestling with doubt. Father Keegans' answer when asked why God allows disasters, is that the bomb on flight 103 was created by man, an act of man's free will. "There is no real answer, though. You could ask the same about cot deaths. I've seen both sides – those who say they can never believe in God again, and those whose faith has been increased by the love and care born out of the experience in Lockerbie."

He was terrified by the memorial service attended by a host of dignitaries including Mrs Thatcher and televised all over the world. "I said a prayer I have which goes, 'God help me, so nothing can happen today which You and I can't get through together'. That and 'Help!' were my only prayers at that time, but they got me through a lot of days."

Before the disaster, Lockerbie had perhaps suffered from that sense of apathy that affects many small towns. The community council, once short of members, now has a surplus of volunteers. The primary children's club is thriving. And most residents take a lively interest in the re-development of the town.

Christine Hannah, who lives in the centre and was evacuated on the night of the disaster, says, "I think we have all realised how much our town means to us this year. I would like to see a real celebration of Lockerbie next year, with more flowers to brighten the place up. Maybe we could compete with Moffat to win the Scotland in Bloom contest."

The same spirit animates the new residents' association set up on the Rosebank estate. Now that the rebuilding is almost complete, there are plans to improve the area further. Members want the district council to acquire the site of an old creamery factory and turn it into a park and adventure playground. The council is keen to back the plan.

Maxwell Kerr, chairman of the Rosebank residents' association, says, "We would never have had an association if it were not for the disaster. We will probably disband eventually, but it has meant that we may have tackled a real eyesore, and if we get our park it will be marvellous for the whole town."

In Sherwood Crescent, the crater has been filled in and a new tarmac road laid on top. But only a sparse growth of grass covers the soil and much of the area is still mud. The houses in the immediate area look sadly battered now. At least a dozen people will still be in temporary accommodation this Christmas. "They are the forgotten victims," says Tom Carson, owner of a chemist's shop in the High Street and chairman of Sherwood Crescent residents' association. "With the best will in the world, no one can tell them when they will be able to go home."

Homeless residents who were still suffering from shock had to deal with insurance companies' loss adjusters, many of whom behaved as though they were dealing with an ordinary accident. Eventually, members of the residents' association complained to the insurance industry and claims were treated rather more sensitively.

Far more upsetting, and far harder to deal with, was the constant flow of sightseers. Some even came in minibuses. Father Keegans, who moved back to his home at the edge of the crater on December 31, has spoken to many of the unwelcome visitors. "They come because they want to touch death at a safe distance," he says.

The invasion of hundreds of reporters, cameramen and photographers provoked reactions ranging from irritation to disgust. No one was prepared for the photographers who stood on doorsteps to get a good view of the house next door, or hustled local children off the pavement. Others saw photographers lifting the cloths placed over the heads of corpses. One reporter even pretended to be a priest in order to gain access to Stephen Flanagan, the boy whose family perished in Sherwood Crescent.

Later media coverage continued to cause anger and distress. Many people feel journalists have been interested in reporting only controversy, whether real or imagined, and they want to challenge the impression of carping and division which has been created.

Community Support responded to fears about media coverage of the anniversary and a training course was set up to prepare locals for a new surge of interest. "I think it has been one of the most successful things we have done," says Alex McElroy. He believes the course is a world first.

The Lockerbie disaster was the work of a very few men or women. Ironically, the good that has come out of it is the work of thousands. Letters and donations, offers of gifts and holidays poured into the town for weeks. A party of teenagers were the guests of the Dutch town of Middelburg in the summer, and older residents have enjoyed free breaks in Cromer and Jersey.

Some gifts were large-scale – a food firm donated playground equipment for the main public park. Others were smaller gestures of compassion. One resident vividly remembers receiving a letter a few days after the crash. On the back of the envelope was written, "Deepest sympathy, Milton Keynes postmen".

In the town itself there is a new closeness. "I never knew so many people before," says Val Moloney. Although they yearn for normality, no one will ever shirk giving hospitality to the relatives of those who died. A friendship group was set up to offer support to visiting families. Members have relatives to stay and will even accompany them to the exact spot where their son, daughter, husband or wife was found. Some townspeople will share their Christmas with grieving relations.

Gideon Pringle, Elma's husband, who recently took over as chairman of the friendship group, says, "The relatives want to know what it is like here, and they find it easier to talk to somebody in their own home. It may seem strange to us if they want to take a photograph of the place where someone died, but these are their ways, and we are learning all the time about different creeds and nationalities." He expects relatives will return regularly. "There'll always be a welcome for them."

There are special links between Lockerbie and Syracuse, the university town in New York state, which lost 38 students in the disaster. A scholarship has been set up which will enable two Lockerbie school-leavers to attend the university every year.

As the first anniversary approaches, Lockerbie's goal is to recover its old tranquillity. "People want to get back to normal," says Maxwell Kerr. "It amazes me how well we have coped, but I doubt that we can ever be quite the same again."

Only time can heal the emotional scars. For many, the nightmare continues. Sarah Campbell will never forget those terrible few minutes. "Even now I sometimes close my eyes at night and see the engine falling... just pirouetting to the ground."

December 17, 1989

Are you an orange person?

Joanna Blythman

Oh what a tangled web we weave when first we practise to be public relations consultants. Sorry, let me rephrase that. This still qualifies as the season of goodwill, PR is an honourable profession and, of course, we are all colleagues.

I'm indebted to the useful information and helpful advice that helps keep us in touch with the goings-on of our food producers and retailers: the release I received from Struthers PR on the newly-launched Gourmet Pasta shop at 54 Morningside Road, Edinburgh, is a case in point. Here you have two absolutely charming and delightful Italians, Anna and Maurizio Meoni, dispensing an endless stream of variations of magnificent pasta made before your eyes. One look at their sparkling emporium, or taste of their wild mushroom-filled mezzeluna or parsley fettucine, and everyone is convinced.

Now, not every PR firm has similarly excellent raw materials with which to work. It is however, amazing how inventive the PR and marketing brains can become when the account is at stake.

Casting charity aside, here are my hype awards for the best food (and wine) clangers of 1989.

The Weird Award must go to Alan Compton-Batt Associates (better known for promoting the entirely excellent grande marque Taittinger champagne) who presided over the launch of Champagne Marquis de Sade, "a new luxurious champagne packaged in marbled red and black with the original signature of D.A.F. de Sade in gold...it is evocative of the refinement and culture which surrounded the life of the Divine Marquis." (Just the drink for ruthless city yuppies?)

The Environment Award goes deservedly to Chambers Cox PR on behalf of Beefeater Steak-houses for managing to turn the greenhouse effect into a virtue. "As temperatures soar, the last thing a housewife wants is to slave over a hot stove...the greenhouse effect means that a sweltering summer is predicted. Sunny skies call for imaginative light and tempting dishes...look no further than your local Beefeater restaurant."

In the exceptionally tough category of **Best Recipe Award**, (no shortage of competition here), the clear winner is the U.S. Rice Information Service for its circa 1960 offering of broccoli and brown rice casserole. "Take 1 onion, 3 sticks celery, (so far so good), 1oz butter or margarine, 1lb cooked American long grain rice (borderline), 10oz frozen broccoli (help!), a can of condensed cream of chicken soup (yuck!), 4oz processed cheese spread" – but no more, lest it spoil your Hogmanay.

The outright winner of the **Remodelling Reality Award,** is the much-berated Outspan organisation under its user-friendly guise of the Summer Orange Office for its venture into colour analysis. "Are you an orange person, do you love being sociable...and enjoy well-being, togetherness and a sharing of pleasures? If the answer is yes, then, according to Marie Louise Lacy, a leading authority on colour analysis, you are undoubtedly an orange person. What better way to illustrate these qualities than by looking at one of the most enjoyable fruits on earth – the orange." Nice one, Marie. Try black next time.

The Most Attractive Breakfast Invitation Award goes to John McCann's Canned Porridge Oats for inviting journalists along for a 9am start to taste the eponymous ready-made porridge out of the tin, "only 125 calories per serving, low sodium, etc. etc." followed by a full cooked hotel breakfast (high caloric, high sodium, high cholesterol by any chance?).

The Sexist Codswollop Award goes to D.J. Edelman for work on behalf of the Meat and Livestock Commission for the campaign titled "Why your butcher is learning to be mum: There used to be a time when virtually all young women learned to roast, stew and braise to please their man and feed their family. If they got stuck, mum was just around the corner to ask. Now in the age of the independent working woman...the MLC has been training the friendly high street butcher in his striped apron to become stand-in for mums! These naturally cheerful men are learning how to help the busy working girl..." (Keep smiling ladies, you are in capable hands!)

The Get Them While They're Young Processed Food Award goes to H.J. Heinz for its Halloween introduction of Haunted House spaghetti shapes. "Children will love these spooky shapes in a tasty tomato sauce including witches, bats and ghouls...to celebrate Halloween, Heinz have got 2,000 Haunted House kits to give away free. There are nearly 50 great glow-in-the-dark stickers and a chart to stick them on to..."

The Up-Market Packaging For Down-Market Product Award goes to Paragon Communications for dreaming up the notion of commissioning Gallup research and a learned psychologist to sell cup soup as follows: "Take care as you sip your next cup of soup – the variety you choose reveals more about you than you may think. According to Batchelors, the soup people, soup snackers generally fit into four categories: Traditionalists, Experimentalists, Gourmands or Ecologicals. These portraits, revealed by Dr Furnham – a psychologist from the University College of London – show that your type of soup also reveals what type of foodie you are likely to be, what type of newspaper you may choose, what type of car you drive or indeed what your bedtime habits might be!"

That leaves a few residual awards. In the **Beat The Big Boys at Their Own Game Category,** the award goes to Whole Earth Foods, for the organic version of Pasta Pots. **The Squeezing The Most Out of Guy Fawkes Night Award** goes again to Paragon Communications for taking perfectly good fish and stuffing it into a filo pastry pudding with sparklers on top to create *Fisherman's Bonfire Surprise*. My final accolade for **The Most Outstandingly Disgusting Microwave Meal of the '80s,** (another hotly contested category) goes again to H.J. Heinz for its ready-to-eat in two minutes microwave LunchBowls: "Imagine a steaming bowl of chicken curry packed with delicious ingredients such as sweetcorn, mango chutney, cream and onions, or a spaghetti Bolognese with all the traditional flavour of pasta, herbs and spicy meat. Designed specifically for microwave use, LunchBowl couldn't be easier to prepare. Simply lift off the plastic cover and place in the microwave (650w) for two minutes at full power. They have a heat protective shield which means that you can eat them straight from the bowl, which can be held in your hand. Because they are fully cooked...with all the goodness sealed in, they do not need storing in a fridge of freezer – you can keep them in a

cupboard, drawer or anywhere handy."
Personally, I'd rather eat the budgie's food...

December 31, 1989

Seasonal greetings

Joyce McMillan

I remember the moment – perhaps 10 years ago – when I first suspected there was something seriously out of joint about this great mid-winter festival of ours. It was during a family Christmas in a small, unglamorous West Midlands town; after a huge Christmas lunch, I felt impelled to take a late-afternoon walk, and went out into the cold streets. At first, it seemed pleasantly quiet after the blare of Christmas TV; but as I drifted past the cricket ground into the centre of town, the atmosphere began to seem more and more sinister. I walked for half an hour, my footsteps clanging in the silence; and during that time I saw no other living soul, not so much as a man walking a dog. One car crawled by, its headlights dim in the mist. But the only other sign of human life was the flicker of a thousand TV screens glimpsed through gaps in front-room curtains; *The Sound of Music* was playing, and the faint, tinny tinkle of the sound-track hung over the town like a mist.

This Christmas Day in the Midlands was a holiday, no question; ordinary life had come to a halt. But festive? Celebratory? A season to be jolly? It looked more like a post-holocaust scene from one of those cheery dramas about biological warfare; the buildings were still standing, but the population might have been wiped out at a stroke.

Nor has the British retreat into an intensely private Christmas been reversed in the 1980s; if anything, it's worse. There are places where people celebrate festivals by dancing in the streets or partying on the pavements; there are perfectly respectable European countries where they actually run extra trains on high days and holidays, so that people can travel in style to visit their relations. But not here.

If Dickens' *Christmas Carol* were set here and now, and the transformed Scrooge were to wake up in Scotland tomorrow morning, he would find himself faced with a world not open to the idea of love and forgiveness, but closed for the duration; churches shut for lack of Christmas-morning customers, shops and restaurants blank-faced, no trains, little traffic, no life in the streets.

A couple of years ago, the prime minister attracted widespread scorn with her remark that "there is no such thing as society, only individual men and women, and families." But the way we handle this great common holiday suggests that she knows us better than we know ourselves. For we do not choose to celebrate Christmas as a brief, joyful transfiguration of the ordinary fabric of our lives. Instead, as Christmas Eve approaches, we bring our normal lives to a juddering halt, and consign ourselves – with varying degrees of affection, resignation, irritation or despair – to days of unaccustomed seclusion in the bosom of the nuclear family.

Which is fine for those of us who love and like our families. For the rest – including that growing army of Britons who have no immediate family to turn to at Christmas – the "festive season" is an unspoken ordeal, an aching void in the normal rhythm of life filled only by food, drink and family tensions. This sense of emptiness is not entirely a matter of declining religious faith; any human being with the smallest feeling for the rhythms of nature can share the joy of a winter solstice celebration. But somewhere in the gap between the old Scottish Ne'erday and the new British Xmas we seem to have lost the will to celebrate this midwinter feast as if it meant something. Of course, we cover our lack of commitment to the event with the universal assertion that the whole thing is "just for the kids". But the truth is that what makes a festival special for children is the sense that the grown-ups around them are involved in some special once-a-year day ritual, full of mystery and importance. Children cannot carry the meaning of the festival alone; they have to learn a sense of midwinter magic from the adults around them.

And all these graceless features of the British Christmas seem particularly sad at the end of a year in which the power of people coming together on the streets to express their faith and hope for the future has been so spectacularly demonstrated across Europe.

A couple of friends of mine are going to Prague this Christmas, and I suggest they'll find a spirit of celebration there that will put our dyspeptic little festival of private consumption to shame; the tragedy is that it seems to take some terrible imposed suffering – a Lockerbie disaster, or the long drawn-out misery of political repression – to shake modern men and women out of their fantasies of individual self-sufficiency.

But our best hope is that the East Europeans, unlike us, will never become so pluralistic and fragmented as a society that they will lose that brave, sentimental willingness to come out in public and talk about the human values they share. For we in the West have now largely lost the habit of confronting our deepest human feelings through public, communal events; and what that means is revealed in the bleak, empty streets of our towns at Christmas.

Unless, from somewhere, we can learn new ways of publicly sharing and affirming the fundamental feelings – about light shining through mid-winter darkness, the birth of hope in the shape of the Christ-child, the promise of the returning sun – that used to cling around this time of year, then I suspect that we can no longer have festivals in the true sense of the word. Holidays, yes; long winter breaks full of pudding and boredom, presents and squabbles. But nothing special, nothing to celebrate, nothing magical; nothing like Christmas at all.

December 24, 1989

Diary of a shop assistant

Ajay Close

Glaswegians have been doing their Christmas shopping at Lewis's for 60 years. In the week before Christmas, Ajay Close signed on as one of the store's 700 staff.

Day One

8.30am
To the morning meeting held by general manager Keith Harmer, a newfangled retailer with a conviction handshake and philosophy to match ("We believe we're good but we could be a lot better.") To someone who has not yet started her Christmas shopping, it comes as a shock to learn that Lewis's has been making plans for the festive season since June. "For us Christmas is almost over." Now all his energies are concentrated on the end-of-year sale: today's tasks include storing the marked-down goods just in from Central Buying, ordering price tickets, and planning press advertisements.

Meanwhile up in the canteen, the staff are steeling themselves for the day ahead with coffee and a quick cigarette, and entering into the Christmas spirit. Snatches of conversation rise above the clink of crockery: "All these people coming in and buying things they don't want..." "I honestly can't think of anything I need..."

10.30am
Santa is busy. "Just-a-present-is-it?-99-pence-please-there's-

a-twenty-five-minute-queue-but-it-won't-get-any-shorter-just-give-the-ticket-to-Santa" busy. Karen, a former air hostess whose chronic flight-sickness has grounded her in Lewis's grotto, repeats her spiel to each customer with remarkable cheerfulness while I take the money.

Lewis's has three Santas. The grotto is cunningly designed to allow two of them to work simultaneously, while maintaining the illusion that, as every youngster knows, there is only one Santa at Christmas; the third stands by to relieve them. It is the only way to cope with up to 1,000 children a day, all wanting to get in their request for the Ghostbusters' fire station or Barbie's caravan (both sold out, naturally). Post Cleveland, the wise Santa works with a chaperone, so there is also a photographer doing a small but significant trade in 16-year-old girls wanting a snap of themselves sitting on Santa's knee.

In a cardboard carton-lined cavern, Santa's elves are making up little bags of presents and grumbling a little, as elves are wont to do when they have been on grotto duty since late October. Santa One is causing a certain amount of aggro with his refusal to give 6-12-year-old girls skipping ropes. We are joined by one of the photographers, who has been carrying out an impromptu time and motion study. "Seven kids in 14 minutes!" he says indignantly. "That's two minutes each; it's supposed to be 2.3 children a minute."

Every child under the age of six emerges from the grotto with a small plastic trumpet. Parents look pained; the staff, murderous. Mutterings of "Who's smart idea was that?" can be heard across the sales floor.

1pm
Outside there is a raging blizzard – although in this thermostat-controlled environment you'd never know it; there are no windows and no clocks to remind you of time passing in the world outside.

3pm
The chief fact to remember in the toy department is that just about everything you will be asked for is sold out. Although the shelves are piled with hundreds of different types of toys, Glasgow children only seem to be interested in Big Red Buses, Barbie's caravans, Mini chefs, Tiny Tears, somersaulting dogs, and Ghostbusters fire stations and backpacks. (The makers of Ghostbusters clearly know a marketing opportunity when they see one, the spin-offs are endless: wristwatches, cars, dolls, board games, ectoplasm...)

Appropriately enough, staff in 'Toys' are famed for their fun and games. Chief prankster is Craig the section manager, a master of high camp who specialises in delivering outrageous one-liners just when the hapless recipient can least afford to laugh. Isobel is serving at the till when he walks over and says, deadpan: "You'd better check when you get home – I think I must have left my tie under your bed last night."

While she turns an unusual shade of puce, I continue wrapping purchases: a more taxing task than it might seem. I seem to have an unerring instinct for the bag which is just too small, too weak, or too large for the toy in hand.

The customers divide into two broad camps: ditherers, and do-or-die commandoes. The former seem to have been deserted by their powers of description and, having no idea of the name of the toy they want, resort to mime. By the time I have worked out what they mean the last one in the shop is just being wrapped for someone else. The latter category can be identified by the vein pulsing on their temple. They bark out the toy they want, and I have a split-second to assess the chances of physical assault if I admit I've never heard of it. Commando couples stare fixedly ahead with identical expressions of mute suffering, apparently on the point of divorce, if not actual murder.

5pm
Even toys lose their appeal after an afternoon of putting them into plastic carriers. As Bruce Springsteen informs us that *Santa Claus Is Coming To Town* for what I estimate to be the 567th time, I am beginning to be abnormally aware of my feet. A shabbily-dressed woman buys a £25 set of Janet Reger-style lingerie for her eight-year-old daughter. A big hit in the housing schemes, this line was walking off the rails by the dozen until security caught the culprit.

5.30pm
The floor is almost deserted, we chat desultorily. Craig and Isobel recall the day they threw out a gang of troublemaking "wee neds". True, one of them protested loudly that he was out with his granny, but then, that's what they all say...To their horror, he was back 10 minutes later with a formidable old lady who marched him up to every assistant on the floor asking "Was it her? Was it her?" Craig and Isobel discovered urgent business in the stockroom.

5.55pm
A sudden rush of table football sales: a really challenging bag job. Santa emerges from the grotto in check cap and carcoat, looking amazingly perky after a hard day's dandling.

6pm
The bell rings, but the customers keep coming. Someone uses a credit card to pay for a £2.99 game. We assume expressions of saintly forebearance.

6.10pm
The last purchase is rung up on the till. I go home to dream of putting toys into bags for Bruce Springsteen.

Day Two

10am
To Perfumery, where the entire staff look as if they have just returned from a fortnight in the Bahamas. Department manager Rita Brown asks me: "Do you want your make-up done? We can totally transform you." After a pause she adds: "If you want transforming that is." I get the impression I have little choice.

10.30am
I emerge from the Elizabeth Arden counter fully made-up, a process which only seems to have emphasised the gulf separating me from the exotic species behind the counters. YSL are spraying the air with Opium: a high-risk strategy (Lewis's legend has it that a beauty consultant once sneezed, popping two buttons, and her skirt fell down). Apparently, it is a scent which inspires strong passions. "If I spray it around the counter you can guarantee that the men will say 'that's nice', but women either love it or hate it. And you know that some of them will open it on Christmas Day and say 'Oh no'..."

Chanel warn me to expect customers to come in asking for Channel No. 14, while Dior's Poison tends to be known as poisson. Opinion is divided over which name is more apt: I was given a squirt and, several hours later on the train home, was seriously worried that the man in the next seat might ask me to move.

12.30pm
Staff can eat under the bright yellow sun umbrellas of the customers' coffee shop, The Meeting Place ('Benidorm' to the girls), but most opt for the unadulterated cholesterol of the canteen: fish, sausage, egg, chips, white bread and world-class fudge doughnuts. With a week to go, everyone is looking forward to 5pm – closing time – December 24. "We're open 71 hours this week but there'll still be people who haven't finished on Christmas Eve," someone predicts gloomily. "You're talking about half past five." Perfumery expect to take £100,000 in the one day. "There's nothing on the shelves by then and people will take anything. They're desperate."

2pm
Back on the floor, I have yet to perfect the art of spraying testers; but the customers are very understanding about the wet sleeves. The entire population of Glasgow seems to be in Lewis's, and at least half

of them are buying from Estee Lauder. Some fragrance houses do 40% of their business in the six weeks before Christmas. To create the right ambience, we have our own ghetto blaster belting out *Do They Know It's Christmas*. I am taking huge amounts of money, effortlessly; the computer till singing to my touch, the other beauty consultants jigging on the spot good naturedly as they wait for me to master the intricacies of electronic wand and magnetic strip.

3pm
Dutiful teenage sons and love-struck boyfriends are handing over wads of notes without demur (but there is always one who comes back to return a £150 gift box after Christmas because he's broken up with his fiancee). The department has achieved its sales target for the day and rumours of staggering takings fly across the floor (rivalry between the different fragrance houses is fierce). Giorgio has just rung up £240 worth of skin care and cosmetics to a single customer.

4pm
The tannoy announces the seventh toddler to have lost his mammy today. Two shoplifters are arrested by the store detectives near our counter, but the drama goes unnoticed in the bustle. Later we learn that they had a hypodermic needle and a 6in knife with them.

5pm
Closing time. As the crowds disperse I am aware of a strange prickling in my calf muscles. Incipient varicose veins? Only when I flop on to the train to wallow in blissful anonymity do I appreciate the strain of constantly being in the public eye.

Day Three

9am
Christmas is high season for crime, so I am assigned to Store Security (sensitive to police teasing, they avoid the term detective). As security manager, David Macklin (known among Glasgow's shoplifting fraternity as Carrot) is responsible for everything from ejecting mischief-making children, to arresting light-fingered drug addicts. None of this compares with the trauma of having to shut out the customers at 5pm on Christmas Eve: "Suddenly you're the most unpopular man in Glasgow."

He encounters every type of criminal from Dippers (pickpockets) to professional shoplifters who make a handsome living out of store theft. "They steal anything of value: from top of the range £300 to £400 suits, down to a £20 bottle of perfume. You can pick the good ones, they'll come in clean-shaven, with a smart suit – perhaps Christian Dior – but you look at their shoes and you know," he says.

"Their heels are worn right down." ??? "Have you ever tried to steal a pair of shoes?" Then there are the regulars: Shorty, Gumsy – who takes his false teeth out in a vain attempt at disguise – and the Salmon Man, bane of the Food Hall, who only steals tinned fish. In an average day the team spots 30-35 of them on the video monitors, fed by overhead cameras which a surprising number of thieves assume to be dummies. Drug addicts, known as desperadoes, are a major problem, accounting for 75 out of the 180 prosecutions this year. Every store detective dreads having a needle pulled on him.

Not everyone is prosecuted. "We've got nothing to achieve by putting 60 and 70-year-olds into court. You could kill a person of that age," he says. "It can cause a lot of bad publicity for the store: 'Granny shoplifting takes a stroke and dies – security man last seen heading for the Costa del Sol'..."

12.30pm
I grab my coat and take a tour round the store with Aileen, a former sales assistant who moved sideways into security. Dressed in jeans and an outdoor jacket, she mingles convincingly with the customers, although the regulars aren't fooled. On the streets of Glasgow it is not unknown for them to say hello and offer to buy her a drink.

Since Lewis's insists on three months training before security staff are unleashed on the shop floor, mine is strictly a watching brief. I listen for unfamiliar accents and keep my eyes peeled for prams (which can have false bottoms), duvet anoraks (perfect for poacher's pockets), big carrier bags and sports holdalls. Amazingly, given this list, they insist they have never stopped a genuine customer. A common trick is for men to take two suits into the changing room and come out with one (embarrassing if you're caught in the cubicle next door, peeking under the partition to see if the suspect is tucking a pair of trousers into his socks). Hiding booty up a jumper is another favourite. ("You get women coming in and the next time you see them they're nine months pregnant.") "Watch their eyes and their hands," Aileen advises. "Everything else about them is normal."

Unfortunately, I find it difficult enough to negotiate the crystalware displays and avoid toppling shelvesful of stuffed hippos in wedding dresses without having to spot shoplifters as well. After countless top-to-bottom tours of the store, all I have to show for my efforts is a mysterious ache in my kidneys.

3pm
Christmas Stationery. Underneath a speaker blaring out jazzed-up carols, I am instructed to tidy the card racks. I soon know just how Sisyphus felt. For some reason, no slot contains an equal number of cards and envelopes. In the time it takes to straighten one row,

another three are messed-up. Periodically I am asked if we have a card specifically for a boss/nephew and wife/cousin and husband. I rifle through cards for mothers, fathers, brothers, sisters, aunts, uncles, in-laws – every permutation of human bonding except the one the customer wants.

If by some miracle I find the right relation, the rhyme inside is unsuitable. One woman looking for a card 'to a special brother and his wife', isn't keen on: *Here's a Xmas wish for you/ With more love than before/ To bring you happiness on this day/ And throughout the year in store.* I take her point. Still, it's preferable to *It's Xmas so let's make music together: you shake your maracas and I'll play with my organ.*

I go home to a nightmare about mismatched envelopes and awake with a stabbing pain between my shoulder blades.

Day Four

9am
Doing the rounds with Pat Campbell, the display manager, we are horrified to spot an elegantly-dressed mannequin in the window, warmly-wrapped against the December cold in red wool coat with black velvet collar, immaculately made-up and bald as a coot.

We stop to tidy one of the mountains of white nylon teddy bears with red knitted hats dotted around the store (*Take me home for £12.99*), this year's special promotion. Lewis's is selling 400 a week.

An assistant arrives to tell us that a customer wants to buy a black velvet minidress modelled by an aloof beauty in the window opposite Baldy. The mannequin stares disdainfully as Pat strips her of dress, wig, arms and dignity, and changes her into another little black number. Unfortunately it is such a little black number that the hem fails to meet her stocking tops, turning the tableau from a classy cocktail party into a peepshow.

Pat massages her thighs unselfconsciously to eliminate the gap, while I wrestle with her arm, trying to click it into the shoulder socket, horribly aware of the fact that a new mannequin costs £460, and even a respray leaves little change from £100.

11am
Assigned to Lingerie, I spend the rest of the morning putting knickers on the sort of hangers that shed their load as soon as you look at them. A couple of hours of this and I'm doing a passable imitation of a zombie – except that zombies don't get backache.

12.30pm
En route to the canteen I pass the white bears. The way I'm feeling, I tell them, you could take me home for considerably less than

£12.99.
1.30pm
Perfumery again. Business is sluggish, but we sell a mild-mannered type in an anorak *two* bottles of Chanel No. 5. It's always the quiet ones...
5.15pm
I've had enough. On my way out, Laura from Personnel remarks that it's all right for those who *can* walk away. Hobbling a little, I agree, but promise to think of her working until 5pm on Christmas Eve. The sale starts 10am, Boxing Day.

December 24, 1989

List of authors

Derek Bateman	*Sink or swim?*	152
Joanna Blythman	*Mr Lim's corner shop*	42
	The worm turns	99
	Are you an orange person?	176
Rob Brown	*The Wall*	23
Ajay Close	*Lords of the ring*	58
	In search of the hard man	105
	The King and I	126
	Diary of a shop assistant	181
Derek Cooper	*Confessions of a meat eater*	68
	Recipe for disaster	158
Keren David	*Inside Barlinnie*	80
	Lockerbie: a year on	167
Neil Drysdale	*Trial at Titwood (2)*	114
Rob Edwards	*Scotland 2050*	91
Roddy Forsyth	*Disnaeland*	66
	Lucky breaks	120
Neville Garden	*Pipe down*	12
	Discordant notes	87
Michael Fry	*The Forsyth saga*	161
Brian Groom	*Royal soap*	163
Allan Hunter	*Bette Davis eyes*	19
Sue Innes	*May stands by her man*	44
	The surplus sex	134
Kevin McCarra	*Playing for time*	14
Alexander MacLeod	*Tyranny and after*	54
Joyce McMillan	*Scandal*	21
	Caught on a train	64
	The new morality	89
	Tartan special	144
	Seasonal greetings	179
Rennie McOwan	*Small but beautifully formed*	78

189

Julie Morrice	*The Big M*	75
James Naughtie	*A woman's work*	101
Calum Neish	*The Campbells keep mum*	29
William Paul	*Week of judgment* (with Kenny Farquharson)	36
	Hands across the sea	70
	War games	121
	The last sleeper	156
Robert Philip	*Extraordinary Joe*	31
	Trial at Titwood (1)	112
	GoGo and BoBo are missing	140
Kenneth Roy	*Urban Voltaire*	47
	Everlasting Sunday	76
	Poetic justice	94
	Brigadoon revisited	132
	Now for the Rumba	142
Trevor Royle	*The trial of John Buchan*	146
Graham Spiers	*Sexy's City*	51
	Grandstand finish	154
Alan Taylor	*Hangovers*	11
	Framed	33
	Peace, imperfect peace	56
	A pow-wow of Helmuts	103
	Ghost ride	116
	Sex at the festival	165
Jeremy Watson	*Dying for a smoke*	130